For the Love of the Game

MATTHEW MORRIS

DEDICATION

This book is dedicated to all of the amazing people I met during my trip.
The baseball community is one of the greatest on this planet, and it was
getting to know some of these people, not the games themselves, that made
these travels so special. Keep spreading your love of the game!

CONTENTS

ACKNOWLEDGMENTS

With great thanks to the many amazing people who helped me on my journey and made it one to remember. Joel, Ryan, Tyler, Yakub, Dave, Paul, Ryan, Masato, and so many others. You all made the trip possible.

PRELUDE: THE LONDON SERIES

The UK is arguably one of the most influential sporting nations in the world. A huge number of sports were supposedly invented on our shores, including football, rugby and cricket, and despite our limited population we continue to punch above our weights at the Olympic Games. A significant proportion of the population pay big money every month to watch sports on television, and similarly large numbers either attend live events or take part themselves. It is curious, therefore, that some sports which are incredibly popular worldwide seem almost niche in this country. Ask a Brit to name a curling or volleyball team and they'll probably look at you in confusion, and that's before we even start talking about baseball.

Often derisively compared to rounders or compared with cricket, one of the world's most popular sports doesn't seem to exist in the minds of the British. A small but dedicated community notwithstanding, it seems as though there's vast room to grow the sport in the UK, and that's exactly where MLB saw potential. Several years ago, the league announced a deal to bring two games a year to London – following the huge success of American Football's NFL games – and just nine months before Covid struck, the New York Yankees and the Boston Red Sox played out their iconic rivalry in front of a combined total of nearly 120,000 fans at West Ham's London Stadium.

The 2019 games were a success, but the impact of the pandemic meant that any impact that Major League Baseball was hoping to make lost all momentum for an extended period of time. First-time fans that had come to see the Yankees and the Red Sox were starved of an opportunity to see any more action, and with there still being a paucity of baseball on British television it was difficult to see the game growing. There was an attempt to re-engage fans in 2022 with *Home Run Derby X* in Crystal Palace Park, but shambolic organisation and a relatively alien style of concept made it difficult for even the more avid baseball fan to digest.

All of this goes some way to explaining why 2023 would be such a monumental year for the sport in the UK. It started in the best possible way – with Great Britain competing in their first ever World Baseball Classic, and giving a good account of themselves to boot. Drawn into an incredibly tough pool containing the United States, Canada, Colombia and Mexico, even the most optimistic of fans had low expectations, but the side started their campaign by taking a shock lead against a US side containing Mike Trout, Mookie Betts, Pete Alonso and reigning MVP Paul Goldschmidt (more of him later). A shock win against Colombia two days later was enough for them to finish fourth in the group and automatically qualify for the 2027 tournament. This not only generated significant media coverage back in the UK, but also ensured significant funding for the sport for years to come.

It was with this in mind that the timing of the 2023 London Series was so crucial. It was an opportunity to build some momentum just three months after some success on the international stage, and importantly it felt as though the media were beginning to pay attention to what would be going on in Stratford.

The league made sure to make this year's event a lot bigger than back in 2019. They had announced a "takeover" of Trafalgar Square over the weekend, which was my first port of call. I was curious what it would entail, as details were sparse. After a rare stress-free train journey from the West Country, I arrived to a resplendent city enjoying a heatwave, and following a short queue (it was nice to see that baseball had embraced our national pastime) entered what appeared to be a small inner-city festival site.

What immediately struck me was how many American visitors there were. Far from being filled with curious locals, fans from Chicago and St. Louis had flocked to the takeover and were making the most of what was on offer. The highlight was a scaled-down version of *Home Run Derby X* – a fully-netted stage with snazzy computer tech providing the targets and tracking, and more former players on display than in the dedicated event offered last year. I even managed to get a photo with the indomitable force that is Nick Swisher after his turn hitting dingers.

The man is an absolute force of nature. He approaches everything in life with a positive energy that sets a shining example to us all, and despite being the most popular man in Trafalgar Square he had an almost unlimited amount of time to chat to fans and pose for numerous photo opportunities. Most importantly, he was clearly enjoying himself, and managed to spread real enthusiasm for the entire event to everyone else there.

After deciding not to queue for the quoted three hours for the merchandise stands, I made a mental note to check back in the morning before the games and headed back to my parents' house in Hertfordshire before it got too late. There were two big days coming up!

The following day can only be described as one of the best days of my life. The sheer number of amazing people that I spoke to and the activities on offer were second-to-none, and actually make me slightly worried that my trip around the US will struggle to meet the same highs. I started off back in Trafalgar Square, in a mercifully shorter queue at the Topps booth to get a free personalised baseball card made. This was a really nice addition to the event and could have easily been a paid-for activity, so I was grateful that there was no charge at all. There was also a chance to take some swings in the HRD cage (it turns out that I'm not actually very good at playing baseball), and better opportunities to check out the merchandise on offer. I ended up leaving just after midday to head to the stadium, a full six hours before first pitch.

It was at the tube station that I got talking to the first baseball fan of the day. Rick, a Cubs fan, was just one of the amazing individuals that was happy to chat all things baseball and America, and although we got slightly lost walking around Stratford it was great to introduce him to certain parts of London. As a keen historian, he was planning to stay for a few more days, so I was able to recommend places to visit, and after exchanging numbers I went off to queue to buy some memorabilia.

I would not consider myself particularly financially prudent, despite the fact that I had spent years saving up for my 30 in 35 Challenge (an unsurprisingly costly endeavour), so such a well-stocked merchandise booth was pretty much my kryptonite. I'm not sure if it was intentional that we queued for so long in full view of what was on offer, but I could have spent hundreds on a huge range of items. In the end, I settled for a relatively modest haul of a programme, a new cap, a pint glass, a commemorative ball and a set of Topps cards (believe me, I could have bought ten times as many items). The queue was also a chance to chat to some Cardinals fans, who I'm sure I will keep in touch with after adding them on social media.

You could tell that excitement was growing for the games at this point, with gates due to open imminently. Despite the lengthy queues, entry was surprisingly quick, and I made a beeline for the Cardinals dugout for an optimal spot to watch batting practice. Upon entering the stadium bowl, I was immediately struck by how different the field was compared to the 2019 games, and indeed other ballparks. Foul territory had been substantially reduced by bringing the seats closer to the action, which made the place feel a little more suitable for MLB action, although the overall shape of the stadium was still very different to what Americans would expect from their home parks. One of the best things about baseball is how every location is different, so I was pleased to realise that London Stadium had kept its unique feel whilst simultaneously being adjusted to provide a better spectator experience.

It wasn't long before the St. Louis Cardinals team were out on the field and swinging for the fences. A plethora of legends were also standing nearby watching the action, including Albert Pujols and Lord Coe (I'm not sure anyone has ever written a sentence including both of those names before). It was also pretty cool to get autographs from pitchers Jordan Montgomery and Gio Gallegos, who were very generous with their time. With batting practice over, I decided to head back to the concourse and see what was on offer.

Another big difference between British and American sports is the range of food available. In the UK, you're usually lucky to get a stale burger, and you have to stay out of view of the action to drink a lukewarm beer, but in the States creative and high-quality catering is one of the highlights of attending a game. MLB had promised to bring some of the most popular options over to London, and true to their word they had delivered separate fan zones for each team including various grills and fried delicacies. As I was on a diet, I was hardly going to be eating the two-foot-long hot dog or enormous portions of nachos, neither would I be drinking beer out of a full-size plastic bat, but it was certainly fun to see others making the most of what was available.

I also took the time to check out the view from various seats. I headed up to the back row on the first base side (I was a little disappointed that there were no sherpa guides or oxygen tanks available, as it may well be the steepest and highest view available in the sport), taking in the panoramic views of the field (breath-taking in more ways than one), as well as the location I would be watching from the following day in centre field, before heading to my designated seat much closer to the action down the third base line. I arrived just in time to see the teams emerge from the central tunnel to resplendent pyrotechnics, and the line-ups to be read out.

Then it was time for the pure Americana to kick in. Another big cultural difference between the two nations is the patriotism. Whilst the UK had something of a resurgence in the 1990s, most Brits seem to be somewhat reluctant to show belonging to the country. Maybe this is the norm worldwide, but it is completely different to the America, where the national anthem is performed before every major sporting event and flags are regularly flown outside houses. With the anthems played and the ceremonial first pitch thrown by cricketers Jimmy Andersen and Nathan Lyons, the game finally got underway.

I'll spare you a detailed description of the game, because many words have been written by much better sports journalists than myself, but it's safe to say that it was very different to the 2019 matches. With the fences moved further out, it was never going to be a slugfest, but the first of three home runs were scored by Ian Happ in the top of the second as Adam "Uncle Charlie" Wainwright began to lose control of the game, giving up another homer to Happ in the third and eventually exiting in the fourth inning having given up a total of seven earned runs. The bullpen performed significantly better (despite a poor start, letting the runners Waino had allowed on base to score), and the next four-and-a-half innings saw just one run scored (by the Cardinals, after reigning MVP Paul Goldschmidt hit a single in the bottom of the sixth) and only three hits in total.

In hindsight, it was important for newer fans to see both sides of the game, so it was lucky that they could experience a handful of runs and home runs followed by something of a pitcher's duel. Brits would also have enjoyed seeing the entertainment that took place between innings, including a surreal mascot race in which a gigantic Winston Churchill narrowly beat Freddie Mercury and Henry VIII. Fans also took to the field to try and field fly balls, and youngsters were picked out of the crowd to name songs in order to win bags of baseball merchandise. The absolute highlight, as always, had to be the seventh inning stretch, where Nick Offerman led over 50,000 people in a rendition of *Take Me Out to the Ball Game* before Bill Murray was shown on the big screen waving to the crowd. You'd never get that at a football game.

Dansby Swanson then blasted a two-run homer in the top of the ninth to put some gloss on the scoreline, and a scoreless bottom meant the Cubs took the game 9-1. Fireworks and blue smoke blasting over the stadium's roof meant it was time to leave, and I was able to head into the MLB Superstore just outside before leaving, managing to pick up an incredibly cool art print (signed by the artist and numbered to just 300) on the way out.

There were, of course, significant queues on the way to the station, but even these were good-natured compared to a typical British crowd. We counted down until the "STOP" signs changed to "GO", cheering when they did so, and the thirty-minute walk flew by. It was just after 10pm by the time I got back to my parents' house, and I was absolutely shattered, having walked seven miles and become so emotionally invested in the game, but I was completely ready to do it all over again just a few hours later.

If Saturday was a perfect day, then the start of Sunday was anything but. Waking up to news of train cancellations and lines being closed, I had to frantically work out an alternative plan to get me into London, which meant I was already behind schedule before I even started. Thankfully, there were minimal dramas after getting on the train and before long I was back at Trafalgar Square, queueing to enter in some of the hottest weather of the year so far. After getting a custom Chicago Cubs card made on the

Saturday, I opted to get a Cardinals one for the second matchup before heading back to Stratford for the game itself.

Whilst I had met a lot of new people during the first game, the Sunday was mostly given over to meeting up with those that I already knew. After taking my seat in the top level of the stadium early on, I met up with fellow British Giants fan Richard to chat about my upcoming trip to the States. Shortly after, he messaged me saying that there were empty seats next to him in the bottom tier out in centre field (in a traditional ballpark, these might have been described as bleachers, but because of the layout of a football stadium they were proper seats), and after watching the pre-game ceremonies and the Cubs take a commanding four-run lead in the first inning I moved down to the significantly better vantage point.

It was in these seats that I experienced the familiar joy of an MLB game. Sitting in the baking sun, watching a slightly more casual game take place, and chatting all things baseball with like-minded individuals is the perfect way to spend a summer afternoon, and Richard was excellent company during this time. We watched the Cardinals claw back the lead after hitting well against Stroman (who exited early in the fourth) before he had to leave to get back to his family. It was perfect luck after this that saw me checking my phone to see a message that had just come through from Flynn, another one of my San Francisco Giants friends, inviting me to come and sit with him for the rest of the game. He was close to home plate, and sitting in the shade with him was an excellent way to round off the game.

Overall, the London Series was an absolute triumph. On the face of it, one of the greatest sports in the world came to the UK in a two-day celebration of baseball, but it was so much more than that. Entire communities came together, friendships were formed, and the teams put on one hell of a show. Yes, I saw the Cubs and Cardinals split a series, but more importantly, I made memories that will last a lifetime.

THE 30 IN 35 CHALLENGE

"I'm going on an adventure!"
Bilbo Baggins, The Hobbit (J.R.R. Tolkien, 1937)

I'm not quite sure how old I was when I decided that I liked watching sports. One of my first memories was from the 2002 World Cup, when time differences meant that a lot of the games kicked off early in the morning. I would have been in primary school at the time, and I vividly remember being part of a large group crowding around a CRT TV in the tiny dining hall to watch England's quarter-final match against Brazil. I don't have any memories of the game itself (although I've seen the clip of Ronaldinho lobbing the ball over David Seaman countess times since), but it definitely taught me the lesson that football (and sports in general) was a really big deal. I'd like to think that day was the beginning of a beautiful obsession in my life.

It probably helped that I was terrible at playing sports myself, so the only option I had was to watch and live vicariously though others. At one point, having been dropped off at a football ground early while my parents went to visit my brother, I decided to have a kickabout with some friends in the car park. After deciding that I was good enough to do some skills (I wasn't), I went head over heels on the rough gravel surface and broke my wrist and my ankle simultaneously, resulting in a trip to A&E which caused my entire family to miss the game. I don't think I was the most popular person that day. I also managed to fall over playing hockey during the one appearance for my school, and so when we were given options, I picked cross country running instead. The only issue there was that I was an extremely slow runner. I knew that I couldn't embarrass myself falling over if I was sat in a seat watching other people play sports, so I ended up becoming more of a spectator than a player.

I've always had an addictive personality. From the early days of watching Reading FC, I started to think about somehow "completing" a goal. First it was attending every home game of the season, and soon it grew to seeing as many away matches as I could, before I eventually settled on the holy grail of football fans – visiting all 92 league grounds. Trying to tick off the yet-to-be-visited stadiums became an absolute obsession for years, before I eventually managed to complete the mission in 2017. Having graduated that morning, I frantically drove back to my parents' house near London before travelling up to Sunderland with my dad to watch what was ultimately a brilliant match of football. Mission complete. But what would be the next thing to aim for?

Well, unlike in American sports, where franchises are fixed, English sports leagues are based around promotion and relegation, so as soon as I'd been to every ground in the top four divisions, new teams appeared and I had more places to visit. Trips to the glamorous locations of Sutton, Hartlepool and Barrow-in-Furness did little to dampen my enthusiasm, and it wasn't long before I was starting to look at other sports for another goal.

A few of you might be wondering why I chose to start a book about baseball with some football stories, but I think it gives a bit of an insight as to why I began my challenge in the first place. In 2016 I had enjoyed an epic road trip through France following Wales at the European Championships, and I wanted to celebrate finishing my teacher training course the following year with another big summer holiday. After some careful planning I settled on visiting three parts of the United States. San Francisco had always appealed to me, and after British Airways launched a new route to Oakland with some cheaper fares it became the first stop on the trip. Having finished watching Breaking Bad the previous year, my addictive personality forced me to visit Albuquerque, and my interest in space led me to conclude the trip in Houston.

Wanting to fill my evenings, I'd booked a trip down to San Jose immediately upon arrival to watch the Earthquakes play in the MLS. I also decided that it might be fun to watch one of the major American sports, but with it being the wrong time of year for American football and hockey and the Golden State Warriors of the NBA being out of town, I settled for a baseball game. Tickets were cheap and Oracle Park (then AT&T Park) was a short walk from my budget hotel, so after a morning spent on an open top tour bus I attended my first ever MLB game. And so, on June 25th 2017, when the New York Mets beat the San Francisco Giants, I became a baseball fan.

Little did I know how much I'd enjoy watching the game. I was confused by a lot of what I saw (I didn't understand why there were coaches on the field wearing uniforms, or what the different types of pitches were), but I remember the crack of the bat hitting the ball, the speed that outfielders could throw it back, and above all else the sheer Americana of it all. Food vendors walking up and down the stands selling popcorn and beer, the seventh inning stretch, the organ player; all of it reminded me of the classic movies and cartoons, and I *loved* it. In fact, I loved it so much that as soon as I got back to my hotel that night I went straight onto the Giants' website and bought tickets to the next two home games. My second day in America, and I was already hooked.

I'd always planned to visit New York the following year, but when I realised that the Giants would be there on a road trip at the end of August I knew I had to time my holiday to catch those games as well. In a poetic sort of way, my second visit to the United States meant I saw exactly the same matchup as my first ever game, except this time I knew what was going on. Another year later, in 2019, Major League Baseball brought the show to me – the London Series being an exciting opportunity to see superstars like Aaron Judge and Mookie Betts in the UK, and suddenly I was a full-on fan. A subscription to MLB TV followed, and waking up at 4am to catch a game began to become a routine before work.

And so, with the Covid pandemic starting to wind down, the obsessive side of me began to take over and I started to plan another epic road trip. 30 teams in the Major Leagues seemed like such an achievable number to visit – after all, I'd done 92 different stadiums in the United Kingdom, which was over three times as many. Being a teacher, I knew that

I'd have a limited time to visit (about 6 weeks during the summer holidays), so some intensive planning was needed. I knew 2021 would be a write-off thanks to continuing pandemic restrictions, and the potential work stoppage in 2022 would also shelf those plans. That meant that 2023 would be the target date, which seemed a long way off at the time. 2 years of saving up followed, before the season's schedule was released in late 2022. After hours of routing and re-routing, I had a plan in place.

There's something iconic about a great American road trip. So many movies and books have been made about crossing this massive country, taking in the cities, the deserts, the mountains and the swamps. When I was still completing the 92 I thought nothing of driving halfway across England, but these 4-hour drives to Yorkshire were nothing in comparison to the size of the United States. People in Texas could drive twice as long and still be in the same state, and flying from New York to Los Angeles requires over 6 hours in a plane – further than London to Baku, a flight that crosses almost all of mainland Europe, or about the same as a flight from Boston back to London. The sheer size of the country is difficult to grasp for a non-American like me, so perhaps I didn't know what I would be getting myself in to, but it would be one hell of a challenge.

And this is where you join me. I realised that some people might be interested following a hapless Brit navigate the United States for a month, taking in all 30 Major League ballparks along the way. This book is a collection of my experiences and stories, from meeting wonderful people to wasting hours at airports waiting for flights. I hope you enjoy the story, and maybe you might be inspired to attempt a similar trip yourself. Either way, this is the tale of the 30 in 35 challenge.

1

YANKEE STADIUM

"You can observe a lot just by watching"

Yogi Berra

As the son of a former military nurse and a director in an aviation company, good organisation is probably in my genes. Our family have always been on time to everything (in fact, we're usually the people that are irritatingly early – sorry about that!) and I don't think I've ever been anywhere without at least some element of planning. Perhaps this is why a once-in-a-lifetime trip, visiting all 30 ballparks in a little over a month, was the kind of organisational challenge that I was always going to relish, or perhaps it was the collector trait in me that wanted to cross them all off in one go. Either way, it would be impossible to understate the logistical puzzle that I had to solve.

In the days leading up to the trip, it became all-consuming. Having finished work for the summer half a week before I was set to fly out to the USA, I was able to put the final touches in place. And yet I was becoming more and more anxious; what if something were to go wrong? What if my flight from London was cancelled, and the challenge was over before it began? I knew that once I was sitting on the plane and the journey was underway this would all leave my mind, and I could begin to enjoy it, so it couldn't come soon enough.

Heathrow Airport is one of my favourite places in the world. It's a gleaming, cavernous hive of activity; a place through which thousands of people pass hour to start an adventure. Terminal 5 is its crowning jewel, with the gigantic space dedicated entirely to British Airways flights. So many of my trips have begun there in recent years; whether it's flights to Newcastle to watch football or my baseball pilgrimage to Fenway Park the previous year, entering the terminal always meant the start of something incredible.

Thanks to British Airways, I had the opportunity to make the journey to New York City in business class – or, more accurately, their (relatively) new Club Suite. Having only made transatlantic flights in economy before this, the opportunity to have so much desk space, plated meals and a fully reclining seat offered a huge upgrade, and it will be difficult to ever go back to normal seats again. This also meant I had access to a lounge at Heathrow, and with it a (pretty good) free breakfast and views of the runway to start off the journey. I was relaxed before even stepping onto the plane.

In the weeks before the trip, the weather in the UK had been awful. As a Brit, I love talking about the weather, but even I was getting fed up of discussing the constant rain and low temperatures. This had become especially frustrating knowing that I would be encountering almost perfect conditions in the US, even if Arizona and Texas would push my limits with their heatwaves. With this in mind, I'm sure you could understand my joy when I stepped off the plane at JFK Airport in New York to blue skies and temperatures approaching 30 degrees Celsius (that's closing in on 85 Fahrenheit if you prefer).

This wasn't my first visit to the city, so I didn't feel the need to do all the cliché tourist attractions – in fact, with previous experience of jetlag in mind, I decided to head straight to my hotel to get some rest before the game that night. Having previously stayed in budget hotels for extended trips (some of the motels I stayed in during my EURO 2016 experience still haunt my dreams), I had made sure to book places which were a little nicer, although budget would be a concern considering I needed to book 35 nights at nearly 30 different hotels. The Midtown West would definitely fall into that "budget" category, but the location – directly next to the iconic Penn Station – couldn't be beaten. After a short rest, it was off to watch the Yankees in the first of many games!

Although I had been to Yankee Stadium before, it was for a football match – when I visited New York in 2018, the Yankees were on a road trip and the stadium was used for NYCFC's local derby with the Red Bulls. I had spent the day doing typical tourist things with my friend Ben, so we got there with little time to spare, which meant I had barely explored the ballpark and what it had to offer.

And I quickly realised that I had missed out. The place is an absolute cathedral of baseball. Although it might not be as historic as Fenway Park or Wrigley Field, it's certainly the most iconic ballpark to a global audience. Ask a Brit on the street which baseball teams they know, and odds are the Yankees will be the only answer they can give. They've probably heard of Babe Ruth and Mickey Mantle too. Yankees caps are worn worldwide – even by people who have no awareness that baseball even exists as a sport – and the story of Aaron Judge chasing the home run record in 2022 was reported on British sports networks. With that in mind, I couldn't think of a better place to start the journey.

You could feel the history within the ballpark. I loved that the concourses had huge banners hanging down with the names of some of the legends that had worn the pinstripes over the years. There were some cool easter eggs too – including giant bobbleheads of Babe Ruth and Mickey Mantle hiding in one of the corridors, and a Yankees branded Mickey Mouse standing next to a Statue of Liberty decked out in team gear. You wouldn't get that at the football!

When doing my research and planning this trip, I'd read a lot about how expensive tickets were at Yankee Stadium. I never want to be negative about a sports team, but I would have to agree with the many voices online about this. Close to 85 dollars for a seat in the top level felt a tad excessive when selecting seats, especially when you consider that most teams sell those tickets for a fraction of the price. In the Yankees' defence, I probably picked one of the worst games for value (a Subway Series game against the Mets), but in an era where the sport is trying to engage younger fans I do worry that many must be priced out of watching one of its biggest teams.

However, that seat, whilst high up and far away from the action, did afford me a fantastic view of the ballpark. And one of the best things about sitting up high is that you're guaranteed to be near people who love the game. Quite often, seats behind home plate are filled with corporate guests or influencers who are more interested in being seen at a game than actually following along or talking about baseball, but instead I was sat next to a couple from Arizona who had spent a few weeks back in their birth town to catch some games.

The game flew by. Carlos Rodon was starting on the mount for the Yankees – a former Giant, who left at the conclusion of the the 2022 season after only signing a one-year contract. He had been injured for most of his time in New York, but you could see that he was starting to get back to being the ace that he was capable of giving, only giving up one run through this start and earning his first win for the team. The Mets, started with Jose Quintana, another established pitcher who had played minimal baseball in 2023, and similarly had a fairly good start before giving up a couple of earned runs. The scoring was finished after the fourth inning, and despite the Yankees' famously slow pace of games we were done in a little over two and a half hours, with the home side winning 3-1.

With that, it was time to head back to my hotel after an extremely long day. It was about 10pm by the time I got through the door, but of course in UK time that was 3 in the morning; I'd been up for 23 hours. That said, it was absolutely worth it.

Of course, with my trip covering so many different locations, it's only human to want to somehow rank them. People love to find a favourite – in fact, when telling others about this adventure the most common questions asked in response are about which ballpark will be the best, or the stadium I'm looking forward to the most. Therefore, it seems prudent to score each ballpark in an attempt to come up with some kind of league table at the end. There doesn't seem to be a standard system for these rankings, so I'm going to create my own criteria. You may find them useful, but I make no apologies if you don't…

Location:

This is something that I don't really see mentioned when others visit ballparks. There are two key consequences of where a stadium is located – the backdrop (think PNC Park and the bridges, or Oracle Park and the bay) and the ease of access. I'd rather visit somewhere that's a breeze to get to on public transport than have to travel miles out of town. Arguably, the two factors go hand-in-hand; a central location helps with the backdrop.

With that latter criteria in mind, Yankee Stadium scores strongly, as it's right on a subway line. New York is a huge place, and whilst it can be daunting for a newcomer to get around it's probably the only major city in the US with a truly substantial subway network. It's a breeze to get from Manhattan to the Bronx, and that's something that really should be valued. However, there isn't really a view of the Big Apple from any part of the ballpark (I appreciate the size of the place makes that tough, even if it were closer to the iconic skyscrapers that dominate the New York skyline), so I'm limiting the score to 7/10.

Concessions:

As a football (OK, soccer) fan, one of the things I've watched with great interest in the past 12 months is the rise of "footy scran", a Twitter account which highlights the best food on offer across the world of football stadia. Out with the dry burgers and stale hot dog buns, and in with genuinely tasty and innovative meals.

Except American sports got there first. Many words have been written by fans and journalists alike about the food options at various venues across baseball, basketball and American football – more than I could ever hope to replicate. It may be expensive, but you're never going to leave a ballpark hungry. As an extremely picky eater, I'm never going to experience the full range of what every stadium has on offer (and even if I wasn't, there's only so much one man can eat), but this score is for the range available.

At Yankee Stadium, there are a few well-known dishes that were recommended to me. The limited edition "99 burger" paying tribute to Aaron Judge sells out every game, and English fans loved the innovative bowl of chicken which fits over their drink. I really liked the idea of having a steakhouse on site, but ultimately I went to Lobel's for their steak sandwich following a raft of recommendations. It was absolutely incredible. Despite costing over $20, the steak was juicy and melted in my mouth, and it was perfectly filling. Possibly the best food I've ever eaten at a sporting event, it set the bar high for the rest of the trip. I also had the relatively standard ice cream in a mini helmet, but bonus marks to the Yankees for selling scoops in a variety of flavours rather than the ubiquitous soft-serve variety. Setting the bar high, I'm going to have to score the Yankees 10/10.

Atmosphere:

Partly down to the fans at each ballpark, and partly down to how friendly and welcoming the stadium employees are. The United States has a varied reputation for this, and like many major world cities New York is not globally regarded as a particularly friendly location (especially compared with the famed southern hospitality that I would hopefully experience later in the trip). However, everyone I spoke to was happy to take photos or have a quick chat.

Perhaps the Yankees had an advantage on the former count as well – the Subway Series is one of the bigger rivalries they have (albeit nowhere near as fierce as that against the Red Sox). A healthy number of Mets fans had made the trip, so there was chanting for both teams, but it was strangely subdued for a large portion of the game; possibly due to neither side having an outstanding season so far, with the Yankees sitting bottom of their division at the time of writing. Because of this, I'm going to have to give them a score of 6/10.

Weather:

OK, this one is outside of any team's control – to an extent. But the weather is important. You don't want to be watching a game in freezing conditions, and if it's unbearably hot an enclosed, air conditioned ballpark is a welcome bonus. I'm about as pale as they come and I appreciate any form of shade or temperature control.

New York seems to be fairly middle-of-the-road as American weather goes. It might not have the blazing heat of Arizona or the sheer humidity of Florida, but as a Brit with limited experience of good weather I still find it a little too hot (give me San Francisco any day!). There was a good amount of cover in the ballpark for any potential rain, and despite it becoming a little chilly later in the evening it was a surprisingly pleasant set of conditions for watching a ballgame. Yankee Stadium therefore scores 8/10.

Additional Features:

This is something that may well be unique to baseball. Certainly in the UK, football traditionalists reserve a certain level of contempt for anything that may be in a stadium which distracts fans from the game. But in baseball, it's nice to have something else in the park that you can visit before or during the matchup – whether that's the stingray tank at Tropicana Field or Eutaw Street at Camden Yards.

For someone visiting a lot of ballparks in a very short space of time, I think it's essential to have a standout feature to remember the place by, which is why this category has as much weighting as the food options or the friendliness of the staff. Yankee Stadium did have a few things – the aforementioned statues in the concourses and a museum in the 200 level, but I was slightly struck by how functional a lot of the ballpark was compared to what I had seen elsewhere. Considering this was built relatively recently at a significant cost, I was expecting a little more. This one has to go down as a fairly low 5/10.

Overall:

With a somewhat middle-of-the-road score of 36/50, Yankee Stadium became simultaneously the best and worst ballpark of the trip so far! Read on to see how the others compare...

2

CITI FIELD

"The Mets have shown me more ways to lose than I even knew existed"

Casey Stengel

Fifteen years ago, there was a seismic shift in the position of power in English football. The Abu Dhabi United Group – effectively the sovereign wealth fund of one of the wealthiest nations in the world – completed the purchase of Manchester City. Up until this point, City were a side that had been established in the Premier League, but far from a superpower; indeed, they had been relegated multiple times, and were some way off challenging for even the secondary European competitions.

However, within a matter of months, everything changed. Immediate financial support allowed them to sign Robinho, at the time one of the biggest transfers in the country, and ever since they have invested heavily to build the strongest possible squad. Under some of the most respected managers in world football, they've gone on to achieve unbelievable success, including a historic "treble" in 2023 after winning the Premier League, the FA Cup and the Champions' League within the space of a month.

Perhaps most significantly, though, this was against the backdrop of sharing a city with arguably one of the most recognisable and best-supported sporting institutions in the world. Manchester United are a powerhouse not just of football, but of sports and business. With some estimates that nearly a tenth of the world's population following the club at their peak, even those who are not interested in sport are aware of their profile, and under Sir Alex Ferguson they achieved a period of unparalleled success. They still hold the record for most Premier League titles, and were the first club to achieve a treble back in 1999 – not to mention a similarly successful spell in between 2007 and 2009 where they won everything there was to win in the European game.

The Manchester City takeover, therefore, has added huge significance to a historic rivalry across the city. In the past, it was something of a one-sided affair, with United always the favourites and City rarely challenging for anywhere near their level of glory. Indeed, Ferguson famously described the blue team as "noisy neighbours", and it was seen as somewhat petty when City put up billboards of star signing Carlos Tevez in 2009 after signing him from the Red Devils. As time has gone on though, the Abu-Dhabi backed side have blown past United's achievements (perhaps helped along by the decline the club has experienced since Ferguson left in 2013).

There are some parallels that can be drawn between the United-City rivalry and that shared by the Yankees and the Mets. Both pairs of teams are based in one of the biggest cities in their respective countries; ones that are passionate about sport as well. They both feature one historic side with unparalleled levels of success (just as United have the most league titles, the Yankees have won an incredible 27 World Series in their history) against another who have less history but are willing to spend to succeed. It remains to be seen, however, whether the New York rivalry evolves to the same extent.

In 2020, during the pandemic that shut down sport for so many fans, Steve Cohen acquired a 97.2% stake in the New York Mets – a side that only came into existence in 1962 as an expansion side following the relocation of both the Giants and the Dodgers across the country to California (more on that soon). The Mets had experienced a reasonable amount of success in their short history – two world series, a smattering of pennants and division titles as well as a few hall of fame candidates – but nothing beyond what would be considered ordinary in the world of Major League Baseball. However, Cohen would go on to invest heavily in the side in an attempt to make them superpowers in the sport, building one of the most expensive rosters in history.

With Max Scherzer, Justin Verlander, Jose Quintana and Kodai Senga all signed to extremely well-paying contracts since Cohen took over (with the first two earning over $40 million per year each), the payroll increased significantly in an attempt to build an all-star starting rotation – and that's not to mention the side acquiring Francisco Lindor and re-signing slugger

Pete Alonso and closer Edwin Diaz to similarly large deals. The Mets were clearly aiming to consistently challenge for the World Series moving forward – something that could potentially push the Yankees to perform even stronger, and in turn drive standards across the city.

Except it didn't quite work out. Baseball is a funny sport, where building the best team doesn't always guarantee you success. Perhaps the closest parallel to this was in Los Angeles during the 2010s and early 2020s, where excellent player development through the Minor Leagues coupled with big-name trades such as Mookie Betts and Albert Pujols had led to a grand total of one World Series despite leading the division for the best part of a decade. In particular, pitchers only tend to play one out of every five games, leading to inconsistent results if too much money is thrown at individual players. From the hitting side of things, the very best players tend to only get on base somewhere between 30 and 40 percent of time time. Simply put, baseball is a very difficult game with a lot of randomness involved, and Cohen was discovering this after spending the best part of a billion dollars chasing success.

None of this could possibly detract from my 30 in 35 tour though, which had got off to an incredible start the previous night. Ironically, I had seen the Mets play just across town, where they went down 3-1 to the Yankees in a game that tied the Subway Series for the year. Perhaps the power was finely balanced, or perhaps both sides were just having extremely poor seasons. I had struggled during the night, with both jetlag and a very noisy hotel combining to rob me of many hours of sleep, but I woke up to an unbelievable outpouring of support on social media for the trip. It looked like this challenge had resonated with hundreds of others, and I was hugely grateful to see so many people comment with their own experiences and messages of support. The baseball community does genuinely seem to be the most welcoming and encouraging that I've ever come across, and it reassured me that I had made a good choice to embark upon this challenge.

First on the agenda for the day was finding a traditional American diner for some breakfast. Thankfully, Andrew's was a short walk from my hotel, and offered up a simple but tasty meal of eggs, potatoes and toast for a little under $10. For a relatively central location in one of the busiest cities in the world, I thought that this was a bit of a bargain, and I made a mental note to drop in the following day if I was awake in time. Checking the weather for the day made me a little nervous – rain was forecast, and this had been something I had completely forgotten to check so far – meaning I quickly tried to sort out some contingency plans. In the worst case scenario, I could accept that I'd visited Citi Field in the past, but it would make the challenge a bit of a damp squib to reduce it to 29 ballparks so early on.

Having been on holiday to New York City a few years ago, during which I visited all the key tourist sites, I elected to make today a more restful day. I had covered eight miles on foot the previous day, was still adjusting to the time difference and was aware of the excessive heat warning, so I thought it would be prudent to spend some time preparing for the upcoming days rather than simply revisiting famous sights for the sake of it. In fact, I had walked through Times Square the previous day, and it had reminded me how underwhelming it was during the daytime (and, indeed, how it had suffered the same fate as much of central London, with plenty of tourist trap souvenir shops popping up and blighting the landscape). This isn't to suggest that New York is a bad place for a visit, however – I truly enjoyed my trip five years ago, but I was acutely aware that 35 days of intensive sightseeing and long distance walking would more than take its toll on me.

After several relaxed hours spent planning, updating my blog and organising to meet other like-minded baseball fans later in the trip, it was time to head to Citi Field. It was more down to luck than judgement that I was staying so close to Penn Station, but it worked in my favour as it made the trip extremely easy. The New York subway is regarded as one of the most confusing in the world, with its multitude of routes and stopping patterns which change depending on the time of day, but I was able to take the Long Island Railroad straight to the ballpark, which had a station on its doorstep. Not every city has such well-integrated public transport, so it's important to recognise that New York does well here. Just as the news had predicted, it was extremely hot, so I was grateful to enter via the air conditioned Jackie Robinson rotunda. Robinson never played for the Mets, retiring only four years after the team had even come into existence, but his story is firmly rooted in the city (his entire career was spent with the Brooklyn Dodgers). Every team has retired his iconic number 42 (and I'd recommend watching the excellent biopic of the same name, featuring the late Chadwick Boseman), but it's nice to see a club going even further in recognising the man's enormous impact on baseball.

Citi Field opened in 2009 – the same year as the new Yankee Stadium – and replaced the much-loved Shea Stadium that was home to the Mets for much of their history. Some fans long for the older ballpark, but as someone that had visited the newer location a few years ago I liked the progress that had been made. Newer sporting venues often attract criticism for being large corporate structures compared to the older places which seem to be filled with history, but Citi Field seems to incorporate a lot of the team's history and traditions into a more modern design. I particularly liked the home run apple in centre field, which raises and gives a visual representation of the city's nickname every time a Mets player hits one out of the park, as well as the previously mentioned rotunda that represents one of the most memorable entrances to any ballpark in the Majors. They had also managed to incorporate the old stadium's bridge into the outfield, giving some character to an often neglected area of ballpark design.

This game was also my first experience of a staple of baseball – it was a giveaway game. Numerous times each year, teams give free items to all (or the first few thousand) attendees – it depends on how cynical you are whether you consider this to be a welcome sign of appreciation from the management or an attempt to get fans through the gate for an otherwise unappealing matchup. The most popular items to give out are bobbleheads, which are hugely collectible in their own right (as a Brit, I always find this astonishing, since they seem to barely be considered a novelty in the United Kingdom), but for this particular game they were handing out Mets soccer jerseys. I'm not quite sure how they decided on this for a giveaway, but it was certainly a welcome souvenir! This meant that there were huge queues a full two hours before the game – it's certainly an effective way to get people in early.

After getting into the ballpark, my attention was immediately caught by the Mets' authentics store, where they were selling game-used memorabilia. Specifically, they had grab bags – or, to be precise, a tombola where you picked a slip of paper corresponding to a mystery item. I couldn't resist, and ended up with an autographed photo of all-star Daniel Vogelbach, who was starting that night as the designated hitter. After that success, I went to get the Pat LaFrieda's steak sandwich that had been so highly recommended to me, and found my seat for the game.

Much like the previous night, this one was a pitcher's duel, with both Kodai Senga and Josiah Gray giving excellent performances, with the visiting Nationals 1-0 up going into the eighth inning. Despite this, the crowd was in good spirits, making lots of noise and really getting behind their team. However, after the Mets had levelled things up in the bottom of the eighth, the teams left the field before the ground crew pulled out the protective covering. Initially I was confused – there was no sign of rain – but it suddenly dawned on me that the flashes I had noticed earlier weren't from the stadium lights. A thunderstorm of truly epic proportions was rolling into Queens, and the game was delayed for nearly two hours to let it pass. The vast majority of the crowd headed for the exit, and recognising that I had still seen the bulk of the game I decided to join them – albeit after the worst of the rain had passed. After all, I had an early start in the morning to catch a flight...

And of course, we need to rate the ballpark. I'm not going to let the storm at the end of the game dampen my spirits, so these are based on everything up to that point.

Location:

This one is a little bit tricky. Citi Field is a bit more out of town than Yankee Stadium (it's fairly deep into Queen's, and only really accessible by a subway or train ride that takes you a fair way out of the city), but it's in an area steeped in sporting pedigree. The iconic Flushing Meadows is almost next door, providing something interesting for tennis aficionados, and the original site of the World Fair is only a little further away. It's also near the location of the team's previous home, Shea Stadium, so at least the team is staying close to its roots. Despite all this, the area feels a little bare, and there's no real reason to get here early unless you're going straight into the ballpark. There are plans to build more nearby, and I'm sure this will improve it, but for now I'm giving it a 7/10.

Concessions:

Perhaps this is one of the downsides of visiting both ballparks in the same city on consecutive days – sporting venues usually try to reflect the local cuisine, and having already had a breathtaking steak sandwich at Yankee Stadium I was faced with more of the same here.

That said, I had been recommended the fillet mignon sandwich at Pat LaFrieda's – and as I was in New York, who was I to turn down a steakhouse? As with any ballpark food, it wasn't cheap, but I firmly believe you have to ignore the pricing at a game and just enjoy what you're eating (and enjoy it I did, with the ciabatta-style baguette more than making up for the slightly less flavourful meat). I also noticed a stand specialising in chips (if you're British) in the outfield, and they offered up some superb cajun fries later in the game. Bonus marks to the Mets for having a deli on-site as well as the standard options of pizzas, burgers and hot dogs – but it didn't quite measure up to the Lobel's at Yankee Stadium, which looks like it will become the standard against which everything else is measured. I think a fair mark here is 9/10.

Atmosphere:

With the Mets arguably being the second most popular baseball team in the city, they're going to need to offer something a bit different to attract fans – and friendliness is usually an easy way to go about that. I found the ushers and fans to be very helpful and chatty, with several wanting to talk about my challenge. The actual atmosphere once the game had started was incredible, especially when you consider how poorly the team had been performing. There's also a bonus point awarded for the presence of the Cowbell Man, who went around each block making some noise and encouraging fans during the later innings. It might not have been a sellout crowd, but the fans made a lot of noise and really made Citi Field a special place to be. It's not quite the electric atmosphere of Fenway (or English football) though, so it's earning a score of 9/10.

Weather:

It feels harsh to score this any differently to Yankee Stadium, despite the heat and thunderstorm warnings in effect; if I had done these two ballparks the other way round, I would most likely have been a lot more harsh towards the Yankees. It's in the same city, and has a similar amount of shade (but still no retractible roof, albeit for understandable reasons). I don't think I can blame the ballpark for the thunderstorm, and up until that point it was a perfect set of conditions to sit and watch a game. With that in mind, I'm going to be boring and give Citi Field an identical score of 8/10.

Additional Features:

As previously mentioned, I love the home run apple – it's the sort of fun feature that could easily define a park and provide a landmark for fans. However, it's a little understated in the context of the ballpark, and something that could easily be overlooked. The rotunda, however, gives visitors a truly iconic first impression of the stadium, and is surely worth points on its own. There could be a few more references to the team's history – or, indeed, its planned future, given Cohen's significant investment in the side and the obvious ambitions he harbours. I think, therefore, it's fair to give the Mets a score of 8/10 here.

Overall:

With a total score of 41/10, Citi Field scores more highly than Yankee Stadium (which I think is fair – I genuinely find it a better location to watch baseball, even though the team isn't anywhere near as iconic). Next up is a trip to Toronto, and I was very excited to see how the Rogers Cenrer measures up against the New York ballparks...

3

ROGERS CENTRE

"This is what we dream of doing"

Bo Bichette

One of the biggest criticisms that British people tend to make of baseball – and, indeed, many of the most popular American sports – is that it has limited popularity outside of the US. Almost everyone that follows the game will likely have heard someone complain that the final games of the season are called the World Series despite it being contested between two North American teams; I'm not entirely sure if these people are unaware of the level of enthusiasm for baseball in Japan and South Korea, or if they just think they're being funny. Either way, it's always intrigued me that the Major Leagues have 29 of the 30 teams based in the United States, with one located over the border in neighbouring Canada.

After two days spent in New York City – hardly the most adventurous start to the challenge, considering I'd visited both ballparks in the past and barely stepped outside of the most popular tourist areas – I was looking forward to heading somewhere new. Getting to a different city felt like the real start of the tour; I knew before long I would be getting up early and travelling on a regular basis, so a relatively short journey would be a good way to start this off.

This was to be the first of many flights over the next few weeks, and I wanted to get into the habit of using the extended time waiting at airports to post updates on Instagram, Twitter and so on. One of the major changes to society that I've noticed in the last decade is the effect of smartphones and social media on people. Yes, I grew up with Facebook too, but it never dominated my childhood. Without sounding old-fashioned, it does seem like people spend their entire lives on their phones nowadays, more interested in sharing a perfectly curated selfie with thousands of others that they've never met than actually forming meaningful connections with colleagues or neighbours.

In fact, it might be worse than that. I remember watching a documentary called *The Social Dilemma*, which, despite being overly dramatic (with some very bad acting in certain segments) makes the astute observation that social media allows us to create our own "echo chambers", in which we tend to follow others with similar views to us and become more entrenched in our own beliefs. After all, if everyone we see says the same things, it starts to make us think that it has to be right. The documentary goes on to claim this has contributed to the polarisation of politics, and I'm inclined to agree.

Now, the irony of this rant is not lost on me. After all, I'm writing this with the intention of sharing it with strangers who have found out about my journey online. But that's why I want to highlight the positive side of social media and the connections that the internet allows us to form. Generally speaking, as long as you stay away from politics and contentious issues, you can join like-minded communities and meet some amazing people. And I have to say I'm yet to find a friendlier group of people than the online baseball community.

I started out fairly cautiously in sharing this challenge with the world, but even with a limited online presence I've been shocked with the response. It seems that every single person that's read about my plans has been excited for me, with many sharing extremely helpful tips about their city or ballpark and others offering help. I've had MLB social media managers follow me, offers of interviews with radio broadcasters, and many many people telling me they're buying me a beer when I reach their city. If the rest of the world were this friendly, I doubt we'd have half the problems that currently seem to plague society.

This is ultimately a long-winded way of saying thank you to one Blue Jays fan in particular. About two months before starting the trip, I joined a few Facebook groups to ask for advice and share my journey. Once again, I was taken aback by the reaction, with hundreds of strangers wishing me well and giving me advice about various aspects of the journey. Amongst a very kind and helpful group, Brian stood out. In an example of how wonderful the internet can be, he offered somebody that he'd never met (and only ever seen post once on social media) his season ticket seats for the game, to save me having to buy a ticket myself. I was speechless, and needless to say very grateful.

They were truly excellent seats as well. After landing in Toronto – it was a real novelty to land on an island just outside of the city, and *walk* to the mainland – and after checking into my hotel, there was a brief chance to freshen up at my hotel before heading over to the Rogers Centre. My first impression of the city was extremely positive. It was located on the scenic shores of Lake Ontario, with some boats moored up on my route from the airport to the hotel, and much of the city felt modern and inviting. Coming from New York, it felt like a different world, and I loved it. The Canadian city was, like much of the United States, experiencing a heatwave, but it wasn't uncomfortable and it was a particularly pleasant place to walk through on my way to the game.

The Blue Jays' ballpark was one of the stops I was most looking forward to during the trip. I really got into the sport during the COVID pandemic, and collecting baseball cards was my gateway drug. I learned a lot about the best players on each team, and how to read and understand the statistics printed on the back. Many an evening was spent staring at the slugging percentage of Mike Trout and the earned run average of Clayton Kershaw, but there was one card that stood out in particular to me. Bo Bichette's 2020 Stadium Club rookie card was absolutely gorgeous.

It was a panoramic shot of the shortstop, taken from an extremely low angle with the CN Tower in the background. I was captivated by the photography, the player – it was such a cool name, and it helped that he was having a genuinely good year – and the ballpark itself. The sliding roof, the vivid blue seats, and the iconic background all combined to give the only Major League Baseball venue in Canada a sense of intrigue that left me longing to visit.

With it being another giveaway game – this time a Caribbean themed bucket hat as part of a party night – I got there early, and took the chance to explore. My initial impression was that this ballpark was very different to the two that I had already visited, with more enclosed concourses but significantly better team branding all around the park, and a much more modern shop. I picked up a Blue Jays cap and logo ball, and was able to get an exceptionally cool Vladimir Guerrero Jr baseball card with a piece of an actual baseball that he hit earlier this season. An added bonus was that I had become so used to American currency, I was looking at the prices and expecting things to be much more expensive than they actually were, so it was a welcome surprise to see that a smaller amount of money than expected had left my account after picking up the memorabilia.

Kevin Gausman was starting for the Blue Jays – and so for the second time in three days, I would be watching a former Giants ace take to the mound. Gausman was arguably one of the catalysts of San Francisco's hugely successful 2021 season, in which they won a franchise record 107 games and beat the Dodgers to win the NL West. Over that season and the previous one, he had been the best pitcher on the team, and losing him to the Blue Jays that summer was a huge blow. Gausman was a player that I had never seen live, so I was delighted to see that he was playing during my time in Toronto. Up against him was the Angels' newest pitching acquisition in Lucas Giolito, who had joined from the Chicago White Sox just two days earlier. Unfairly on Giolito, most fans were disappointed to see that he was starting, as Shohei Ohtani was originally meant to be the starting pitcher before a hastily-arranged doubleheader in Detroit the previous day altered the rotation, but he was a competent player and it let into an appealing matchup for my visit.

And Ohtani started the game with a bang. The man is having quite possibly the greatest season of any baseball player ever, and he carried that form into this game with a home run to right field on the first pitch he saw. Gausman didn't have a chance. Such is the popularity of the two-way phenomenon, the Blue Jays fans applauded the shot as if it were their own team that had gone ahead. However, the home side fired back quickly, and after Matt Chapman (in the second) and Danny Jansen (in the third) also hit solo shots the Blue Jays had taken the lead. To an extent, this game summarised the Angels' season; moments of absolute brilliance by the talismanic Ohtani getting fans off their feet, but the rest of the team failing to build upon it and the side ultimately falling to defeat.

There was some hope late on, with the Blue Jays' closer Jordan Romano getting into a jam in the top of the ninth and loading the bases. Yimi Garcia had the unenviable task of taking over the situation and trying to record the final out – and he managed to do so in just two pitches, as the entire ballpark breathed a sigh of relief.

And so, that was the ballgame. It was a truly memorable evening, with the home side being in control for the vast majority of the game, and the slightly more relaxed nature of the match meant I was able to spend some time exploring various parts of the park and checking out different vantage points. I was able to meet a few other ballpark chasers who were at various points of their journeys, and there was an excellent opportunity to check out the new Ballpark Social area in the top deck.

But how did the ballpark hold up in my estimations?

Location:

Toronto is a much more compact city than many in its neighbouring country, and this makes the Blue Jays' home a more attractive place to visit. Situated within walking distance of the majority of the city's landmarks and a short subway journey from the rest, it was easy for me to do a few tourist activities before catching the game. There's a reasonable amount of parking nearby, and you're less than a mile from an international airport. I'd struggle to think of a more perfect location to put a ballpark. It doesn't hurt that the city itself is stunning as well. 10/10

Concessions:

Did you really go to Canada unless you get some poutine? In my case, yes. After two days of steak, I was craving some chicken, and I managed to find a branch of local fast food staple Mary Brown's in the ballpark. It might have been the boring choice considering what was on offer, but sometimes a meal of chicken strips and potato wedges is precisely what you need. It didn't stand out, but that's on me for choosing chicken strips at a baseball game when there's so much else on offer.

I also headed over to the value section in the outfield; personally I don't mind stadium prices, but they are a bone of contention to many others, so having a simple menu of the most popular items at extremely reasonable prices was a great move by the Blue Jays. I grabbed some mini pretzels for less than $5, which worked out as less than £3 – you really can't argue with that! Even more impressively, they were selling some beers for what converts to less than £3.50, and water for under £1.50.

The ballpark also had a huge amount of options in the newly renovated outfield section, including a pick and mix candy wall and other value options. Honestly, I couldn't fault Rogers Centre in this regard, so it scores another 10/10.

Atmosphere:

The stereotype of Canadians is that they're polite almost to a fault, and I was keen to see how this would translate into a sporting experience. Some might assume that this would create a sterile atmosphere, but it was absolutely electric throughout the game. The Blue Jays fans showed up in numbers and made some incredible noise, and this added to the friendliness of the staff made it a memorable occasion. My only criticism was that there wasn't a vast amount of fan engagement between innings, which means it won't be a perfect score, but I think 9/10 is pretty fair.

Weather:

Time to clarify a ruling on this category – does a roof on the stadium negate a city having truly unbearable weather? It makes the hottest climates somewhat tolerable, but it also takes a lot of charm away from the ballpark. I'm not going to penalise any venue that takes steps to ensure the comfort of fans (especially considering the extreme weather that certain parts of North America experience, and that's before we see the effects of climate change over the next few years), so Rogers Centre scores strongly here. Toronto seems perfect to me – it gets warm but not uncomfortable, and even during the heatwave it didn't feel ridiculous. Being on the shore of Lake Ontario probably helps – I'm sure with some of the cities I have coming up I'll be desperate to be back in Toronto! It's just a shame the roof was closed on my visit when the weather was so nice – so I'm going to be a little mean and give it 9/10.

Additional Features:

I've already mentioned it a couple of times, but the renovations at Rogers Centre have made a huge difference. At Yankee Stadium, the fans I spent the game chatting with told me that the old seats in Toronto had you facing away from home plate, and the place felt a little sterile. The addition of Park Social seems to have transformed the ballpark into an exciting place to be, and strangely enough it made the cheaper seats more desirable than the premium areas. That said, a lot of the concourses felt slightly empty, and it does appear that more could be done to give the stadium some Blue Jays branding; this was a similar issue I found at Yankee Stadium. The newer areas rescues the score somewhat, and it scores 7/10.

Overall:

This might be a surprise to some, but Rogers Centre finishes with a score of 45/50, making it the new leader and an early contender for best ballpark of the entire trip. One of the favourites is up next though, so it may not last long at the top...

4

PNC PARK

"Any time you have an opportunity to make a difference in this world and don't, then you are wasting your time on Earth"

Roberto Clemente

It's been interesting to see the reaction that I have been getting as a Brit in America. When I'm abroad, I always feel a little self-conscious when starting to speak, as if my accent will make me sound like an outsider, especially in a setting like a ballpark where British people might be rarely seen. However, the reactions have been overwhelmingly positive; everyone I've spoken to has taken a genuine interest in where I'm from and my reasons for visiting their city, and people have been incredibly welcoming. A common stereotype is that Americans love English accents (I guess it comes from old movies), and from what I've seen so far it seems to be true.

Another stereotype that seems to come up a lot is that British people love talking about the weather. I imagine it comes from the fact that, in the United Kingdom, it offers so many talking points; it's not unheard of for us to experience four seasons in the space of a few hours. In the weeks preceding the trip, I had gone through days of gorgeous sunshine followed by weeks of rain, and the unpredictability was beginning to both frustrate me and leave me longing for my first flight to the States to draw ever closer and escape the cold and damp conditions.

Conditions in America were looking good – several days of hot and sunny weather, with a few heatwaves thrown in for good weather. To tell the truth I was slightly anxious about how I would cope with the extreme warmth in places such as Texas and Arizona (not to mention the humidity and potential stuffiness of Florida), but I had decided that it would be better than the forecast back in England.

One thing I hadn't banked on, however, was thunderstorms. In hindsight, it was an obvious concern, but I had naively assumed that the US only experienced this during the spring. I was given a powerful reminder of this on just the second stop of my trip, when the Mets game had been paused for nearly two hours after a storm had rolled through New York and generated a level of rainfall that would be unheard of in the UK, and during the delay I had decided to check the forecast for some of my upcoming stops. What I saw concerned me. Pittsburgh was due similar storms for most of the weekend I was scheduled to be there, including the entire evening of my planned Saturday evening game.

Thankfully, I had a backup in mind – my flight to Seattle on the Sunday would not leave until early evening, and the Pirates had an early game that day, so as long as there was some break in the storm I would be able to catch the majority of a game at some point over the two days I was in Pittsburgh.

I woke up on Saturday morning in Toronto, sad to be leaving what had proven to be an incredible city. It felt as though my tour might have already peaked at Rogers Centre, but I was keen to see what PNC Park had to offer; regarded as one of the most scenic parks in all of baseball, I would be lucky enough to walk across one of the iconic bridges that paint the backdrop to the stadium.

I had booked a two-legged flight to get from Toronto to Pittsburgh, which would be a new and slightly stressful experience for me. It was nice to pre-clear US customs and immigration in Canada, which gave me some peace of mind for my connection in Washington DC. In the end, things worked well and I even had time during my short layover to get some food for the second leg of the journey. The flight to Pittsburgh included a flyover of the city, which looked beautiful from the air. Having spent my time in much larger locations so far on my trip, it was surprising to see such a compact city centre. It only made me more excited to get to the game later that evening.

After a short Uber ride to my hotel, it was time to walk to the stadium. Thankfully, the storms that were forecast to plague the evening had passed through earlier, leaving a damp but sunny city behind that showed off its full beauty as I crossed the bridge over the Allegheny and down North

Shore Drive to the park. I was stunned at the huge queues over 90 minutes before the game was due to start – once again I had selected a giveaway game. This time, the Pirates were handing out bobbleheads (arguably the most collectible commodity in baseball circles) of their closer David Bednar, which even played out the song *Renegade* in tribute to his entrance song. After an extended wait to get in – and one of the security scanners going down – I was in the ballpark.

The stadium announcer proudly proclaimed that PNC Park was "American's favourite ballpark" – a bold claim, but one that had been backed up by a number of voices when planning my trip. I have to admit that my first impression was slightly underwhelming though – the concourses were extremely busy and felt slightly too small (although this was almost certainly down to the fact that fans had arrived early to secure a bobblehead), and it felt a little dated. All of my reservations disappeared the minute I entered the seating bowl, however, and saw the stunning view of downtown Pittsburgh from inside the ballpark. PNC is regarded as the most scenic stadium in baseball, and I found it hard to disagree. They also had, in my opinion, the best team store, if just for the Topps booth where you could get your own custom baseball card made.

Rookie Quinn Priester was on the mound for the Phillies, offering up three scoreless innings to start the game, up against Phillies star Aaron Nola. It was a brisk beginning, with both pitchers retiring hitters quickly before the game opened up in the bottom of the third as Liover Peguero hit a home run to put the home side ahead. That began a back-and-forth game as the visitors responded with a four-run fourth inning, and the Pirates hit back with two of their own in the bottom before recording another four runs in the fifth to go 7-4 ahead. The Phillies chipped away at the lead with runs in both the sixth and the eighth, before Bednar joined the game to wild celebrations and gave an extended appearance to shut down the visiting side and give bragging rights to the Pirates.

And with such an incredible game over, it was time to head back to my hotel. Just like the previous night, it was nice to be staying so close to the ballpark and have a short walk with hundreds of other fans rather than sitting on a subway for an extended period of time – after four days of non-stop travelling and sports, I was simply glad to be able to get to sleep at a sensible time! Overall, it was another great day, but one that's not complete until we give PNC Park its scores…

Location:

There's only one word for it – perfection. Pittsburgh benefits from being a city located at the point where the Ohio River splits into the Allegheny and Monongahela, which conveniently places various districts into distinct locations. PNC Park was built on the north shore of the Allegheny River, forcing the vast majority of fans to travel over one of the city's many bridges to get to the game. This gives rise to one of the most scenic approaches in baseball, and it's only a taste of what's to come.

Many words have been written in the past about the view that PNC Park offers up – often regarded as the best in all of sport – and I'm not sure I can do any better than the hundreds of others that have already commented on it. The financial district is located just over the river, meaning fans lucky enough to be sitting in the upper deck get a glorious view of the city's famous yellow bridges (including the iconic Roberto Clemente bridge, which was closed during my visit) and a multitude of skyscrapers. When I mentioned Yankee Stadium lacking a view, this is what it could have been. I could happily have spent my entire time there just looking in awe at the scenery rather than watching the game, so this stadium scores an easy 10/10.

Concessions:

Pittsburgh is perhaps the first stop of the trip that doesn't have any truly famous dishes – or at least to a Brit. Whilst New York is famed for its steakhouses and bodegas, and Canada is well-known for poutine, very few people over here would be aware of Pittsburgh's reputation for pierogis. That said, the Pirates had tried to integrate a range of options, including some local institutions such as Quaker's Steak which served up some excellent fresh chicken wings and onion rings with a variety of sauces. I had also planned to try the crab fries, but the wings had filled me up so much that I didn't get a chance to try them. There wasn't a huge amount that stood out over and above the obvious options though, so I'm going to give PNC Park a somewhat harsh score of 6/10.

Atmosphere:

I was lucky to catch a game featuring two local rivals, but boy was it loud. Both sets of fans combined to sell out the ballpark (a sign of baseball's recent spike in attendances following the pandemic) and created a fantastic atmosphere. The scoreboard operator was having a ton of fun too, putting up a number of "facts" to taunt the Pirates' cross-state rivals and amuse the home fans. I also loved the complete contrast between the somewhat intense atmosphere of the main seating bowl and the relaxed nature of the outfield riverside area – the first time I had seen such a range of environments within one ballpark. If I had one criticism to make, it was that the game had a fairly quiet start before the atmosphere grew in the closing innings, which will prevent the ballpark from getting a perfect score, but it still earns a mark of 8/10.

Weather:

Ignoring the storms that had been forecast – something that had been plaguing the Eastern United States for a while – Pittsburgh seems to have great weather. Being located along several rivers means a slight breeze blows through, reducing the impact of the heat, although the high humidity prevents this from being a perfect score. There wasn't anything that concerned me or made me feel uncomfortable during my visit, so I think a fair score would be 9/10.

Additional Features:

The Pirates have used the ballpark's location to their advantage. Most stadiums use the large space behind the outfield to put something interesting in – Citi Field had a foot court and Toronto offered up new social spaces, for instance – but PNC Park took it to another level. With the stadium located right against the Allegheny River, the team had incorporated a riverside walk with casual dining options into the right field line. There were several oversized bobbleheads and a children's play area alongside bars and restaurants, with multiple tables closer to the river than the field and several screens showing the game so fans didn't miss any of the action.

This was, however, the only real standout feature. There were some downsides too – I wasn't keen on how you couldn't walk around the park on one level; you needed to go up or down stairs to complete a lap, since the field level was raised up above the riverside walk, and the upper decks didn't offer a vast amount beyond simple access to the seats. I did like how the park incorporated spiral ramps by the left field foul pole to allow increased standing room viewing points, but it did feel like the team could offer a little more. It's not going to be the lowest score though, as the view and the riverside area were so good that on their own they earn a score of 7/10.

Overall:

PNC Park is regarded as one of the nation's favourite, and with a total of 40/50 it ranks as the highest-scoring American ballpark so far – but a little behind the Canadian Rogers Centre. The location and view do a lot of the heavy lifting here, but it's by no means a bad park as the score shows.

5

T-MOBILE PARK

"As long as I have fun playing, the stats will take care of themselves"

Ken Griffey Jr

The United Kingdom is regarded as one of the most sports-crazy nations in the world, and with good reason – it is claimed that a number of them were invented there (football, rugby and cricket to name but a few are alleged to have been invented in Britain). Participation across all levels is high as well, but perhaps the best indication of how much Brits love their sport is the level of interest at all levels of the football pyramid.

Sure, the Premier League is regarded as one of the best divisions on this planet – and sell-out crowds almost weekly demonstrate this – but attendances are extremely healthy several divisions below that. Take, for instance, Bradford City, who play in the fourth tier of English football (equivalent to Single-A in the Minor Leagues of baseball), and draw more than 10,000 supporters on a regular basis; a level of support which many top-tier clubs in other countries could only dream of. Indeed, Wrexham, who played their most recent season in an even lower-ranked league, sold out every single home game and are having to expand their stadium to accommodate all their fans.

As a result, the standard remains high throughout the league system. The vast majority of the England national team have played some football outside the Premier League, with a number starting their careers at lower-level clubs (for instance, James Maddison began at then-third tier side Coventry City, and defender Tyrone Mings started out at seventh-division

Yate) before earning moves higher up the pyramid. This rich depth throughout English football is perhaps undervalued by many, but if you go to any lower league stadium local fans will often take great pride in telling you about the time they watched a future superstar play for their team.

This is a complete contrast to the way that baseball – and, indeed, the majority of North American sports – handle player recruitment. Each franchise is a huge organisation with affiliated teams at each level of the Minor League Baseball structure, which are treated as feeder teams rather than sides in their own right. Rather than working their way through various lower league clubs, players are drafted out of high school (not a million miles off joining an academy system in England, albeit at a much older age) and sent to the minors to develop.

This does mean that, by going to a Minor League game, you're almost guaranteed to see players who will end up playing for a Major League team, but it is simply an opportunity for the individuals to develop rather than teams that play for their own success. Some fans do closely follow the standings and successes at various levels, but to nowhere near the level of support for non-league football in England; players simply don't stick around long enough to become key parts of their teams, since anyone doing particularly well is promoted to a higher level and fast-tracked to the big leagues.

Given the time differences between the United States and England, it's hard enough to follow Major League Baseball, so you'll struggle to find many Brits who have a deep interest in the Minor Leagues. That said, I had begun to take a slight interest in the Mariners' affiliates after watching Great Britain in the World Baseball Classic. Their star player during the tournament had been Harry Ford, who was drafted by the Seattle Mariners in 2021. After hitting a couple of huge home runs for my home country, I had decided to follow his progress and support him throughout his career. He started the season with the high-A side the Everett Aquasox (seriously, I wish UK teams had such cool names), and whilst I knew there was little hope that he would make it to the big leagues in time for me to see him play on my trip, it was good to see him working his way through the system.

Inevitably, following the Mariners' affiliates meant I had become slightly invested in the team itself, and they had become an exciting team to keep an eye on, thanks largely to the emergence of Julio Rodriguez who had won the 2022 Rookie of the Year award. The side had a great track record in recent years of developing superstars, such as Ken Griffey Jr and Ichiro, and I was hopeful that Ford would follow in their footsteps and become a true success in Major League Baseball. Clearly, 2023 was a little early for him, but nevertheless I was looking forward to visiting Seattle and seeing the team play.

I landed late on the Sunday night, after catching a second game at PNC Park. After previous experience of domestic US flights, I was surprised how long it took to get out of Seattle-Tacoma Airport, and I arrived at my hotel extremely tired; with the time difference taken into account, it was effectively 1am. Thankfully, my schedule was clear the following day, with the obvious exception of the game in the evening, and so I was able to have my first lie-in of the entire trip – much needed with a full week of early flights up ahead.

I took the opportunity to spend the early afternoon exploring Seattle. It was a beautiful city, and extremely walkable, with very few cars in the centre of the city. The weather was perfect as well – it was warm, but not uncomfortable, and the lower humidity levels made it almost chilly in the shade, which after some extreme heat was a welcome surprise.

I had arrived early, as the Mariners opened up the doors to the T-Mobile Bullpen area two hours before the first pitch. It was a nice place to watch the Red Sox take their warmups, and allowed me to be in prime position to access the seating bowl once the rest of the stadium opened 30 minutes later. I took the opportunity to explore the ballpark, which was dominated by the sliding roof structure that loomed over right field. Uniquely, this roof doesn't make the park fully enclosed when it's shut, with the right field remaining open in place of a wall, making the stadium feel airy and arguably making it more attractive. The team had also placed a number of smaller merchandise stands around the park rather than packing supporters into one larger store – with a number of them offering discount lines including up to 75% off hats commemorating the previous year's postseason run.

After exploring and getting some customary photos, I went to my seat in the top deck – which was much closer to the field than a lot of the previous ballparks I had visited – and settled down to watch the game. It started badly for the home side, as the visiting Red Sox plated a run in the top of the first, although the Mariners responded with a run of their own – courtesy of a Cal Raleigh home run – in the bottom of the second. Raleigh had come through the Mariners' minor league system himself, and had written himself into the team's history books after being responsible for the run that secured their first playoff appearance in 20 years. Between him and Julio Rodriguez, the Seattle side had created an excellent young core for the future.

As the game went on, the atmosphere became incredible. A spectacular 4-run eighth inning for the Mariners got the crowd on their feet and making a huge amount of noise, and made the game something of a foregone conclusion heading into the ninth. The Red Sox made them work for their victory though, and a late scare led to an electric atmosphere for the final out, as JP Crawford made an acrobatic diving catch to finish the game in dramatic fashion. The crowd were buoyant as they left the ballpark, and it was an easy journey back to the hotel, where I tried to get straight to sleep ahead of my early flight the following day.

Overall, it was an enjoyable trip to T-Mobile Park, so it's time to score it...

Location:

Seattle is a relatively modern city, and so I feel like they missed an opportunity to place their ballpark in the downtown area. Instead, it's over a mile out of town in a small complex with the Seahawks' stadium. There is a light rail line that takes you straight there, but it was fairly crowded getting back, and the walk from the station to the ballpark involved crossing some extremely busy roads. It could be worse – it wasn't a struggle to get there from the city centre – but compared to the last few places I had visited it was a little inconvenient. I think a fair score would be 6/10.

Concessions:

The Mariners really lean into Seattle's reputation for seafood; several stands offer up fish and chips (they get a bonus point for calling them chips rather than fries) and clam chowder, whilst other local business are well-represented. Starbucks, for instance, have concession stands within the ballpark, and Amazon – who are establishing a large presence in the city – have placed a few of their "Go" stores in the lower bowl, which allow fans to pick up food without scanning anything and simply leave by tapping a payment card or their smartphone. It's creative, but the food they offer up isn't anything particularly inventive. Extra credit for offering up a value menu – although a number of items were out of stock, as were several ice cream options despite the crowd being far from a sellout. Maybe this is harsh, but I don't think any of the food available stood out, so T-Mobile Park gets a score of 7/10.

Atmosphere:

The bar has been set high for atmosphere on the journey so far; most games have almost felt like playoffs with the level of noise that fans have made. Seattle was no different as much as the later part of the matchup was concerned, with the atmosphere becoming incredible as the team piled on runs towards the end of the game. This was particularly impressive since it was my first game with a lower crowd; those who didn't attend certainly missed out. However, the atmosphere was somewhat muted to begin with – perhaps an indication of the side's stuttering form so far this season and the presence of a large number of visiting Red Sox fans – which took a while to grow into the impressive level of support later on in the game. Therefore, the atmosphere at T-Mobile Park scores 7/10.

Weather:

Being located on the Pacific coast, Seattle experiences milder weather than a lot of the country. Whilst it was warm in the sun, temperatures didn't reach above what would be considered a typical British summer, making it a comfortable place to explore. Indeed, in the shade it almost became chilly during the game – a welcome surprise, but one that caught me out as I had only packed shorts for the trip! It's hard to give this ballpark anything less than a 9/10 here.

Additional Features:

This is perhaps where T-Mobile Park really stands out. The unique take on a retractable roof gives the ballpark some character as well as an airy feel even when closed, and the bullpen social space offers up a great opportunity to watch a game from a standing room location in the outfield. The team have also installed a hall of fame museum in the field level concourse, offering an interesting opportunity to see unique memorabilia from some of the franchise's greatest names, but on the whole there didn't seem to be anything that screamed "Seattle" at me during my visit apart from a view of downtown from the right field seats. This seems to be one area that could be improved, and so I think it's reasonable to give the ballpark a score of 7/10.

Overall:

The Seattle Mariners put on a good show, and the overall score of 36/50 is certainly respectable, even if it doesn't reach the highs of Toronto or Pittsburgh. It's by no means a bad ballpark, but there were certainly some things that could have been done to make it a little more unique and set it apart from others. T-Mobile Park probably suffers from being visited directly after PNC, giving it a tough experience to measure up to, but it will be interesting to see how it compares to some of the smaller market teams later on in the trip…

6

KAUFFMAN STADIUM

"I never say it can't get worse"

Buddy Bell

Baseball is a game which has close ties to other sports. The easy comparison to make is softball, which is similar in many ways, but there are a whole family of others which are grouped into the family of bat and ball sports. Indeed, baseball has no confirmed origin story (the pervasive myth of Abner Doubleday inventing the game is entertaining – and led to his birthplace of Cooperstown in New York becoming the home of the Major League's Hall of Fame – but sadly is believed by experts to be untrue), but it could be argued that it evolved from the quintessentially English sport of cricket.

Just as baseball in the United States is undergoing a minor revolution with the introduction of the pitch clock and a ghost runner in extra innings, cricket in the United Kingdom is experiencing a similar shift. The appointment of Brendon McCullum As the English national team's head coach led to the adoption of "bazball" tactics – a new approach to the game which forewent the traditional wisdom and preferred much more aggressive tactics. Players now aimed to hit the ball for boundaries every time, and bowlers went for outs rather than avoiding any form of risk.

It's debatable whether these tactics are any more effective – the side fell to two consecutive defeats in their attempt to win back the Ashes during the 2023 series, before the balance of power shifted and they were on track to win the series but for rain delays) – but the approach generated much discussion amongst pundits, and opened a debate with more casual fans about the use of tactics in cricket. I'm not a great lover of cricket, so this was my first real insight to the tactical approaches used, but it made me realise how others may view baseball through a similar lens.

To an outsider, there may not be much need for tactics in baseball. The game, on the face of it, it very simple – if you're a batter, you try and hit the ball as hard as you can, and if you're a pitcher you try to strike them out. Except those who have watched even a handful of games know that it isn't quite that simple. One of the beautiful things about the sport is how it's accessible on a number of levels; a first timer can simply enjoy the crack of the bat, someone with a slightly deeper interest can follow the game through the nine innings, and more advanced fans can analyse pitches and defensive alignments.

From a batter's point of view, there are two main approaches that can be taken – the slightly more traditional "small ball" tactic to hit singles or draw walks to slowly advance runners with significantly lower risk of outs, or the more modern attempt to hit a home run (or strike out trying). That alone offers a few possibilities during a game, but is nothing compared to potential fielding tactics.

There is so much data available in baseball that sometimes it can be difficult to know what you're looking at. Nowadays a player will most likely know exactly what to expect when they're fielding – whether the opposition hitter is likely to go for a home run or a bunt, and whereabouts in the field they're most likely to hit it. This has led to some significant defensive repositioning mid-game – and this became so extreme (known as the "overshift", or "shift" for short) that the league placed heavy restrictions on it beginning with the 2023 season.

Players still need to practice this though, and with games taking place nearly every day during the course of the season (162 games being played in 6 months simply doesn't allow for much time off) baseball players don't have days dedicated to training, unlike many other sports. Instead, they report to the park extremely early – often six or more hours before the start of a game – and spend an hour or two practicing in the early afternoon. This phenomenon is known as batting practice, and it's an extremely popular thing to watch for those fans who are keen enough to get to the ballpark as it opens.

Some teams have become more aware of this as time as gone on, and sell tickets that allow fans in even earlier to watch both teams take batting practice. This allows those who are willing to pay the opportunity to see their favourite players in a more informal setting, and offers up the chance to catch a ball hit by their team's star (or maybe catch them for an autograph when they're finished warming up). In the planning for my trip, I had noticed that the Kansas City Royals were one of the teams that did this; for $15 you could enter an hour earlier than other fans and see the home team take to the field and take batting practice. I jumped on this offer, and ticked another item off the bucket list.

Tuesday morning started with an extremely early flight out of Seattle thanks to the difference in time zones between the Pacific Northwest and Missouri, and my extreme tiredness made the extensive queues at Tacoma Airport all the more frustrating. Thankfully, I was able to catch some sleep on the plane, and after landing in Kansas City just after midday I was able to get an Uber over to my hotel near the ballpark. They were able to let me into my room early, and I was grateful for the opportunity to rest up before the game. As I was so far out of the city, I decided not to head into downtown and instead walked to the stadium to check out the area.

I must have timed it well, as I noticed a bus pull up as I approached the ticket office. A handful of Mets players got off, including Brandon Nimmo who stopped to speak to a few fans that were hanging around. I was able to have a quick chat with him and got him to pose for a photo with one of the signs explaining my trip, which I was delighted about. Nimmo could not have been any nicer, and he made a fan for life with his actions.

After getting a few photos of the stadium's exterior, I headed round to the early access gate to get in and watch batting practice, which meant standing in the blistering Kansas City heat for a while. It was at this point I became aware that this was yet another giveaway game, with all fans entering Kauffman Stadium receiving a Royals t-shirt. This was an unexpected bonus, since the hot and humid conditions meant a change of clothing was a welcome opportunity to freshen up once inside the ballpark and in the shade. In the queue, I got chatting to a few Mets fans who had also paid for the early entry, and were taken aback by the friendliness of the staff member manning the queue. I think it's fair to say there's a big difference in culture between New York and the Midwest!

It was interesting to watch both teams take batting practice. There was an almost rhythmic beauty to it; players lined up in the cage, the coaches gently lobbing a ball across and the satisfying crack of the bat as each batter inevitably hit the ball far into the outfield. The time flew by as we saw a succession of Royals and Mets hitters take to the field for this warm-up, with those not taking swings standing in the outfield to practice making routine catches and pitchers shuttling to and from the bullpen to prepare for the game ahead.

After both teams had finished, it suddenly hit me how much the heat had taken its toll on me. With such an early start to the day, I had not eaten since having a quick bag of crisps at the airport that morning, and standing in the sun for so long I was starting to struggle a little. After changing shirts and buying a Royals hat, I made a beeline for a food stand and grabbed a quick but dependable meal of chicken strips and two litres of ice cold water, which made me feel significantly better. With that, it was time for the game to start.

Both teams were fielding significantly depleted teams – it was the day of the trade deadline, and the Mets had moved Justin Verlander and Tommy Pham on for future prospects, whilst Scott Barlow and Ryan Yarbrough had left the Royals. In addition to this, Nimmo had been scratched from the lineup after feeling soreness warming up, leaving the Mets with a bare-bones team. To tell the truth, it showed on the part of both sides, with a slight lack of quality on display, although they still put on an entertaining game. The Mets took the lead in the second before the Royals responded in the bottom of the fifth to tie the game at 1-1. After the seventh-inning stretch, the game was blown wide open as the Royals scored two more runs to take control. However, the Mets responded in devastating fashion in the top of the eighth, exposing Kansas City's defensive frailties and capitalising on a bases-loaded situation to go 4-3 up. Ultimately, the Royals were able to fight back in the bottom of the same inning with a sacrifice fly, tying the game after the ninth.

This meant that the game would become the first of the trip to go into extra innings, and an opportunity for me to see the "ghost runner" on second base that had become so controversial since its introduction. The Mets took advantage of this to score 2 runs in the top of the tenth, seemingly giving them a good chance to take the win, but the Royals responded with two of their own in the bottom of the inning before a somewhat bizarre end to the game. The rule around balks is confusing at best, and fans often disagree with umpires when one is called, so when Mets pitcher ___ stepped off his position due to an apparent issue with his communications system it seemed a little harsh for it to be ruled as such. However, this meant that every Royals runner could advance, and with the bases loaded this meant they won the game with a walk-off balk – a baseball occurrence rarer than a complete game.

It was a strange way to end a fascinating matchup, and the crowd were jubilant as I walked back to my hotel and went straight to sleep ahead of another very early flight the following day. It had been a surprisingly enjoyable day, and the ratings should reflect that...

Location:

Kauffman Stadium has one of the more awkward locations in the big leagues, being placed far out of town in a sporting complex surrounded by parking lots. On one hand, this is convenient for those wishing to drive to games – and sharing the parking facilities with the NFL Chiefs is a good way to cut down on space required – but when travelling by public transport it's a pain. I had to book a hotel by the ballpark to be able to get back at a sensible time, and as a result I didn't get any opportunity to see the city at all. It's a real shame, and as a result the score is a pretty low 4/10.

Concessions:

This was a pleasant surprise. With Kauffman being one of the oldest stadiums in the league, I was expecting a basic offering, but the Royals had made a real effort to serve interesting and unique options. In particular, I loved the dessert shop behind home plate, which not only made fresh ice cream using liquid nitrogen for each customer but also had a range of baked goods such as brownies and cupcakes.

Kansas City is also known as one of the homes of the barbecue, so of course they had a wide range of meats available as well. There was a restaurant-style location on the 200 level – open to everyone – that served up interesting barbecued food – it looked incredible. Add to that the various stands serving the typical ballpark classics dotted around the concourses and it was an unexpected highlight of the trip. Here, Kauffman scores 9/10.

Atmosphere:

With the Royals having a miserable season, they've been struggling to draw crowds – this game drew around 16,000 fans, representing a touch over 40% the stadium capacity. It might have been the lowest attendance of the trip so far, but those who did attend caught a classic. Thanks to staff members making an effort to get the atmosphere building, the fans did make a good level of noise, and in what's becoming a running theme so far it felt like we were watching a playoff game by the end of the game.

In terms of friendliness, it could best be summed up by a Mets fan that I overheard – "this is why I hate the midwest, everyone's so damn friendly". Staff at Kauffman were the nicest I've encountered anywhere on the trip. The man monitoring the early entry queue made sure to speak to everyone and ask where they'd travelled from (managing to lead the crowd in a rendition of *Happy Birthday* to a young fan and getting us to all sing *Take me out to the Ballgame* before entering the stadium), and ushers were relaxed about fans moving around before the game to get photos. I can't give a perfect score because of the lower crowd, but it was still an enjoyable experience, so the Royals earn an 8/10.

Weather:

If I said it was warm at the K, that would be an understatement. With temperatures approaching 35 Celcius and humidity that increased the "feels like" temperature by another few degrees, it was a blazing hot place to be. The concrete construction of the stadium doesn't help that, but once the sun went down it became a significantly more bearable place to watch a ballgame. It became pleasant later into the game, but it was still a little warm for me early on, so I'm giving it a score of 7/10.

Additional Features:

I thought the Royals would be somewhat hamstrung by the age of their stadium – at 50 years old, it's the 6th oldest in the big leagues. Whilst it did feel a little dated (the exposed concrete was far from modern), the team had made a real effort to modernise it and put some interesting features in place. Kansas City is known as the city of fountains, and the vast range of them in the outfield gave it an attractive view, as well as the unique shape of the scoreboard (the first vertical screen that I had seen on the trip) providing a slightly different experience.

I also loved the Authentics store in the concourse – whilst it's fairly standard for teams to sell game-used memorabilia at the stadium, Kauffman went even further by operating a ticketed queuing system for fans to pick up balls that had been used in the game that day. After picking up a ticket before first pitch, I came back after the seventh-inning stretch, at which point a range of baseballs were placed on a table and fans were called by number to pick up a piece of unique memorabilia from the game they were watching. Additionally, the presence of a free-entry restaurant in the 200 level was a welcome addition, and an excellent hall of fame within the ballpark gave fans another thing to do before the game. It can't quite make up for the fact that the stadium is so far out of town and lacking a true outfield district, but it was by no means bad – and I think a fair score is 9/10.

Overall:

Kauffman Stadium is slightly let down by its location, meaning a total of 37/50 places it slightly lower down the list, but it was an enjoyable place to watch a ballgame – it picked up 33 out of 40 possible points outside of that particular area of scoring. It's with mixed emotions that I read about plans for a new ballpark in Kansas City; whilst it will undoubtedly be better located than the team's current home, it will inevitably lack Kauffman's charm and history.

7

COORS FIELD

"I love hitting there. Who doesn't?"

Kris Bryant

It's hard to comprehend just how big the United States of America is. The country is the third largest in the world, and over 40 times the size of the UK; indeed, the entirety of Great Britain could fit into many individual states (many times over, in some cases). This was something that I knew of, but I wasn't quite familiar with the sheer scale of the place. A flight of a little over 5 hours (from Pittsburgh to Seattle), not that much less than the journey from London to New York City, didn't even take me across the entire country, and some of the long drives later in the trip were slightly intimidating.

But it wasn't just the size that sets America apart from England. Many Brits might scoff at Americans saying that they plan to visit Europe, without being specific about which country or city they might be travelling to, but it's probably fair to compare the continent with the United States, and not just for its land mass. The cultural differences across the nation – and sometimes even between neighbouring states – are significant, ranging from the hustle and bustle of the northeastern region to the more relaxed and friendly midwest. The southern states have a significant Mexican influence (Texas, after all, was much more closely affiliated with there than it was with the US over the course of history) that would be a completely alien concept in Washington, and California's famous liberalism contrasts deeply with the Upper Midwest.

Similarly, the country has a fantastic range of geography. The southwestern states feature some of the largest regions of deserts in the world – as well as the location of the hottest temperature recorded in human history (Furnace Creek in California's Death Valley national park), whilst Alaska reaches into the arctic circle and is home to stunning glaciers and wildlife. There are mountain ranges, swamps, rivers and salt plains – sometimes all in the same state – and the vast range of geographical features gives rise to a contrast in climate as well. Florida is hot and humid year-round, making it a popular vacation spot over the winter, whilst the northern California Bay Area is regarded as being so mild that Mark Twain famously claimed that "the coldest winter I ever spent was a summer in San Francisco".

Perhaps the most scenic area that I had seen – from an airplane window at least – was the Rocky Mountain range in Colorado. Despite having to wake up extremely early in Kansas City to catch a 6am flight, it looked stunning on the approach to Denver. Located in the Mountain West region, the city is located nearly a mile above sea level – one of the highest in the country, along with Albuquerque in New Mexico – and is home to mountain lions and bison towards the edge of the city. This was a complete contrast to Missouri the previous day, and an even bigger shift from the hustle and bustle of New York City, which I had left only a few days previously.

One of the key consequences of Denver's high altitude was how games in the team's ballpark tended to play out. With the stadium being located so high above sea level and the air being so much thinner, balls travelled a lot further; the air resistance simply wasn't as powerful to slow things down. This meant that Coors Field was regarded as a true hitter's park, and visiting fans tended to travel in large numbers in the hope that their team would hit plenty of home runs during the game.

After landing at the airport very early – I opted to stay in the terminal and get a good breakfast before heading to the hotel to drop my bags off – I investigated options for getting to the ballpark. It turns out that Denver offers free travel on the local train system during the summer months in an attempt to tempt residents away from their cars, and it made me willing to walk the 15 minutes from my hotel to the local station rather than getting an Uber into downtown. Once again, this was a giveaway game – I swear I'm not actively seeking them out – and I got a pack of Topps baseball cards upon entering the stadium. It immediately struck me how many Padres fans were around, having travelled around 1,000 miles to watch their team on the road. That's true fandom.

I was on a slightly ridiculous streak at this point of only seeing the home team win on the trip – including a rare win for the Royals the previous night – but this was to come to an end with the Rockies struggling to cope with San Diego's lineup of powerful sluggers. The Padres had found the 2023 season struggling despite having a star-studded squad featuring young stars like Juan Soto and Fernando Tatis Jr as well as future hall-of-famer Manny Machado, but it looked like they had found their groove at Coors Field as players lined up to knock balls out of the park. It started early on, as leadoff man Ha-Seong Kim hit a home run on only the second pitch of the game, and the brutal display concluded late on with Tatis' 100th career homer – making him the fifth fastest player in the modern game to reach that milestone.

After a devastating top of the ninth inning, in which the Padres piled on 7 runs to inflate the score to 11-1, the vast majority of fans elected to leave early, not believing that any form of comeback would be possible in the final inning. They were correct, of course, and the game finished at that scoreline as I took advantage of the lower crowds to have a hassle-free walk back to the station and catch a free train back to the hotel. I was in bed by 7, as I had a 6am flight the following day, and with warnings of extensive TSA queues at the airport I was keen to leave the hotel by 3. Thankfully, it would be the last day for a while where I would have to be awake so early, and I fell asleep excited for the days ahead.

Location:

I had limited time in Denver, with another early flight the following day necessitating getting to sleep before the sun went down, but I had a brief opportunity to explore downtown due to the ballpark's location right in the centre of the city. It was easy to step off the train and walk to Coors Field, and even during the brief walk there were several bars and restaurants to visit. There were major roads at a different elevation, allowing easy vehicular access as well as making it safe for pedestrians, and this contributed to it feeling like the ballpark was in an ideal location. There was perhaps a lack of parking lots for those who do prefer to drive, but beyond that I couldn't find any criticisms, so on this count the Rockies score 9/10.

Concessions:

There's one local delicacy that you simply have to try when you visit Colorado – Rocky Mountain Oysters. They don't sound particularly appetising when you realise what they are (finely chopped bull testicles, coated in flour and deep fried), but they really weren't all that bad. They had very little flavour – they've been described as a mix between chicken, venison and calamari by various others – but I couldn't really taste that much; the chewy texture was more overpowering. If that's not your cup of tea, Coors Field also offers up all the standard ballpark classics as well as a wide range of specialty hot dogs (I'm sure I saw a sausage made from rattlesnake on offer) and even a separate booth offering a menu especially for children.

I also liked the fact that there were sit-down restaurants located near home plate, with a (limited) view of the field available whilst you ate, and there were a large number of bars scattered around the park – perhaps to be expected when the stadium is named after a brewery. Dessert options were good too (I had a "kebob" made of chocolate-drizzled strawberries and brownie bites, which was divine) and there were perhaps more merchandise stands dotted around the concourse than I'd seen at any ballpark so far. Even more welcome was the fact that the Rockies had a huge number of items on sale, offering value as well as variety. It was impressive, and earns Coors Field another 9/10.

Atmosphere:

The Rockies really deserve a better team. The National League West is a brutal division, with the LA Dodgers dominating every year and their California Rivals in the Giants and the Padres regularly challenging for wildcard spots behind them. This year, the Arizona Diamondbacks have begun to challenge, thanks to a revolution sparked by rookie Corbin Carroll, meaning the Rockies have been stuck in last place for pretty much the entire season. This isn't new for them either; the side are on track for their fifth consecutive season finishing either fourth or fifth in the division, and there are no signs of them improving in the immediate future.

This inevitably has led to a decline in attendances, but it hasn't been as stark as in some cities. Colorado draw fairly middle-of-the-road crowds, boosted in part by visiting fans and those keen to experience the high-altitude ballpark. The atmosphere in this game was understandably muted – when you lose 11-1 there isn't much to cheer about – but it struck me how everyone at the stadium was so friendly. The ushers clearly took pride in their jobs, with the man in charge of the upper deck taking the time to talk be through Coors Field's history and key features, whilst the fans were excited to talk about baseball to visitors. This boosts the score to a very respectable 7/10.

Weather:

This one is perhaps more subjective than any other ballpark, if just for the fact that everyone adjusts to high altitudes differently. It's estimated that roughly one in ten visitors to Denver will suffer from altitude sickness (usually with a headache or mild shortness of breath), and this would inevitably impact upon their experience visiting the city. Personally, this wasn't something I noticed, but it's something to be aware of if you are planning a visit.

Other than that, the weather was pretty good. Denver has cooler mornings than many other locations in the US, but does still get warm in the afternoon. It felt a little less humid than, for instance, Kansas City, although later on in the game it did become slightly muggy – though it did start to drizzle pretty soon after. The mountainous location does give rise to some brief storms (the previous day's game did get halted for rain) and makes it less predictable than other towns, but on my visit there wasn't much to complain about. Considering the risk of altitude sickness and rain on any given visit though, Coors Field scores a slightly more limited 6/10.

Additional Features:

The Rockies lean heavily into their "mile-high" reputation, and have installed a row of purple seats in the upper deck to mark the place where fans would be precisely one mile above sea level. It's a popular photo location, but it also offers some pretty good views of the ballpark. They've also installed a garden in the outfield, with trees and fountains acting as the batter's eye instead of the traditional black or green wall, which offers an attractive and serene alternative viewing location.

I also loved the interactive experience areas in the concourse, with fans having an opportunity to throw pitches or take swings in a cage, as well as the children's area featuring somewhere to play and their own concession stand. As one of the first retro-classic ballparks, the Rockies had something of a blank canvas to work with, and they've done extremely well in making it an interesting and unique place to watch a ballgame, so on this front they score 9/10.

Overall:

In total, Coors Field gets a score of 40/50, making it one of the highest-ranking parks of the trip so far. Next up is a stadium that is also regarded as many people's favourites, so it remains to be seen where the

Rockies' ballpark finishes in the final rankings…

8

BUSCH STADIUM

"You grind it out all year for the chance to do something special…the opportunity to achieve something great"

Matt Carpenter

Sometimes, it's obvious which sports teams will be successful. Major cities draw large fanbases, which in turn drives revenue and increased chances of success. Even in the days before most sports became money-driven, the allure of playing in a large city attracted the best players. For instance, in European football it's little surprise that some of the biggest sides are based in cities such as Madrid, Milan, London and Paris, whilst few would argue that New York and Los Angeles are home to some of the most recognisable franchises in North America.

But every now and then, you get a less well-known city that develops as a sporting powerhouse. Newcastle, in the north east of England, might be fairly large compared to the rest of the UK, but is a city that few outside of the country will be aware of. However, they have some of the most dedicated fans in all of football, regularly recording attendances of over 50,000 even before they were taken over by the Saudi state investment fund and propelled to greater success. This included some years of turmoil, but historically they have been a successful side, having won over a dozen major honours and been regular competitors in European competition in the past.

There are several sides of this ilk dotted around the world, where a relatively provincial city has become known for its sporting pedigree. It is often said that success drives further success, and this is certainly true in this area, as teams become popular for their trophies, and in turn attract more fans and a higher calibre of player to push them to further glories. I love seeking out these sides – usually they are relatively well-known teams, but occasionally one goes under the radar enough that only dedicated fans of the sport will be aware of their successes.

The St Louis Cardinals are arguably one of these teams. If you were to ask a Brit to name the most successful baseball sides, they would almost certainly be aware of the New York Yankees – their 27 World Series wins put them way out in front of anyone else – but beyond that they would probably answer with the Boston Red Sox or the Los Angeles Dodgers. The Red Sox rank joint-third (with 9 trophies, tied with the Oakland Athletics) and the Dodgers are sixth (pleasingly just behind their rivals the San Francisco Giants), but very few casual fans would be aware of the Cardinals' position in second place, with eleven World Series trophies to their name. It might be some way off the Yankees' gargantuan haul, but it's still incredibly impressive in its own right.

Having seen the Cardinals play in London just a few weeks ago, I was interested to see how the side had changed and was looking forward to my trip to Busch Stadium. What I wasn't looking forward to, however, was the 6am flight I had booked onto departing Denver that morning – the flight schedules not quite lining up for anything more convenient. After a 2:30 alarm, I quickly got myself ready for the hotel's shuttle to the airport and found a quiet space to work before the early departure. Irritatingly, the plane was an hour late taking off, with most of that time being spent on the tarmac, but once we were in the air I was able to doze off for about an hour and catch up on some lost sleep.

Upon landing in St Louis, I caught the relatively modern subway into the city centre. Whilst researching this trip, it was noticeable how many people had tried to argue that most American cities were dangerous and that public transit should be avoided; I had not found this to be the case on the trip, with my experiences being that subways and buses were generally safe, cheap and convenient. However, the red line in St Louis was noticeably different, with a number of individuals displaying erratic behaviour during the journey, and a lack of staff providing reassurances. It's something to bear in mind if you're planning your own trip to the city – I never felt in danger, but it may make others feel uncomfortable.

Thankfully, my hotel had a room available when I arrived at midday, and the check-in staff were extremely accommodating in allowing me to access this early, giving me an opportunity to drop my bags and rest for a few hours before freshening up. The Missouri Athletic Club was somewhat dated – opening in 1916, the rooms were originally built as opportunistic accommodation for members rather than as a hotel – but it was good enough as a place to rest up and spend a night. Given my previous experience of the subway system I opted to take the 15-minute walk to the stadium rather than utilising my day pass, and it was a pleasant walk through downtown.

Upon arriving at Busch Stadium, I was instantly captivated by the ballpark village located just to the north. This area had plenty for fans to do before the gates opened, with food and music stands as well as plenty of bars and a team store. I was surprised that other teams hadn't incorporated similar social spaces in the vicinity of their ballparks, especially those located out of town with plenty of land nearby to work with. I headed into the store and made my customary purchase of a hat, team ball and pin badge, and the cashier was able to apply a discount to the purchase as well.

Once I headed inside the ballpark, I met up with two Cardinals fans who I had originally got to know in England. Dave and Janet had travelled over for the London Series a few weeks previously, and after chatting to them outside the stadium we had kept in touch, offering to host me at Busch for the game. Incredibly, they had secured three tickets in a luxury suite section behind home plate, and I was blown away by their generosity in letting me sit with them for the game. It was really nice to sit in an air-conditioned area and talk all things baseball before the game, and I will forever be grateful for their hospitality and kindness during this visit.

Busch Stadium is described by many as baseball heaven, and I can certainly understand why they say that. Holding a little under 45,000, it stands out with its red seats and superb view of downtown St Louis. The fans are regarded as some of the best in the game – they certainly have a lot to cheer about, although with this being a Wednesday evening matchup after the team had traded away six players at the deadline (including star Paul DeJong) it was a game for the diehards rather than the casuals.

Things did not start well for the Cardinals. A pair of two-run homers in the second inning gave the visiting Twins a 4-0 lead early in the game, from which the home side never really recovered. Dylan Carlson did provide Tommy Edman with a run courtesy of his double in the bottom of the same inning, but Minnesota pitcher Sonny Gray only allowed one more run during his seven inning start – in the bottom of the sixth, after the Twins had added another run of their own, making the score 5-2. More efficient pitching made the result of the game something of a foregone conclusion; whilst Carlson ground out to allow another Cardinals run in the bottom of the ninth, it was too late to make a difference, and St Louis slipped to another defeat in what had been a poor season for them. With the team selling at the deadline, it looked as though the front office had given up on 2023 and were preparing for the future.

It was time for me too to look to the future as I said goodbye to Dave and Janet, picked up another game-used ball in the memorabilia store and headed back to my hotel ahead of yet another flight in the morning. It had once again been a great evening, and I was unsure how this night could be topped later in the trip. Busch Stadium was a superb location, and the scores were bound to be high:

Location:

Busch Stadium is placed at the edge of downtown, and right next to the ballpark district. It's walkable from a wide range of hotels, and its location right next to a subway station makes it extremely easy to access. The ballpark district, bordering the stadium to the north, is a bustling hub on game days, with bars, restaurants and social spaces open to fans before they enter the ballpark. The stadium is oriented such that the outfield offers views of the city centre – you can see a range of skyscrapers as well as the iconic arch and courthouse. Being on the edge of downtown instead of the very centre also allows fans to access a number of parking lots as well, giving Busch the best of both worlds. There's very little (if anything) to criticise here, so it gets a score of 10/10.

Concessions:

St Louis is known for a few things when it comes to food – barbecue (it's in Missouri after all, although it's not as famous for this as Kansas City), toasted ravioli and frozen custard. All three are on offer at Busch Stadium, as well as the standard ballpark classics and the option to get bacon wrapped around your hot dog. As Dave and Janet had so kindly bought me a ticket in a suite area, there were a few other options available, such as chinese and carved roast beef. In the end, I went for a slightly more boring option of chicken tenders, and they were the best I'd ever had – juicy and flavoursome, which is more than most ballparks offer. Bonus marks for the Cardinals bringing in Ben and Jerry's for their ice cream stands, giving a nice twist on the sundae helmet. Busch Stadium scores 9/10 for its food offerings.

Atmosphere:

Cardinals fans are regarded as some of the greatest in all of North American sports, and despite their team having one of its worst seasons in a long time they still turned up in reasonable numbers to cheer them on. They're knowledgable about the game, cheer current and former players and, most impressively, don't need endless scoreboard gimmicks to make some noise and get behind their team.

On top of this, they're friendly. The team employees were proud of their jobs and and keen to give fans the best possible experience, and I cannot fault the hospitality of my friends Dave and Janet. They went above and beyond to provide me with an excellent seat and food, and represented the very best of their city. Once again, I can't find any negatives here, and this gives the Cardinals another perfect score of 10/10.

Weather:

I had been reliably informed that I avoided the worst of the Missouri weather; a week before I had arrived temperatures were well over 100 Fahrenheit. The Midwest seems to get extreme heat in the summer as well as humidity, and this mugginess did make even the reasonable 30 degree heat somewhat uncomfortable in the early afternoon. Thankfully, the suite was air conditioned and so we were only outside when it began to cool down – but walking around the ballpark earlier that day was still an extremely warm experience. Busch Stadium suffers a little here, with a score of 6/10.

Additional Features:

I mentioned it in the location section, but it really is worth repeating how great it is to have the ballpark village located just across the street. Whilst it's not technically inside the stadium, it's an essential addition to anyone's visit to St Louis, and only enhances the experience. The team have also sought to add various elements from their history into the ballpark – one of my favourite touches was the installation of the old scoreboard from the original Busch Stadium above one of the entrance gates, offering nostalgia to fans of a certain age as well as keeping out some of the noise from the adjacent highway.

I also loved the terrace bar area on the upper deck – at many ballparks this top level seems to be an afterthought, with fewer concession options and limited facilities, but at Busch it felt like the organisation had carefully considered how to give fans in these cheaper seats an experience just as good as those down below. The entire ballpark is brimming with history, and the team's position as one of the traditional powerhouses of baseball makes it an essential visit for any self-respecting fan, but the Cardinals haven't rested on their laurels and have made a real effort to make it a unique place to visit. With that in mind, Busch Stadium scores a strong 9/10.

Overall:

In total, the St Louis Cardinals have got an extremely strong score of 44/50. It was a perfect evening of baseball, and with slightly later starts on the horizon I was looking forward to continuing with my trip...

9

TARGET FIELD

"When things are said and done, I want to be remembered"

Joe Mauer

Whilst baseball had been a fairly new part of my life, I had held other interests for a much longer period of time. For instance, I love music. The UK has one of the best histories in this area, having produced countless successful bands over the years, and practically invented some genres. Indeed, the musical cultures of the UK and America are deeply intertwined, with the Beatles "breaking America" and becoming a cultural phenomenon on both sides of the pond. I love attending gigs, and could only imagine how cool it must be to stand on a stage and have thousands of people cheer and sing along to your work every single night.

But behind the facade of a rock and roll lifestyle, I've often thought that being a musician must be a tiring and somewhat lonely existence. Whilst you might spend several hours every day on stage living the dream, performing your music to thousands of fans, when the show is over and the buzz wears off you're sitting backstage without a great number of others who know exactly what your life is like. And then you have the demands of travelling to a different city every night just to stand on a stage that could well be anywhere.

This was best explained by Matt Thompson, lead singer of The Amazons, during their show at Cardiff's Great Hall. He explained that life on the road is great, but you're not really visiting cities, merely passing through. His band had made the effort to connect more with each stop on the tour, and had tried to immerse themselves with the local musical scene – this, he surmised, was the difference between touring and travelling.

And this was something I had always tried to keep in mind with this challenge. The start of the trip had been like many previous holidays – a few days in New York (where I had already spent a week in the past, so there was little need to do the typical tourist things) followed by a short stay in the centre of Toronto and close to two days each in Pittsburgh and Seattle, which gave me the chance to visit some landmarks and make me feel like I had truly seen the cities. But inevitably the endless flights and early starts had begun to take their toll, and I was beginning to feel a little disconnected from the cities I was visiting. It didn't help that many ballparks were named after sponsors, making them feel a little corporate.

For the last couple of stops, I had merely travelled from the airport to a hotel, then gone directly to the ballpark. This was a combination of trying not to exhaust myself and the cities themselves not exactly being tourist hotspots, although it did mean that I could have been anywhere in the world at those moments in time. The early starts had really taken it out of me, but with my flight to Minneapolis being my last airport experience for a full week I knew I would be able to spend a little more time exploring the city.

After landing, I took the tram to the centre of town. My first impression of Minneapolis was that it was a relatively modern and clean city, although there was a fairly heavy police presence. This surprised me considering the turbulent events in 2020, when the death of George Floyd and subsequent demonstrations became a symbol of the nation's fraught relationships with their police force. I dropped my bags at the hotel and walked back into town, noticing a good number of British and Irish pubs nearby. I resisted the urge to drop in to one of them – I was going for the true American experience, after all!

After spending some time in the city, I took the short walk over to the Twins' Target Field. The team are one of the lesser-known sides to casual baseball fans, despite the fact that they are regularly one of the strongest sides in the American League Central, and have a roster containing some extremely good players. After watching them beat the Cardinals the previous evening, I was keen to see how they would cope against an Arizona Diamondbacks side that had made huge strides in the past twelve months, thanks in part to the emergence of key rookies such as Corbin Carroll and Cal Mitchell.

I was also very interested to watch Carlos Correa for the Twins. A key member of the Houston Astros' World Series winning team back in 2017, he was close to signing for the Giants at the start of this season. San Francisco were keen to add a big name to their roster, and had attempted to sign Aaron Judge as a free agent a few weeks previously before he opted to sign a new contract with the Yankees. Correa would have slotted into the side perfectly, and had agreed terms (he would have made $350 million over the space of twelve years) before a medical examination revealed some lingering injury issues. The same problems prevented him signing with the Mets, and so he returned to the Twins on a contract that would net him just over half the amount he would have made in San Francisco.

The first thing that hit me about Target Field was just how friendly everyone was. After picking up a team hat, I went to get some photos of the ballpark from different angles, and fans were keen to speak to me after realising that I had travelled from England. Even better was the usher in the top deck; after overhearing me talking with some other people about my trip, she gave me a free programme and asked another staff member to collect an autographed ball from their authentic memorabilia stand. I was blown away by this act of generosity, which made me feel extremely welcome and instantly made the Twins a team that I will keep an eye out for in the future.

Having picked up a ticket for this game for just $4 – the Twins were selling standing room only tickets in an offer just before Christmas – I was keen to see how possible it would be to enjoy a baseball game on a budget. I had heard that some of the social spaces in the outfield offered excellent value, and so I went up to the second deck and found the Town Ball Tavern, where I was able to sit down and order food. I was delighted to see they offered fish and chips – whilst I was trying to avoid home comforts, this was too good to turn down – at a price that matched local chippies back in England. It was great, with the walleye having a slightly stronger flavour than the usual cod.

By the time I had finished my meal, it was time for the game. Scoreless first innings were becoming a theme on this trip, and sure enough neither side put any runs on the board this time around. Lourdes Gurriel Jr hit a home run in the top of the second, however, putting the visitors ahead for a while, and begun an enjoyable back-and-forth match in which the Twins were always quick to counter the Diamondbacks' runs – Jorge Polanco hitting a solo homer of his own in the bottom of the third to tie the game at 1-1, and Max Kepler in the bottom of the sixth similarly hitting a home run to counter the visiting side's play in the fourth that had put them ahead for a second time. Michael Taylor sent the crowd wild immediately after the seventh-inning stretch with another home run to finally put the home side ahead, and ultimately they never let this lead slip as they saw out the game with a 3-2 win.

Postgame firework shows are somewhat common in American sports, and the Twins were offering this as part of the ticket price. Somehow, after catching Harry Potter night in St Louis the previous evening, it was once again the theme of the game in Minneapolis, and accordingly the display after the match was to the soundtrack of the film series. It was an enjoyable (and loud) end to the night, and it was great to see so many fans stick around after the game had ended to see them. Perhaps British sports could learn a thing or two from this – as they could from the whole experience.

Location:

Target Field is another ballpark that's located on the edge of downtown – albeit a slightly further walk from the city centre than some others. The area around the stadium has some character to it, with a number of bars and live music venues, but it does feel a little out of the way. It does have a tram stop right outside though, as well as a number of parking lots and easy access to the highway. A fair score, therefore, is 9/10.

Concessions:

The Twins offer quite possibly the most comprehensive range of food and drink that I've seen at any ballpark so far. I noticed specialty fried chicken stands, an Australian meat pie kiosk and some premium sausages instead of the basic hot dogs. Most impressive of all was the range of restaurant options inside the ballpark that were open to everyone. It was nice to sit down before the game and have food brought out to a table, and the fish and chips was even better than back in England. Best of all, the price was extremely reasonable – at $14.50, it was actually cheaper than a lot of the grab-and-go options at other ballparks.

There were plenty of dessert options – most fans seemed to flock to the mini donut stand, where they were fried whilst you queued and served in either a bag (containing a dozen) or a bucket (containing 36). I'm not quite sure how anyone can consume that many donuts in one sitting, but plenty managed it during the game! Add in the ubiquitous merchandise stands – although it was also nice to see sponsors giving away free Twins gear – and it was clear that Target Field had something for everyone. There wasn't really anything I could fault, so it scores a perfect 10/10.

Atmosphere:

This is the friendliest ballpark I've ever visited. The phrase "Minnesota nice" is usually used in a somewhat pejorative manner, but I found everyone was unbelievably welcoming and proud of their state. Ushers wanted to talk about my trip (one even giving me a free autographed ball) and fans were happy to chat about the game.

Considering the crowd was some way off a sellout, they made a lot of noise too. Two of the Twins' three runs were scored via solo home runs, which were cheered as though the team had just made the playoffs. I did think that they could have drawn a bigger crowd, considering their lead on the division and the fact that it was a Friday night game with fireworks afterwards. I would have liked to see the ballpark with a sellout attendance – if it was this good with a limited number there, how great could it have been with even more watching the game? With that in mind, the stadium scores 8/10.

Weather:

It's the Midwest, so it's warm and humid. However, Minnesota is slightly more bearable than Missouri, and as the sun starts to go down the conditions become almost perfect for watching a ballgame. There was a little bit of rain upon arrival, but it was light – the impression I got was that serious thunderstorms were rare in the area – and even if that does happen most of the ballpark is under cover. The Twins could do with installing some air conditioning in the toilets though – it was sweltering in there. That detracts a little from the rest of the park, so Target Field scores a slightly harsh 7/10.

Additional Features:

The Twins have made a real effort to make Target Field an enjoyable place to watch a game. Usually, the second deck is comprised almost entirely of luxury seating and corporate suites, but this ballpark had a vast number of social spaces up there instead. I really enjoyed exploring the various standing room areas, which in some places is considered an afterthought. I liked the attempts to make the stadium seem different to others, with an almost sandstone-coloured theme around much of the lower level and bleacher seats reaching over the field, and it was enough to give the ballpark a unique feel – although perhaps there could be more around the ballpark to make it reflect the town and state as well. With this in mind, I'm giving it a score of 7/10.

Overall:

With a total score of 41/50, Target Field is an underrated gem of a park. I went in with no real expectations, as it's rarely mentioned as one of the best in the sport, but I really enjoyed my evening there. And with no flights or early starts coming up for a while, I was truly looking forward to the ballparks in the week ahead…

10

AMERICAN FAMILY FIELD

"I led the league in go get 'em next time"

Bob Uecker

One of the most notable examples of American culture crossing over to the UK is *The Simpsons*. The iconic TV show was first shown on BBC Two in 1996, just seven years after it began, and has been a fixture of the schedule ever since. Unlike in the US, where it was originally seen as a cartoon providing a satirical view of the world, it's viewed more as a children's show in the UK, although those who grew up with it still watch it to this day. Arguably, it transcends age ranges, with episodes tackling broader social themes.

And most of all, it's simply an excellent piece of television. Episodes such as *Last Exit to Springfield* and *You Only Move Twice* are regarded as some of the greatest pieces of TV of its era. The show has won 34 Emmys amongst it's haul of over 120 awards, and whilst there has been a gradual decline in quality since the departures of Bill Oakley, Josh Weinstein and Mike Scully few could argue with the significance and cultural impact of the programme's first decade.

Being a programme that aimed to reflect American life, it should come as no surprise that the show features baseball as a central theme in a number of episodes. One of my favourites is *Homer at the Bat*, in which Mr Burns recruits a flurry of former MLB stars to represent his power plant's company softball team – replacing Homer, until a series of freak accidents and injuries leads to him winning the game anyway. As a child, I didn't

69

really appreciate the episode, failing to understand many of the references to the sport (and I certainly didn't recognise any of the guest stars; Steve Sax and Mike Scioscia are hardly household names in the UK), but since falling in love with the sport I have become more familiar with the players and the humour.

One of the other episodes to centre itself around the sport is *Hungry Hungry Homer*, in which the titular character learns of Springfield's local baseball team's plans to move to Albuquerque. Despite the side's cynical attempts to discredit him (a nod to the increasingly corporate nature of American sports), Homer goes on a hunger strike to draw attention to the relocation, and eventually convinces a crowd mid-game that the move is imminent. In a rare example of pop culture crossing into the real world, Albuquerque's minor league team renamed themselves the Isotopes after the fictional side in this episode, and installed statues of the Simpson family around the ballpark.

This is but one example of American sporting sides having interesting names; something that is generally unheard of in the United Kingdom. Indeed, some of the sides in the minor leagues have the most unique names – the Sugar Land Space Cowboys and the Binghampton Rumble Ponies are amongst my favourite – but this extends to the most popular teams as well, with many Brits being surprised that teams have names such as the Detroit Tigers or the Miami Marlins.

The furthest that British teams go tend to be a reference to United, City, Albion or Athletic after the city (usually to distinguish themselves from another side in the same location), but this is some way off the extravagance of American names. Of course, British teams do have nicknames – and some are shared with the actual names of North American teams. Most notably, Burton Albion – who play in the third division of English football – are nicknamed the Brewers after the town's long history of making beer. This is reflected in their crest, and fans often refer to the team by this moniker, but is notably absent from the team's name itself.

This is in contrast with the side that I would be visiting today; the Milwaukee Brewers, who proudly reference the city's similar history in their team's name. Formed in 1969 as the Seattle Pilots, they lasted just a single season in the Pacific Northwest before moving to the midwestern state of Wisconsin, where they have stayed ever since.

This was to be the first city of the trip that I would not need to fly to, as the relatively modest rail network in the United States had a direct service there from Minneapolis. However, I woke up to several emails from Amtrak informing me that the train had been delayed. In the UK, this might mean the service being 20 minutes late; in the US, however, it meant more than 3 hours. This was described as a "minor" disruption – it's not unheard of for trains to be late by an entire day on some long-distance routes – but it would be enough to make me miss the start of the game that night. Thankfully, I was aware of the company's reputation, and had preemptively booked a bus service departing at the same time as a backup in case this happened.

It was, in fact, a shorter walk from my hotel, and after grabbing the seat at the front of the coach we set off on a long journey out of Minnesota and across Wisconsin. The driver was in good humour and made the seven-hour trip bearable, including a comfort stop at a Kwik-Trip which allowed me to eat a substantial lunch and break the journey up. We arrived into Milwaukee at almost exactly 4pm, and a short Uber ride took me to an airBNB near the ballpark. It was certainly a new experience for me staying at a stranger's house, but the host was extremely accommodating and the room was clean.

Due to the length of the journey, I was only in the room for a few minutes before walking to the ballpark. The location of the stadium meant my airBNB was the only accommodation within walking distance – its out-of-town positioning making it another awkward one to get to. However, upon approaching the gates it became clear why this was the case – the people of Wisconsin love tailgating, and the parking lots were full of barbecues, seats and food as people enjoyed the pre-game atmosphere. Even more surprisingly, some of the Brewers players had headed out amongst the sea of cars to mingle with fans (and, in some cases, share their food). I managed to get a quick photo with closer Devin Williams before heading into the stadium – and, in a surreal moment, picking up his bobblehead just moments after meeting him.

American Family Field certainly provided a unique environment for a game of baseball – it had a retractable roof, necessitating a wall in the outfield, but unlike some ballparks such as the Rogers Centre it didn't feel particularly enclosed, thanks largely to enormous panes of glass providing views out of the park (albeit a less-than-glamorous view of the interstate rather than one of skyscrapers or natural landmarks). It felt like a smaller and more intimate place to watch a game, despite being decidedly middle-of-the-road in terms of capacity, and I got a good first impression of the place.

I had once again been gifted a ticket for this thanks to the generosity of those following my trip, and it was an excellent seat. I settled down to watch the game, which featured Brewers ace Corbin Burnes on the mound for the home side and Bailey Faulter starting for the visiting Pittsburgh Pirates. Burnes is one of the best pitchers in the game, having been an All-Star for three consecutive years and the recipient of the Cy Young award (as the best pitcher in the National League) in 2021, and he started the game strongly, keeping the Pirates scoreless – and without so much as a hit – for the first four innings. By contrast, the Brewers were getting players on base, but failing to capitalise on it, with a home player reaching first safely in each of the first four innings, before being stranded as the rest of the side could only record outs.

This was to change in the fifth inning, however, as Llover Peguero got the first Pirates hit of the game before stealing a base, Alek Williams drew a walk and Jason Delay got a double to send both runners around the bases. Suddenly the Brewers were 2-0 down and in danger, and even though runners advanced on a Christian Yelich out in the bottom of the same inning allowing Victor Caratini to score and reduce the deficit to a single run it looked as though I would be seeing my third Pirates win of the game.

Until the ninth inning. Pirates closer David Bednar did not have a good outing as Sal Frelick hit a single and allowed Blake Perkins to score the tying run. The atmosphere stepped up a gear, but the Brewers could not capitalise on this, and the ninth inning ended with both sides level at 2-2. For just the second time on my trip, the game went to extra innings, with a runner placed on second base for added jeopardy. Devin Williams was selected to pitch the tenth, with one of the best entrances I had seen for a closer so far, and threw an excellent inning, striking out two of the three hitters faced and allowing no hits or walks.

It was all down to the Brewers in the bottom of the tenth. With the Pirates having already used their best reliever, it was down to Angel Perdomo to shut out the home side. The visitors took a gamble with Contreras due up, intentionally walking him and opting to pitch against the less accomplished Blake Perkins. In the end, it wasn't to be for Perdomo, with Perkins – the man who scored the equaliser earlier in the game – recording a two-out hit, advancing the loaded bases and allowing Caratini to cross home plate and win the game for the Brewers. Fans were elated as the entire home side ran on to the field to celebrate, and I headed back to the airBNB happy.

Location:

I can understand why American Family Field is located where it is – with the fanbase's preference for tailgating, large parking lots are required – but it's one of the more inconvenient ballparks to get to. I was lucky enough to find somewhere to stay within a 20-minute walk, but if I had stayed downtown, or arrived straight in the city centre by public transit, I would have been in a difficult position. In fairness, those who did choose to drive had excellent access – with a dedicated exit from the highway placing fans immediately in the stadium's footprint – and there are plenty of bars about a 15 minute walk away, but having recently spent time at ballparks with such incredible locations and public transport options this one stood out as having a real weakness. It's not as remote as Kauffman Stadium, so it scores a slightly higher score of 5/10.

Concessions:

Milwaukee is proud of its history of brewing – the team is even named after it – so it was perhaps inevitable that the ballpark features an on-site brewery as well as various bars that serve a wide range of alcoholic drinks. The food options were comparatively limited, although there did seem to be a variety of burgers available (certainly over and above that of other parks) alongside the standard options of hot dogs, chicken tenders and snacks. I also noticed that American Family Field seemed to be the only park so far that didn't offer ice cream, instead choosing to focus solely on serving frozen custard as their cold dessert option. The pizza and loaded fries seemed to be the best option, but having eaten a decent lunch on the way (and being slightly tired of greasy ballpark food) I didn't partake on this occasion. Due to the relative lack of options (perhaps this is inevitable when so many choose to eat outside the ballpark), the Brewers score 6/10.

Atmosphere:

I'm not sure if I'd just had good luck with picking exciting games so far, or whether some sets of fans just happen to make incredible noise on a regular basis. Either way, the Brew Crew created a superb atmosphere in the second half of the game – I wouldn't be surprised if the fanbase was what drove the team on to get the walk-off win. Once again, staff and fans alike were friendly, with ushers taking a laid-back approach to fans exploring the lower seated sections before the game, but nothing stood out like in Minneapolis. A fair score here is 7/10.

Weather:

Milwaukee's weather is unpredictable, but it has a much cooler climate than many other parts of the United States. Summers do not get unreasonably hot, thanks to the breeze coming in from Lake Michigan, but there's an ever-present risk of storms. American Family Field counters this by having a retractable roof (one of the most unique in baseball), and features huge air conditioning vents in the top level to cool fans down if the humidity makes things difficult. This provided ideal conditions for watching baseball (although, incredibly, I felt a little cold later in the game), and so the Brewers receive a score of 9/10 here.

Additional Features:

Like many ballparks, the upper deck of American Family Field is enclosed, but the Brewers have taken care to to paint a number of team-based murals on the walls to prevent it from looking dull and uninspiring. This level of attention to detail is evident throughout the park; I liked the "Autograph Alley" section of the lower level, in which fans had inscribed their names on hundreds of baseballs which made up a section of the wall, and the presence of a kid's area in right field provided an opportunity for parents to let their children blow off some steam. Fans had an opportunity to ride mascot Bernie Brewer's slide before the game, and of course the brewery on site added character to the park. It definitely had a Milwaukee feel to it, which is all I can ever ask in this section, so once again the Brewers score 9/10.

Overall:

The Milwaukee Brewers receive a score of 36/50 for their ballpark – slightly lower than some other stadia, mainly due to its poor location and relative paucity of food options. It was by no means a bad ballpark, but the standard had been extremely high so far. Next up was one of the most historic in the sport...

11

WRIGLEY FIELD

"People ask me what I do in the winter when there's no baseball. I'll tell you what I do. I stare out of the window and wait for spring."

Rogers Hornsby

Baseball is a sport with a rich history, which has allowed it to be intertwined with that of the United States over the past hundred or so years and become known as "America's pastime". Those who have shown an interest in the sport will know about the deep cultural impact of Babe Ruth and Mickey Mantle on American culture, and many movies and television shows have plots based around elements of the game.

It's surprising, therefore, that the vast majority of Major League Baseball stadia are relatively modern. 60% of the ballparks are less than 25 years old, and just five have been around for more than half a century (and one of those looks likely to be replaced before 2030). Part of this is due to the fact that different styles have gone in and out of fashion over time – at one point it was popular for multi-sport stadia to be built, allowing baseball teams to share a home with their city's football side – but another element of this constant rebuilding of ballparks is the evolution of technology and the ability to give fans an upgraded experience with a new location.

All of this makes it even more remarkable that two sides have remained in their current homes for over a century each. Both Fenway Park (home of the Boston Red Sox) and Wrigley Field (where the Chicago Cubs play) were opened before the outbreak of World War 1, and despite the enormous amount of change in both technology and culture in the years since neither side has opted to move to a new stadium. It's often mentioned that these two locations capture the imagination of all who visit, offering fans the chance to step back in time and experience the original era of baseball for a few hours. I had visited Fenway in 2022 before this trip began, and had enjoyed it so much that I planned to finish the tour there, but I could barely describe my excitement for the chance to visit Wrigley Field for a game.

The day began with yet another early start – with it being a Sunday, the game was set to take place during the early afternoon rather than in the evening, and so I had an 8am train to catch from Milwaukee. Mercifully, this one started in Wisconsin, so there were no delays to worry about, and it arrived in Chicago without any delays. Arriving in the windy city I was slightly nervous as it was raining reasonably hard, which I thought could threaten the game, but it reduced to little more than a drizzle by the time I made it to the hotel to drop my bags off. From there, it was a short walk to the city's subway system, which provided a short journey to the ballpark itself.

Wrigley Field did not disappoint. From the minute I got off the subway, I noticed the history of the stadium and the area surrounding it. Unlike modern ballparks, which tower above local buildings even when located in city centres, the home of the Cubs had a somewhat understated appearance, and space was so limited that the team store was actually located in a separate building across the road. Even though it was lunchtime on a Sunday, fans had arrived early and packed the local streets and bars, providing an atmosphere and level of excitement quite unlike anywhere else I had visited on the trip so far.

Despite the restricted space for the ballpark, entry was seamless with no queues at all, and once I was in I took the opportunity to walk the historic concourses and explore different views of the field. There was history in every direction, and I knew it would be impossible to see everything in just one visit. Within the seating area itself the three separate scoreboards stood out – the central one being hand-operated and displaying the scores from other games in the most traditional of ways, and the right one being digital but showing various information on the game in a way that made it look like an old-fashioned display. Only the left screen was modern, but all three worked in combination with each other to provide all the details a fan could need.

The history didn't stop inside the ballpark either. The houses on the streets opposite were tall enough to peek over the outfield bleachers, and many had installed stepped seating on top, forming the famous Wrigley

Rooftops. Largely built in the 1980s as a result of the team's growing popularity and the limited capacity of the ballpark struggling to accommodate everyone that wanted to see the side play, they became an icon and are now marketed as a premium seating option. It takes some doing to make watching a game from outside a stadium a popular option, but to me that sums up the unique nature of Wrigley Field.

The game itself was a classic. Scoreless through two innings, thanks in large part to the the strong pitching performances from Braves ace Charlie Morton and the Cubs' Justin Steele, it exploded into life in the third. After Ronald Acuna Jr – a favourite for the National League MVP award this year – singled to centre field, stole second base and advanced on an Austin Riley sacrifice fly, Matt Olson stepped up and hit a home run which allowed both players to score. The Cubs fans refused to give up though, and in the bottom of the same inning the team almost batted around, with a succession of hits, walks, and in Nico Hoerner's case being hit by a pitch the side manufactured two runs to tie the game.

Despite a good fourth inning neither side could advance the score, and it took a similarly good top of the fifth for the Braves to retake the lead – after Acuna was thrown out at home, Ozzie Albies was more cautious in his baserunning but a succession of hits allowed him to score after Olson's single gave him another RBI. Once again, the Cubs responded in devastating fashion, and put on a show in the bottom of the fifth as former Giant Mike Tauchman hit a single before stealing second base and advancing to third after Hoerner's productive out – and being sent home after an Ian Happ single. Cody Bellinger hit a double to allow Happ to score, and the Braves attempted to remedy the situation with a pitching chance. It was to no avail, however, as a Jeimer Candelario single ensured that Bellinger reached home safely and made the score 5-3.

The Braves responded strongly by loading the bases in the sixth inning before Michael Fulmer came in to pitch for the Cubs. Frustratingly for the home side, it took just three pitches for him to give up a run, as he failed to control his throw and hit Acuna with a 94mph sinker. As the bases were loaded, this allowed the visitors to reduce the deficit without Acuna even swinging his bat, although after two extended plate appearances Fulmer struck out the rest of the side and ensured the Cubs retained the lead.

In the bottom of the seventh former Braves player Dansby Swanson hit a double to allow Bellinger to score, restoring the two-run lead, and some excellent pitching from Chicago allowed them to finish the game without any major drama, securing the win to jubilant scenes at Wrigley Field. The

Cubs mascot entered the field with a giant "W" flag, fans sang along to the traditional song "*Go Cubs Go*", and players high-fived one another on their way off the field. The Cubs had been on a hot streak since the all-star break, and this victory ensured they matched the Braves as the best side in the league during that period, giving their supporters a great sense of pride.

And that wasn't the end of the experience for me. The usher's generosity continued as he gave me a VIP ticket which allowed me access to the field for photos after the game – after joining a short queue I was allowed onto the warning track and another member of staff took multiple shots of me with the scoreboard and bleachers in the background. It was a perfect addition to the experience. I headed back out of the ballpark and got some photos of the ballpark's exterior, amazed at the sheer number of fans who had stuck around to drink in the Wrigleyville bars and generally take in the atmosphere. It only cemented in my mind that the Cubs have a truly special home.

Location:

Wrigley Field may not be a downtown ballpark, but it has its own unique location in a northern district of Chicago. Much like the two New York ballparks, it's easily accessible by public transit, with the red line dropping you right at one corner of the stadium and bus routes running similarly close. Unlike Yankee Stadium or Citi Field, however, there's an established area in the immediate vicinity which lends itself to socialising before and after a game. Wrigleyville is quite unlike anywhere I'd seen so far, as a number of bars and restaurants were situated in the streets around the ballpark and fans gathered hours before first pitch and remained late after the game had ended.

The stadium is old, and was built before the trend of including city views in the outfield – instead bleachers and the famous Wrigley rooftops surround the centre field area. It's just as attractive as the riverside backdrop of PNC Park, albeit in a different way. The only downside is a relative lack of parking options for those who choose to drive to the park – inevitable, given that it was built before cars became ubiquitous – and that prevents a perfect score, but there really isn't anything else wrong with it. As a result, Wrigley Field scores 9/10 here.

Concessions:

Wrigley Field may not have the most exciting or innovative options, but you're at what is arguably the most historic ballpark in the game – your experience isn't really complete unless you have traditional baseball fare. With that in mind, the Cubs could get away with serving a menu comprised entirely of hot dogs, chicken strips and popcorn and people probably wouldn't complain, but they've added a lot more as well. I was saving my appetite for later – Chicago is one of the few American cities that has a Nando's, and I was craving the restaurant after being out of the UK for a few weeks – but I did go for ice cream late in the game in order to get the mini helmet for my collection. Interestingly, the Cubs have opted to serve vegan ice cream only, which had a slightly unfamiliar texture and taste, but hats off to the team for embracing something that also helps the environment and is inclusive to all. There wasn't much more the place needed, so it scores 9/10 here.

Atmosphere:

One word would suffice; wow. The Cubs fans know their baseball, and care deeply about their team. They cheered every strikeout or stolen base as though they had won the World Series all over again, and you could tell that the vast majority of them live or die on every single pitch. It made for an intense (but not intimidating) atmosphere, and one that only enhanced the experience of the historic ballpark.

And everyone was, once again, so friendly. Most of my time before the game was spent discussing my trip with those who saw my sign and wanted to talk, with several asking for advice on planning their own adventure. The usher in my section went out of his way to make me feel welcome, offering to take numerous photos before and after the game as well as giving me advice about the best places to see around the park. He told me about the history of certain traditions, gave me tips for visiting the city itself, and of course handed me the VIP pass to allow me onto the field after the game. The most impressive thing of all was that I got the impression he did this for fans on a regular basis. He was a true credit to his team, and combined with the fans inside Wrigley Field it's hard to give the Cubs a score of anything less than 10/10.

Weather:

It felt like being back in Britain. Midwestern weather is famously unpredictable, and after being lucky avoiding rain earlier in the trip it was inevitable that I would experience some wet weather at some point. It was, mercifully, only a light drizzle for most of the game, but it's worth trying to get some seats under cover – I was in the front row of the 200 level and managed to stay dry throughout. It's warm enough in the summer months (indeed, the wind from lake Michigan makes it cool enough to be comfortable almost all of the time, as long as you're in the shade), but at the start and end of the season it can be cold enough for even a Brit to need a big coat. It's something to bear in mind when planning a trip, and it does hurt Wrigley Field, giving it a score of 7/10.

Additional Features:

Many words have been written about Wrigley Field, and I cannot possibly hope to match some of the better articles out there. Simply put, the stadium has history and character in every square inch; I'm fairly certain that you could spend an entire season exploring the place and still find new things every time. The ballpark might not have all the modern luxuries that other stadia can boast, but with almost all visitors coming for the history it's not really a concern.

In particular, I was wowed by the traditional scoreboard in centre field; normally at a game I'm not particularly interested in scores elsewhere, but I kept finding myself drawn to the hand-operated board during the contest to see updates around the country. Beside this are two flagpoles upon which a "W" or "L" flag is raised after every game – as the usher explained to me, this harks back to the days before mobile phones, when locals would see a flag waving after each game and know whether the Cubs had won or lost.

Add in the Wrigley rooftops, the World Series photo opportunities, the ivy walls and the two-deck structure putting every fan close to the action and you've got an experience like no other. Many ballpark rankings put Wrigley Field close to the top of their list – or even in a tier of its own – and with so many features it's hard to argue with this. I can't give it anything other than 10/10.

Overall:

With a score of 45/10, Wrigley Field ranks highly as expected. The score doesn't do it justice in reality though, with the historical ballpark offering an experience completely unlike the vast majority of the league. It's baseball how it used to be, and the sort of place that every self-respecting fan of the sport needs to visit. It only made me more excited to visit Fenway Park for a similar experience, but that would have to wait until the end of the trip…

12

GUARANTEED RATE FIELD

"Say it ain't so, Joe"

Unidentified White Sox fan

If you've ever been to a school sports day, you'll have heard the phrase "it's the taking part that counts". In many ways this is true; exercise has a myriad of health benefits, and recreational sport is a great way to make connections with others. However, there are some who are competitive to the extreme, and elite sports requires those taking part to prioritise winning, often above all else. This can bring out the worst in people, whether that's through a ruthless streak which sees friendships broken and rules of the game pushed to their limit, or via outright cheating.

It's not a good thing, but there is a long history of cheating in professional sport. In the early days of English football it was forbidden to pay players – the sport was originally intended to be for amateurs only. Team owners (usually, at that point, individuals who ran the factory whose employees made up the team) would therefore occasionally bring in star players under the guise of them working for the company, then asking them to complete no manual work and paying them solely for their sporting performances. The television series "The English Game" portrays this in great detail, and was compulsive lockdown viewing.

Baseball is no stranger to controversy either. In my first full season of watching the sport, the Houston Astros won the World Series against the Los Angeles Dodgers, needing the full seven games to take the title. This in itself was not unusual – the fall classic is often tense – and neither was the fact that it was the Astros' first World Series success. As a Giants fan, I enjoyed seeing the Dodgers lose, but little did I know at the time (in fact, nobody knew) that a huge scandal was about to erupt.

Two years later, the media started to report that other teams had suspicions around the Astros' use of technology to help them. During a game, pitchers work closely with catchers to determine the type of pitch they will throw, with the catcher often using a complex and coded system of hand signals to indicate whether it is more appropriate to throw a fastball or a changeup. Indeed, it is often mentioned that the catcher calls the game, and elite players in this position are given huge credit for this skill, as well as their work in keeping their exact code a secret. Nevertheless, if you watch for long enough you can generally work out what each symbol means – and when there's a runner on second base with a clear view of their gestures they will often switch to another code to make things even more obscure.

The rules of baseball allow runners to try to work out this secret code, and if possible relay it to the batter in order to give them a chance to hit the pitch. By contrast, it's not allowed for any technology to be used to do the same thing. In this case, the Astros used cameras in the outfield to record the catcher, and the operator would relay this to the dugout. A coach would then bang a trash can in a specific rhythm to indicate to the batter what pitch they would be facing, giving them a material advantage against opponents. Upon being uncovered, MLB issued harsh sanctions against the organisation, costing them draft picks and suspending coaches, but ultimately allowing them to retain their World Series trophy. To this day, the team are unpopular amongst the side that they defeated on the way to the crown.

You may be wondering why I'm writing about the Astros in the introduction to the White Sox, but the Chicago side might be at the centre of an even bigger scandal – possibly the most significant in the history of the sport. In 1919, the team accused of fixing the result of the World Series against local rivals the Cincinnati Reds in exchange for money from a betting syndicate. This combined a number of negatives – not only was it clearly a problem to throw a game for money, but gambling on sports has historically been illegal in the United States (and has only recently been allowed).

This scandal had far-reaching implications; not only were all involved banned from baseball for life (including those who weren't involved with the conspiracy, but merely aware of what would happen), but the sport introduced the role of a Commissioner to try and prevent a similar event from occurring in the future. To this day, debate rages on about the involvement of individual players – notably the team's star player Shoeless Joe Jackson, who was allegedly absent from all meetings about the matter, and – being illiterate – would have been unable to sign off on the matter in any case. There is an excellent film about what is now referred to as the Black Sox Scandal called *Eight Men Out*, and the event is referenced in the American classic novel *The Great Gatsby*.

Clearly, I was not expecting this scandal to be referenced at the White Sox's ballpark, and was anticipating the stadium to instead focus on better moments throughout the team's history. They were entering this game on the back of another minor controversy though – just two days earlier, star player Tim Anderson had squared up to Jose Ramirez after a routine play, and promptly lost the fight before earning himself a six-game suspension. Anderson was appealing this punishment, making him eligible to play in this game, but it certainly added some interest to this matchup.

It was nice to wake up that morning without needing to travel anywhere – the week had been brutal with so many early starts, and having an evening free the previous day combined with a full morning was something of a luxury. I leisurely explored Chicago in the day, noting with some delight that the city was home to several branches of Nando's – a reason for any Brit to visit. Before long it was time to head to the ballpark, and once again the red line provided a frequent and fast connection to Guaranteed Rate Field. The stadium was located directly next to the stop, and the short walk over a bridge and around to the gate was almost like a sporting event back in England rather than the typically American trip along a busy highway.

The ballpark itself looked very modern – it certainly felt newer than it was, having been opened in 1991. This was partly down to the black paint covering almost the entire interior, which made the place feel slick and up-to-date in a way that few ballparks had done so far. After entering the park and checking out the team store, I was surprised to be asked to show my ticket again; it transpired that fans are only allowed to enter the level that their seat was in, rather than being able to explore the entire stadium. Thankfully I was in the lower deck, meaning I could enter the outfield and explore the main part of the seating bowl.

The game itself was triumphant for the White Sox. After Dylan Cease shut out the New York Yankees for the first two innings, not allowing so much as a hit, Andrew Vaughn hit a two-run homer in the bottom of the second to give the home side a lead that they would never give up for the rest of the game. The Yankees did look like scoring on a few occasions after that – mostly due to walks that Cease allowed rather than hits – but ultimately it took them until the top of the seventh inning (when relief pitcher Lane Ramsey had entered the game) to earn a run and reduce the deficit to one – Billy McKinney hitting a sacrifice fly to centre field, allowing Aaron Judge to score after the iconic number 99 had hit a single and stolen both second and third earlier in the inning.

Just as the game looked like it might become interesting, the White Sox shut it down. In the top of the ninth, they took advantage of Tommy Kahnle's poor pitching performance and piled on the runs. A routine sacrifice play by Zach Remillard was dropped, loading the bases after earlier singles from Gavin Sheets and Elvis Andrus, and a Benintendi sacrifice fly and Luis Robert double was enough to send all the runners home and make the score 5-1. Aaron Judge did his best in the bottom of the inning, hitting a leadoff double, but three quick outs from the rest of the Yankees ended the game and sent the White Sox fans home jubilant to a celebratory fireworks display. I had enjoyed my trip to Guaranteed Rate Field, but was dreading my first experience driving in the US the following day…

Location:

Similarly to Wrigley Field, the home of the White Sox is not located in downtown Chicago. Instead, it's within the city's notorious South Side – ostensibly a more dangerous area – but still adjacent to a subway station. In fact, it's on the red line, providing a direct link to the their cross-city rivals. If there were ever a day when both teams played at home, it would be possible to catch both games with comparative ease.

Guaranteed Rate Field is also surrounded by a number of parking lots, giving easy access to those who choose to drive to the ballpark as well as spectators arriving by public transit. The result of this is that the immediate vicinity is not as interesting as Wrigleyville, which slightly detracts from the overall experience, but overall it's a fine place for a stadium. It doesn't stand out, but it isn't bad either, so the White Sox receive a score of 7/10 here.

Concessions:

The White Sox definitely had more variety than their cross-city neighbours when it came to food. They leaned heavily into Chicago's reputation for pizza, with several stands offering a variety of deep-dish options, as well as the unique offering of a giant helmet full of chicken strips. Perhaps the best options were, once again, in the outfield – several bars, including a sit-down affair where fans could bring their food in and enjoy a drink, were located here, alongside a number of specialty sausages rather than simply being limited to the standard hot dog. There may have been more in the upper deck, but fans were limited to their own section in this ballpark, so I can't give a fully accurate score here. Overall, Guaranteed Rate Field scores 8/10.

Atmosphere:

This ballpark gave off a significantly different impression to the others so far – instead of being a passionate hub of sport, it felt "cool" to me – somewhere that people went to for recreation and entertainment rather than to support their team. Maybe this was a little unfair of me, or maybe it was just the game I chose, but it was enjoyable nevertheless. The crowd did make some noise towards the end of the game, but it was strangely quiet considering they were demolishing the New York Yankees. The fans themselves were friendly, but there was a slightly strange vibe from the ushers who seemed to be treating visitors as potential problems – they checked everyone's receipt upon leaving the team stores, for instance, which made me feel like I was being accused of shoplifting. Perhaps this is a genuine problem, but it didn't feel as welcoming as other parks so far, and with that in mind it scores 6/10.

Weather:

I can't really give the White Sox a different score to the Cubs here – they're located in the same city and, with a straight line distance of about 8 miles, they're amongst the closest two parks in the entire league. I was lucky to experience better weather here than the previous day's visit to Wrigley Field, but that's more down to the luck of the draw than any microclimates. Therefore, Guaranteed Rate Field gets an identical score of 7/10.

Additional Features:

Upon entering Guaranteed Rate Field, there's an immediate downside. It's the first ballpark I've been to on this trip that restricts access to half the park based on where your seat is; if you have a ticket for the 500 level (the upper deck), you're unable to visit the lower concourse, and vice-versa if you're lucky enough to have bought a seat in the 100 level. Considering that half the fun of going to a game is exploring the park and seeing various attractions, it seems disappointing that half the fans can't see the outfield areas. I was lucky enough to know about this in advance and so bought a seat in the 100 level, which meant I was able to see the statue of Harold Baines that stands in right field, as well as the old Comiskey shower which provides a link to the White Sox's past home.

The other key feature which everyone can see is the iconic exploding scoreboard, another tribute to the team's previous stadium. When the White Sox hit a home run, the spirals spin and shoot out fireworks in celebration, and this – in combination with the floodlights – is also used to great effect in the pre-game show. The ballpark also has a unique entrance due to its position against a busy road, with fans crossing bridges after having their tickets scanned to enter the concourses. On the whole, the team have done a fair amount to make this ballpark memorable, but the fact that half the fans are limited in what they see hurts its score – so it receives a measly 6/10.

Overall:

Combining these scores, the Chicago White Sox's home stadium gets a total score of 34/50. It's perhaps inevitable that this would be lower than the cross-city Wrigley Field – after all, it doesn't have the history or the location – but it's by no means a bad place to watch a game of baseball (in fact, it's significantly cheaper, making it a good option for any visitors to the windy city hoping to catch a game).

13

GREAT AMERICAN BALL PARK

"If the Cincinnati Reds were really the first major league baseball team, who did they play?"

George Carlin

I've written extensively about some of the contrasts between American and British approaches to sport, but certain aspects continue to surprise me. Perhaps the most significant difference in the fan experience is how spectators are treated in each country – in the United Kingdom, those attending a match are generally treated as an inconvenience who are there to spend money and cause trouble, whereas most American teams do their best to accommodate fans during their visit, with every ballpark I've visited so far even having a section of the stadium dedicated to "fan accommodation".

To some extent, this comes from the history of sport in each nation. Over the last 50 or so years there have been significant issues with football fans in particular in England; hooliganism plagued the game from the 1970s, with fights during and after games being a common occurrence. Indeed, some teams outright banned visiting fans from attending in an attempt to curb the problem, and some owners proposed electric fences separating supporters from the field of play to try and keep them in check. It probably didn't help that a number of films glamourised this violent subculture, with movies such as *Green Street* and *The Football Factory* seemingly inspiring others to view this as a tradition rather than a shame.

Whilst this did quieten down over the years, it's rare to attend a game now without some form of trouble; away fans are still given their own section of the ground, and there is usually a line of stewards separating them from the home team's supporters. This is usually the location of any flashpoints; sometimes as mild as chanting designed to wind up opposition fans, but often descending into obscene gestures and occasionally fans trying to cross the gap and physically fight those supporting the other team.

It's a massive contrast, therefore, to see the significantly friendlier culture surrounding baseball – and most other American sports. Whilst hockey can sometimes provoke fans into violence, this is much rarer, but baseball provides the opportunity for fans of multiple sides to mix with each other and enjoy the game as one. As someone who has spent years watching football, it continues to amaze me how easy it is for rival supporters to get along and watch matches together, and this gives me even more enjoyment as part of my journey to visit all 30 ballparks this year.

As I mentioned earlier, teams lean into this as well with their provision of fan accommodation desks at every ballpark. Staff of each team are always happy to help, offering certificates to young fans attending their first game at the stadium, and ushers (rather than stewards) located at each seating section are keen to show others around the park and help give advice and directions to fans. This culture extends beyond the ballpark staff as well; in advance of my trip I emailed each team explaining my challenge and asking for any advice, and a number of back office staff replied with insider tips. The Cincinnati Reds, however, went above and beyond, upgrading my seats to some of the best in the house as well as giving me free tickets to the team's hall of fame and museum before the game.

Needless to say I was blown away by this act of generosity. I was looking forward to visiting Cincinnati, but first I had to get there. So far on this trip I had been relying on flights for the most part – which necessitated long waits at airports and early starts – but for the next few days I had hired a car and would be driving around the midwest. There's so much romance about an American road trip; hitting the freeway for hours on end and crossing the country to reach an exciting new destination, and whilst I didn't want to spend an entire day driving, the next few cities were close enough to justify a rental.

I was slightly intimidated by the five hour run from Chicago to Cincinnati, especially as it would be my first time driving an automatic and it had been years since I had driven on the other side of the road, but I was reassured by many people saying that the United States was one of the easiest countries in the world to drive through. After a shaky start around the Avis parking lot, whilst I was still getting used to the lack of a gearbox and simply using the brake to stop, I grew in confidence and was on the highway in a matter of minutes. It was a straightforward drive through Indiana and into Ohio, and after making a quick stop for food halfway through the trip I arrived in Cincinnati and checked into my hotel.

With parking prices near ballparks being notoriously high, I opted against taking the car into the city and instead got an Uber to the wonderfully named Great American Ball Park, picking up my ticket from the VIP desk and entering the extremely comprehensive hall of fame and museum. It was fascinating to read about the history of the Reds, including that of all-time hits leader Pete Rose; there was a gorgeous display by the staircase showing the sheer number of balls that he hit over his career. Sometimes having a visual makes a number seem more impressive, and this was one of those cases. Rose is conspicuous in his absence from the sport's hall of fame after he admitted to betting on baseball during his career – something that generates debate to this day, after some players who used steroids have been accepted – and now spends his days in Las Vegas sports shops signing autographs for those who visit.

The museum also had some tremendous models of the team's previous ballparks, showing the key differences between historic stadia and the modern ones that offer previously unheard of luxuries. As someone who enjoys baseball cards, I was drawn to the corner dedicated to the hobby, with a complete run of the teams' cards on display as well as examples of some of the more modern ideas introduced by Topps. The museum ended with a truly spectacular hall of fame room, where hundreds of plaques displayed names and faces of those who excelled with the franchise alongside videos of their accomplishments. It was an excellent place to visit, and I would have happily paid the full admission fee to see the displays.

And then, it was on to the ballgame. With the museum located immediately next to the park, I was able to enter as the gates opened, and immediately noticed a number of fans waiting down the first base line as the Reds pitchers finished their warmups. Usually the home side have finished before gates open, so it was interesting to watch this, and it was even better to see reliever Ian Gibaut go down the line to greet fans. Gibaut played for Great Britain in the World Baseball Classic, pitching the final two innings as the side recorded a famous win over Colombia, so it was fantastic to meet him and get a photo.

I then had an opportunity to walk around the stadium, stopping into the team store to buy my customary hat. They had a significantly smaller selection than many other teams so far, and I had to settle for a different brand to usual, which was slightly disappointing. There was an interesting outfield area with an all-you-can-eat section (tickets were $25 – if you like hot dogs, that's a bargain) and the left field section interestingly had a number of chain restaurants. It certainly had a unique feel, although it was perhaps lacking significant references to the team's history, which seemed to be confined to the museum outside.

The game itself was a low-scoring affair, but one packed with significance. The Miami Marlins came into the game on the back of 5 consecutive defeats, during which star hitter Luis Arraez had struggled significantly. Scoreless though the first inning, the visitors took the lead in the top of the second after Jake Burger hit a double to reach second base safely and Joey Wendle did the same and allowed Burger to score. They were unable to capitalise on Wendle being in a scoring position, however, and this came back to haunt them in the bottom of the same inning as TJ Friedl's double sent Kevin Newman home to level things up.

The score stayed at one apiece until a spectacular play in the bottom of the fifth. It's safe to say that Stuart Fairchild has had an unremarkable career; the only reason I had heard of him was his short spell with the San Francisco Giants in 2022, and he's struggled for playing time in the big leagues in the past. However, leading off the inning, he hit the ball far into right field, with the Marlins struggling to get the ball back to the infield. Fairchild rounded third and Arraez failed to throw the ball properly, allowing him to cross home plate and score an inside-the-park home run. It was counted as a triple and an error, but fans didn't care, and the fireworks went off all the same. The atmosphere was electric for a moment that will surely be the highlight of Fairchild's career.

The Marlins were stunned, and it took them until the top of the seventh inning to respond when Jorge Soler hit a two-run homer to give them the lead once again. Arraez then recorded a fly out to end the inning, and the scoring for the game was over. The Reds did try to rally in the ninth inning, with Joey Votto put in for Newman with two outs and earning a walk to offer fans some hope, but Christian Encarnacion-Strand struck out directly afterwards to end the game and hand the Marlins the victory. It was an exciting game in which the lead changed hands a couple of times, and those in attendance would have enjoyed the baseball on display. I got an Uber back to the hotel and got to sleep quickly, being exhausted from the drive and needing to prepare for another long trip the following morning.

Location:

Cincinnati might not be the first name on people's lips when they mention the United States' most famous cities, but Great American Ball Park has a wonderful location alongside the Ohio River. It's on the southern edge of downtown, with a nice district to the west featuring a number of bars and hotels. There's a tram line adjacent to the park, and whilst traffic can be bad in the streets immediately next to the stadium after the game this quickly clears once you enter the highway just a couple of minutes away. The stadium has a slightly strange orientation, meaning you look across the river to Kentucky rather than to Cincinnati and its skyscrapers, but this is the only real negative I could find. With that in mind, the Reds' ballpark scores 8/10.

Concessions:

The first thing that hit me about Great American Ball Park was the choice of concessions – there were a number of franchised food options within the park alongside the more generic kiosks that offered up traditional choices. Chief among these was Chick-Fil-A, which had recently opened along the left field line. It was a slightly surprising choice, given that the company is based in Georgia rather than the midwest, but was certainly a welcome addition (I wonder whether there could be any scope to add a KFC to the park, considering that it's a much more recognisable brand, and is centred just over the bridge).

The biggest disappointment, however, was the lack of range available in the team stores. I have been collecting 9Forty caps from each ballpark – offering a one-size product at an excellent price point – but curiously this was absent from the Reds' stadium, meaning I had to settle for a different style of hat. It might be a minor gripe, but there were other standard items that seemed to be missing from the teams' merchandise lines, which surprised me. Likewise, the game-used authentics store was excellent as usual, and I picked up a ball used in the game for a surprisingly low $30, but they failed to sell lineup cards – an item which every other park had for sale so far. With that in mind, Great American Ball Park receives a score of 6/10.

Atmosphere:

Before the game started, I got the feeling that the Reds had a surprisingly low level of support, such was the emptiness of the park. It did fill up after the first pitch, but this was a little disappointing to see given how much ballparks have to offer outside of the games themselves. Considering the team lost, they still made a good amount of noise, and the feeling inside the stadium was incredible when Fairchild hit his inside-the-park homer. The team has a vast amount of history, and you could tell that many spectators were proud of this, as were the club's staff, who were friendly – not to mention the employee who had gifted me tickets to the museum in advance. The Reds can't quite get a perfect score here, but they get a solid mark of 7/10 for atmosphere.

Weather:

I get the impression that this is becoming a little repetitive, since I'm visiting all the ballparks in the midwest at the same time. Cincinnati was, however, a little warmer than Chicago, since it's not directly on a lake. This made it much more pleasant walking around the ballpark during the evening, although the humidity was still a slight issue. There was some light rain during the game, but I get the impression that Ohio doesn't get storms in sufficient severity or frequency to cause mass disruption to games. This might be close to perfect weather for baseball though – any hotter and it becomes uncomfortable, and any colder would make it unpleasant. The rain did make me move seats though, so instead of a perfect score the Reds get 9/10.

Additional Features:

The designers of Great American Ball Park decided to lean into its riverside location with a sailboat-shaped party deck in the outfield, as well as large foghorns that act as launching stations for fireworks during the national anthem and home run celebrations. It's distinctive enough to make the stadium distinctly part of the city. The ballpark also has a unique gap down the third base side in the upper decks, included in the plans when it was built to ensure a clear view of the river from specific skyscrapers in downtown. It also affords fans a view of the Great American company tower – whilst normally a corporate skyscraper would not be a particular highlight the close affiliation with the park's name and the city itself makes it an interesting feature.

The ballpark also has a fantastic outdoors are behind the first base line, incorporating the hall of fame into the stadium footprint as well as offering spectators the chance to enjoy the sunshine whilst eating and drinking before the game. This is the first ballpark that's really included this, and it makes the place feel bigger and more open than others. With this taken into account, Great American Ball Park has a unique feel and one that represents a historic franchise and a baseball-crazed city well, so it scores 9/10 here.

Overall:

Great American Ball Park earns an overall score of 39/50 – on the high side, but let down by some poorly-stocked concession stands and a late-arriving crowd. It was well worth the long drive to watch a game there, and given the history of the Reds it's definitely worth a visit.

14

PROGRESSIVE FIELD

"The franchise is more than a century old. It's been called the Blues, the Broncos and the Naps. It's also been called a lot worse during hard times when the team wasn't winning"

Tucker Elliot

Whilst the history of the United States is indelibly linked with that of the UK, it's also – in its own ways – completely different. Settled by Brits nearly 400 years ago (and, indeed, by various other European nations as early as 200 years before that) seeking to flee the tyranny of their King, it existed as a colony of the Empire for an extended period of time. Eventually, those who had settled in New England and the surrounding areas became tired of continual meddling from British influences, and arguably the final straw was the levying of taxes from over 3,000 miles away – giving rise to the famous slogan of "no taxation without representation". In 1776, the original Thirteen Colonies (plus the then-Kingdom of Vermont) signed a Declaration of Independence – July 4th, the date of the signing, is still a significant holiday in the States – and a war followed to secure that same independence, establishing the United States of America as a country in its own right.

This is a grossly oversimplified version of events, and there are entire books written on the events from nearly 250 years ago explaining what happened in much greater detail, but it serves to explain how the history of the US is so closely tied to Britain – and also explains links both cultural and linguistic to boot. However, the fact that the United States is so new a nation serves to set it apart from the UK – a country which has existed in some form or another for thousands of years – giving it significant differences as well. For instance, most cities are comparatively modern; America is famously car-friendly, whereas much of Britain was built up before automobiles became a popular means of getting around, and the trend of large business featuring countless skyscrapers is an almost alien concept in much of England, since the city centres were built hundreds of years previously.

However, there's a much thornier issue at the heart of American history. Whilst it was colonised and became independent relatively recently, it was by no means a barren wasteland before that. The indigenous people of the North American continent had inhabited the area for centuries prior to the arrival of European settlers, and despite atrocities committed against them during the arrival of those from Europe – again, many books have been written against this, and I do not possess the expertise to expand upon the intricacies of this – many tribes still share the territory to this day, with vast swathes of land given over as Native American reservations. Much of their language still exists in the names of various rivers and states – Alabama, Kentucky and Tennessee are all words with significant meanings in various tribal languages.

Despite this, there are still many misconceptions about the those indigenous people. The myth famously states that Christopher Columbus had set sail to find India in an attempt to establish trade relations, but instead discovered North America – a land which Europeans were not aware of, and promptly dubbed "The New World" – but, like many stories, this isn't quite correct. Contemporary historians believe that Columbus never actually stepped foot in North America; in fact, the continent had been discovered by Norse explorer Leif Eriksson nearly 500 years before Columbus' birth. Nevertheless, as with many myths, it persisted (after all, it's quite a good story), and unfortunately led to many dubbing Native Americans as Red Indians, a phrase that is now considered to be a racial slur.

As with many forms of tolerance, it took years for this to phrase to be recognised as offensive, during which time it was applied to many parts of American life. Indeed, the baseball team in Cleveland adopted the name of the Cleveland Indians in 1915, and maintained the moniker for over 100 years before a growing movement to reconsider the names of a number of sports teams led to the side rebranding themselves as the Guardians in 2022. The Guardians are far from the only team to have made changes in an attempt to distance themselves from this controversy – indeed, the Exeter Chiefs in English rugby removed a similar mascot from their logo and shifted to one of Celtic origin in the same year – but are perhaps the most notable. This move left the Atlanta Braves as the only side in Major League Baseball to have a reference to the indigenous people in their name (more on that controversy soon).

It's taken time for this change to be accepted – it was, after all, a massive rebranding exercise, and the first significant change of franchise name (not including relocations or expansions) for decades – but by and large fans have accepted the change without an issue. The new name of the Guardians refers to the statues that watch over the bridge approaching the stadium, so still has a significant link to the city, and has the benefit of giving the franchise a pretty cool logo to boot.

After a long drive the previous day, I was ready for another car journey across Ohio – the highway taking me straight across the buckeye state and through Columbus without any issues. I was starting to get used to sitting in the left hand seat and learning to adjust my position in the road, and after navigating an American gas station (they use different colours for petrol and diesel, so I had to be careful to put the correct fuel in the car) it was a pretty easy journey. I managed to pull into my hotel just as check-in began, and was very pleased to be upgraded to a suite.

One of the downsides of the Guardians' Progressive Field was that gates only opened an hour before first pitch – I had gotten into the routine of arriving to stadia as early as possible to give me a chance to see everything. An hour simply isn't enough to explore a ballpark, and after a long queue to get in there was limited time to visit the team store, get some photos and find some food. I did enjoy looking through Heritage Park by the bullpens – a miniature hall of fame area for some of the Guardians' greatest players – but I'm sure there were some other cool areas of the ballpark that I didn't get the chance to discover because of the later opening time.

After watching him pitch in Toronto, Kevin Gausman was back on the mount for the Blue Jays, starting against Logan Allen of the Guardians. Gausman was one of the key players in the Giants' historic 2021 season, and really kicked off the trend of San Francisco having a strong rotation ever since. He had struggled in the home game two weeks previously, giving up a first inning home run to Shohei Ohtani (although that's not really something to be ashamed of), but he had a much stronger start in this game.

To be honest, the game as pretty much over as soon as it had begun. After the Blue Jays' leadoff man Whit Merrifield ground out after six pitches, George Springer stepped up and took part in an extremely long plate appearance against Allen. After working a 3-2 count, he fouled off six consecutive pitches before hitting a home run on the thirteenth pitch he saw. This made the score 1-0, and it stayed that way throughout the game to give the Blue Jays the win. It was good to see Gausman pitch seven scoreless innings – only giving up four hits and no walks in that time – and hopefully he's back to his best.

The game was over in less than two and a half hours, and this allowed me to get back to my hotel relatively promptly ahead of an early start in the morning, with a day game in Detroit next on the agenda. It was an enjoyable experience in Cleveland, albeit one that was brief and didn't quite allow me to visit the entire park, leaving me wondering what else I could have seen…

Location:

This is another ballpark that's located on the edge of downtown, so it once again gets the best of both worlds. I stayed in a central hotel and had a short walk to reach Progressive Field – a safe one, being joined by hundreds of other fans – but it's also got a plethora of parking lots nearby for those who choose to drive. I noticed that, as it was right on a highway ramp, traffic cleared quickly, making it a convenient place to visit by car. There was a noticeable lack of public transport in the immediate vicinity of the stadium, which could be slightly problematic for those with reduced mobility. With that in mind, Progressive Field scores 8/10.

Concessions:

I'm not sure if this is a creative meal or a crime against humanity, but Cleveland's local delicacy is a hot dog topped with fruit loops – yes, you read that right, high-sugar cereal on top of a hot dog. I wasn't brave (or crazy) enough to try it, instead opting to visit the build-your-own-burger stand, having tired of chicken most nights. The queue moved slowly since they made each burger to order, but it was a clever way to give everyone exactly what they wanted the result was fresh and tasty.

Bonus marks to the Guardians for making their prices extremely reasonable too – I paid $14 (almost exactly £11) for my meal, which is on a par with specialist burger joints in the UK. Hot dogs were less than $5, as were most drinks, making the ballpark significantly cheaper than many others in the league. On the downside, the game-used store didn't sell balls from that day, and the store had a few key items missing. That prevents the Guardians getting a perfect score, but they still get a respectable 8/10.

Atmosphere:

It wasn't a game with lots of action, so there was limited reason for fans to cheer, but Progressive Field was by no means quiet. A large proportion of the fans were there to support the Blue Jays – Cleveland being one of the closer cities to Toronto, a mere 5 hour drive separating the two teams – and they made themselves heard during the game.

Guardians fans were friendly and clearly knowledgeable about baseball, although ushers were less proactive in keeping aisles clear during the action, meaning many missed parts of the game as people found their seats. The team could really have done with more support – perhaps this is understandable, given their poor record this season – and this hurts their score with it being a relatively low 6/10.

Weather:

There's not a huge amount to add here – once again, it's a ballpark in the midwest so the weather is pretty similar to the parks I'd been visiting for the previous week. Thankfully, it was another evening which didn't get too hot (and, because this one was further from the lakes than those I'd been to in recent days, didn't get too cool either) and the weather stayed dry, making it another pleasant set of conditions to sit and watch a ballgame. Day games would get very hot though, so I'd always recommend finding a shaded set if possible. I can't score the Guardians too differently to others, so it earns a score of 8/10.

Additional Features:

I'm sure there's a lot to see at Progressive Field, but as previously mentioned I didn't get a chance to see that much because of the gates opening so late. In a sport which prides itself on accommodating fans and offering a great number of attractions at a ballpark, it seems counterintuitive to only give spectators a maximum of an hour to see everything. With long queues to get in, it's likely that fans only get about 45 minutes to explore, and I found a lot of that time was taken up by queuing for food and browsing the team store.

I did get the opportunity to see Heritage Park, which was a calm and green space with statues and plaques dedicated to former greats – a standout feature that would be amongst the best of areas in any park so far. I also liked how a lot of the concourse was divided into "districts", including some excellent areas down the third base side and close to home plate. I would have liked to have spent more time discovering other districts around the park, but there simply wasn't enough time, and with that in mind the Guardians get a low score of 4/10.

Overall:

Late gate opening times and a muted atmosphere hurts Cleveland's score here, with the team earning a total of 34/50. It's a real shame, as with a bit more time to explore the park and a winning team to attract more fans it could be a great place to watch a game of baseball, but it fails to live up to its potential. Next up would be the relatively short trip to Detroit to round off the midwest, and it looked like it would be a much better experience...

15

COMERICA PARK

"When I began playing the game, baseball was about as sentimental as a kick in the crotch"

Ty Cobb

The United States is a country that's gigantic in every sense of the word; home to over 300 million people, it's over 40 times the size of the United Kingdom, and features countless cities that are home to vast populations. The fifth biggest city in the UK is Leeds, with just over 750,000 residents, whereas there are 59 such urban areas in the US. Despite this, there are very few with an identity that's recognisable to those abroad. Most Brits could describe what New York or Los Angeles is like, but if you ask them about Hartford, Raleigh or Sacramento they'd struggle to define the culture.

Detroit is one of those few cities that British people know about. Unfortunately, most know it for its high crime rate, with it often being mentioned as a dangerous place to visit. Interestingly, whilst planning the trip, many Americans pinpointed other cities as being unsafe and spoke of avoiding downtown areas and public transit, whereas my experience of those places had been the opposite, finding a lot of the criticism to be unwarranted.

Further research indicated that there were a small number of neighbourhoods in Detroit – far away from downtown – that had some issues with gang violence, but this was true of most cities not just in the US, but around the world, and so I was relatively relaxed about visiting for the game. I find that approaching cities with an open mind generally gives the best experience, and growing up near London I was used to taking simple precautions in busy areas which tended to avoid the typical tourist traps and scams that make some places feel unsafe.

Indeed, looking beyond the city's unfortunate international reputation, Detroit was a place with a great history in the automotive industry. Known as the motor city, Ford was founded in the city in 1903 and went on to have a global impact on transport, becoming the first company to produce cars on such a large scale. To this day, the company maintains a presence in Detroit, having its headquarters in the suburb of Dearborn just a few miles from the city centre, and is closely linked to the local identity. Add in the region's location as the birthplace of Motown, and there's a huge amount of local culture that firmly embeds Detroit as a significant place in the history of the United States. It just goes to show that when you go slightly beyond scare stories and unfortunate reputations, you really can find amazing places.

It was another early start, with the game in Detroit starting at lunchtime. Day games are common occurrences in baseball; as teams play almost every day, the last matchup of a series often has to start early to allow the teams to get away quickly and head off to the location of their next games the same evening. It meant I had to check out of my Cleveland hotel and be on the road just after 7am, and the final leg of my car hire journey was a relatively brief drive to the drop-off point on the outskirts of Detroit airport (I say brief, but two and a half hours would take you a long way across the United Kingdom). A quick taxi ride took me to the centre of the city, and after dropping my bags at the hotel I walked to Comerica Park.

It was a beautiful day, and the park, which opened just as I approached the gates, was resplendent in the sunshine. The Tigers had put real effort into making the stadium represent the team and its history – there were numerous statues in the outfield alongside a list of retired numbers, and after picking up a hat in the team store this area was my first port of call. There was a wonderful usher in this section, who took great pride in telling me about the franchise's success over the years as well as the achievements of many of these players; speaking to him was a great way to spend time before the game. I completed my lap of the park after this, noticing some very interesting food court areas set some way back from the concourse, being formed of circular outdoor areas. There were rides (a carousel and ferris wheel) in the centre of each area, and various food options surrounding these.

The Tigers gave rookie Reese Olson just the tenth start of his career; the young pitcher had struggled in recent starts, and had a tough matchup against Twins star Kenta Maeda. Both pitchers started strongly – neither team managed to score in the first five innings, with the Twins recording just two hits and three walks in that time, alongside the Tigers' similarly paltry total of two hits and a single walk. In the bottom of the sixth, the game sprung into life, as young star Riley Greene hit a 453-foot home run to right centre field and put the home side in the lead.

Both sides changed pitchers in the seventh, with Chasen Shreve throwing a scoreless inning in just eleven pitches before Dylan Floro had a much more problematic inning for the Twins. After striking out Spencer Torkelson in four pitches, three consecutive Tigers hitters singled and loaded the bases with just one out. The situation was begging for runs to be scored, and Zach McKinstry obliged, hitting a double to right field and allowing both Kerry Carpenter and Javier Baez to reach home safely, increasing the lead to 3-0. No further runs were scored after this, and the Beau Brieske pitched two scoreless innings to round out an impressive victory for the home team. Whilst Cabrera never got on the field, it was still an enjoyable matchup to watch during his final season in baseball.

However, the game itself became almost irrelevant compared to my experience at the park. Unbeknownst to me, the wonderful Yakub – who had reached out on social media a few days before the trip and offered me the ticket – had contacted a few people in advance and let them know about my trip. One of them was his season ticket rep, who had organised a bag of goodies to help remember my time in Detroit, including a wooly hat which will be vital once back in the UK needing to cope with the winter weather!

Yakub had also spoken to Johnny Kane, the TV host for Bally Sports in Detroit – the station that broadcasts Tigers home game in the local area as well as on MLB TV – and let him know about my trip. Johnny then came to interview me in the top of the fifth inning, letting me explain the journey and my love of baseball. It was a surreal experience, with my phone going crazy for the rest of the day after various people had seen the interview on both the TV broadcast and the subsequent Twitter post.

Even better, the Tigers team had seen the interview, and very quickly I was met by someone from the back office and taken to the media section behind home plate, where I was shown around the various studios and camera areas. It was a truly comprehensive VIP tour, and I was able to get some photos holding a microphone, wearing a radio headset and with play-by-play commentator Matt Shepard. The team, as well as Yakub, had gone so far out of their way for me that I was absolutely speechless, and for the rest of the day I almost kept bursting into laughter at how surreal my experience had been. It just goes to show that there are some amazing people in baseball, and I knew it was the most welcoming sport in the world.

Location:

Comerica Park is similar to a lot of the recent parks I had visited, in that it was located towards the edge of downtown. Detroit has a somewhat unfair reputation for violence – whilst it's true that there are some suburbs that are unwise to enter, the vast majority of it is as safe as any other American city – and unfortunately many visiting fans will probably avoid walking around the area, but I found it a very pleasant 20 minute walk from my hotel on the riverfront. There are a number of bars surrounding the stadium, as well as a range of hotels for most budgets. It's also worth noting that Comerica Park is right next to the NFL stadium Ford Field, forming something of a sporting district.

The people mover has a stop next to the park, allowing access to other parts of the city – although the scope of this form of public transport is slightly limited. There are also a number of parking lots (including two multi-storey garages) in the immediate vicinity, but with road closures getting away might be a little trickier than in a city like Cleveland or Milwaukee. It therefore can't score quite as highly as those cities, but the central location helps it out, and so the Tigers' ballpark scores 7/10.

Concessions:

There are a couple of areas behind the main concourse which offer the full range of food options – mostly ballpark classics, such as pizza, hot dogs and chicken. This means the concourse itself is fairly limited; the vast majority of kiosks only sell a range of hot dogs and pizza slices, meaning you have to walk a little further to get something different. The ice cream was scooped rather than soft-serve though, and featured some of the largest portions I've experienced on the trip so far (three giant scoops which completely filled the helmet; I couldn't finish it), and there was a wide range of flavours available rather than the limited choice of chocolate, vanilla or strawberry that seems to be the de-facto range at most parks.

Comerica Park also seems to have more large merchandise stores around the ballpark than other stadia; an excellent range of items were available, and there was an extensive selection of merchandise for Miguel

Cabrera's final season with the Tigers. The game-used store was disappointingly limited, however, with the side unable to offer balls from that day's matchup (as someone spending just a day in each city, it was impossible to wait until the following day to collect one). What was on offer around the park was good, but the range of food and authentic memorabilia was slightly limited, meaning Comerica scores 6/10.

Atmosphere:

I can't fault the welcome I received – even ignoring the unbelievable experience offered to me by the broadcast team, staff and fans alike were incredibly friendly. Before the game started, I had long conversations with both the usher in the bleachers (who took the time to talk about the team's history and take photos of me with the Miggy Milestones signs) and fans in the outfield, all of whom were proud of the team and represented their city well.

The crowd was somewhat limited – but considering it was a midweek day game when local schools were back, it was pretty respectable. Those that did attend certainly made a reasonable atmosphere, and were rewarded with a good display from the Tigers. The scoreboard operators used various prompts and music to get the crowd going, and I could imagine the ballpark would be extremely loud during evenings or playoff games. Spirits were understandably high after the game, and fans stuck around to savour the win rather than leaving early, which is always nice to see. Taking the inconvenient game time into account, it was a reasonable atmosphere, and so Comerica Park scores 8/10 here.

Weather:

This was my final ballpark in the midwest, so you'll be pleased to learn there will be some variety in this score coming up soon. Detroit is situated on the river with the same name, and close to Lake St Clair (part of the Great Lakes, but not one of the five usually listed), meaning the heat rarely becomes unbearable. The ballpark does, however, lack shade during a day game, with only the very back rows of the lower section getting any respite from the sun, which can still burn despite the lack of extreme heat, so it's worth spending a bit more for those seats or packing a lot of suncream.

Like Chicago, Detroit can get extremely cold during the first and last months of the season – it's not unheard of for April evenings to reach zero degrees Celsius, so it's definitely worth packing a coat. There was some rain on my way back to the hotel, and thunderstorms are somewhat common during the summer, so even a light coat is recommended during July and August. It's pretty standard for the midwest though, and so Comerica Park gets the typical score for the region of 7/10.

Additional Features:

This is where Comerica Park really shines. The ballpark was clearly built with the team's history in mind, and there are statues galore in the centre field bleachers, as well as a counter to track Miguel Cabrera's hits and home runs as he rounds off his career. In fact, the park leans heavily into Cabrera's career, with the concourse being home to a couple of giant bobblehead statues of him alongside a throne where fans can get a photo celebrating his triple crown from 2012. It's a good way to spend some time pregame, and I learned a lot about the franchise's history whilst looking around. The team have also placed some interesting displays throughout the concourse celebrating each decade of the franchise, cleverly disguised as carts from a distance.

The Tigers have also got the unique distinction of having fairground rides within their stadium – behind the first base line was a carousel at the centre of a food hall, and a barbecue in left field was located next to a ferris wheel (featuring miniature baseballs as the seats). Combined with multiple tiger statues – including a gigantic one outside the right field gate – the ballpark has a fun feel to it, setting it apart from the others. Add in the "happy hour" where fans can get cheaper drinks between gates opening and the game starting, and there's very little to fault about the park itself, with it earning a score of 10/10.

Overall:

Adding all these scores up, Comerica Park gets a total of 38/50 – the relative lack of variety in food options preventing it from becoming a truly elite place to watch a baseball game. I enjoyed the day much more than the score suggests, and I'll always remember the exceptional way that the team, broadcast crew and fans treated me. There was little time to reflect on that, however, as it was on to the nation's capital for stop number 16 the following day...

16

NATIONALS PARK

"Maybe it's finally our turn"

Ryan Zimmerman

Capital cities are often home to the most famous attractions in any given country. Mention the United Kingdom and people will think of Big Ben or Buckingham Palace, and talks of France will evoke a mental image of the Eiffel Tower. Rome's Coliseum is perhaps the most notable sight in Italy, and Africa's most famous attraction – the Pyramids – are just on the edge of Egypt's capital Cairo.

The United States is no different – with the nation's capital hosting some of the most well-known sights in the world. Washington holds a unique status in the country – the only city that's not located in one of the fifty states that make up the US, instead being part of the District of Columbia – and is notable for having perhaps one of the most densely-packed collection of landmarks in the entire continent (if not the world). The iconic Capitol building is a stone's throw from Union Station; the home of the country's legislature and, of course, the scene of dramatic events in 2021 that are still being investigated to this day.

From there it's a short walk to 1600 Pennsylvania Avenue – better known around the globe as the White House, home to the President of the United States, regularly referred to as leader of the free world and the most powerful man on the planet. It's an even shorter trip to the iconic Washington Monument and Lincoln Memorial, and on the way you pass countless museums and sights that you will have inevitably seen in countless movies over the years.

You'd think, therefore, that such a location would be ripe for sports teams. The endless flow of businessmen and tourists create an ideal market for any side – and, after all, the majority of teams based in capital cities tend to be successful. I've previously mentioned how sides such as Chelsea, Real Madrid and PSG dominate European football, and the natural fanbase and wealth that comes from being in a city such as Washington DC would clearly make the side strong year after year.

It comes as a surprise then that the American capital has struggled to host baseball in the past. In fairness, the Washington Senators were one of the eight founding teams of the American League back in 1901, and stayed in the city for nearly 60 years before moving to the Midwest and rebranding themselves the Minnesota Twins (you've read about them already) – claimed to be the result of falling attendances at the time, such was the dynamic of the city at the time, but later reports suggest that the team's owner was motivated by racism and a "whiter" population in Minneapolis.

The District of Columbia didn't have to wait long for another team, as an expansion team – also called the Senators – were formed in 1961, but they were arguably even less successful at putting down roots in the nation's capital, lasting just ten years before moving to Texas and becoming the Rangers. They were similarly unsuccessful at baseball, failing to win so much as a division title during their time in Washington (in fact, it took the franchise until 1996 to win their first division, and they remain one of six teams to never win the World Series).

Despite frequent additions to the Major League roster, Washington DC then went an extended period of time without a team – in fairness, having two separate sides fail to establish a fanbase and move out of the city is hardly a vote of confidence – and it took over thirty years before the capital would once again have a baseball side to call their own. The Montreal Expos were formed in 1969 – one of the many expansion teams of the era – and became the first MLB side to be based in Canada (and the only one for the first eight years of their existence).

Financial challenges, broadly centred around broadcast rights in the United States, limited the team towards the end of the century, and in 2005 the team moved out of Canada and found a new home in Washington DC, becoming known as the Washington Nationals. This remains the only instance of a Major League team moving to another country as part of a relocation – and, at the time of writing, the most recent move in baseball (more on that later).

The Nationals were due to play against a side who were looking increasingly likely to become the next side to move – and you'll read more about the struggles of the Oakland Athletics in due course – but this was also shaping up to be a game between two sides with extremely poor records (the Nationals and the Athletics had the 26th and 30th best records out of 30 respectively). This inevitably led to predictions of a poor crowd, despite the game being scheduled during the prime time of Friday evening, and the team had put on a few promotions, including the option to purchase special tickets to watch batting practice from the field.

I had jumped on the chance to do this; I had enjoyed the opportunity to watch the teams warm up in Kansas City, and being on the field itself was a rare opportunity. It was a relatively late start that morning, having finished visiting all the parks in the Midwest and needing to catch a lunchtime flight out of Detroit to get me to Washington. It was my first flight in a week, and I quickly realised how little I missed the long TSA lines and extended hours waiting in departure gates, but mercifully it was a short trip and before long I had arrived in the capital, and checked into my hotel slightly early.

I had received an email from the team asking me to be at the ballpark just after 4pm; 3 hours before the game was due to start. It was a pleasant enough day, and I was determined to enjoy the weather before heading to the oppressive heat in Texas the following day, so I took a leisurely trip to Nationals Park and walked from a nearby subway station to the VIP entrance, where I was given a very official-looking field access pass. The group of us that had gathered were led down in a lift to the service level, where we walked down a long tunnel and on to the warning track behind home plate.

The Nationals were out on the field practicing defensive routines, and I was lucky enough to have a quick chat with birthday boy Michael Chavis. I had seen Chavis hit two home runs in London a few years ago, and he was astonished that I remembered this; we shared a quick chat about the game and my challenge, and he very kindly posed for a photo with my sign. It was then time for the Athletics to take batting practice, and as with before I loved seeing the entire thing unfold. It was especially nice to see rookie Zack Gelof on the field less than a month after making his debut – a large contingent of his family had made the journey to Nationals Park to support him, and it was touching to see them so proud of his achievements.

After both teams had finished hitting, we were led back to the 100 section of the park, at which point I met up with Joel and his wife, who were regulars at the ballpark. They showed me into the luxurious club level and gave me a tour of the small museum-like area behind home plate, with a large display of items from the team's successful run at the World Series in 2019. Much of the team had left since then, including star slugger Juan Soto, and others had struggled to reach the same heights since. They introduced me to the ushers in their frequently-visited section, and gave me some very good seats to sit in.

It provided me an excellent vantage point for the game, which pitched the Nationals' Joan Adon against Paul Blackburn of the Athletics. It was not a good start for the hosts – after leadoff man Esteury Ruiz flied out to centre field, JJ Bleday hit a single and Zack Gelof drew a walk from Adon to put the visitors in a strong position early on. After Seth Brown struck out swinging, rookie Jordan Diaz hit a single to send both Bleday and Gelof home and put the Athletics 2-0 up. Tyler Soderstrom then hit a fly ball straight to centre field and was out to end the inning, leaving the hosts with a mountain to climb after just the first inning.

The game remained scoreless for the Nationals until the bottom of the second, when three consecutive singles from Dominic Smith, Ildemargo Vargas and the brilliantly named Stone Garrett allowed them to level the score at 2-2. Two innings later, a sacrifice fly from Jake Alu allowed Vargas to score the go-ahead run, and a Keibert Ruiz homer in the fifth put the Nationals 4-2 up. Three innings later the Athletics crumbled; Vargas hit a three-run home run and put his team 7-2 ahead, with Alu hitting a moonshot of his own in the bottom of the eighth to put some gloss on the score at 8-2. By that point, I was incredibly tired – the consecutive days of travelling (this was my seventeenth consecutive day of watching baseball as well, having caught two games in Pittsburgh) was taking its toll – and I was glad that the game ended shortly later, allowing me to make a quick getaway and get to sleep before it got too late ahead of another early start the following day.

Location:

Given that Washington DC is a densely packed area, and the team (and park) are relatively new, it was always going to be a challenge fitting Nationals Park into the city. They've done a good job, however, with a busy sporting district (DC United's stadium is a short walk away) housing the stadium as well as multiple bars lining the walk to the subway station. As a city on the busy East Coast, there's a frequent, efficient and cheap public transit system, making it easy to access the park from any of the capital's landmarks (I stayed just outside Union Station, and was back in my room within 30 minutes of leaving the ballpark at the end of the game – including time spent getting to the subway and waiting for a train).

Nationals Park has multiple parking garages surrounding it (two are actually built in to the corners of the stadium), although it looked like police closed the roads in the area for games, so getting away seemed tricky. The only other downsides I noticed were that the land to the east of the ballpark was somewhat undeveloped, and felt less impressive than the rest of the surrounding area, and the lack of distinctive view behind the outfield. The side had cleverly built up the area around it, giving a nice view of the bars, but it didn't scream "DC" to me, meaning Nationals Park loses some marks and ends up with a score of 7/10.

Concessions:

Capital cities are generally the most expensive places to live in each country – indeed, many jobs in London offer a higher salary than elsewhere in the UK to counter this increased cost of living, and other nations likely do similar. That said, the prices at Nationals Park weren't that much higher than the rest of the league, and were actually below some parks that I'd visited so far – although $10 for an ice cream helmet felt a little excessive.

The bigger problem was the lack of range. The best ballparks had unique items (even if they were questionable choices, like Cleveland's slider dog or Denver's rocky mountain oysters), but the Nationals seemed to stick with safe options such as pizza, hot dogs and chicken tenders. The outfield area didn't seem to be home to any different choices, unlike other parks, but there was a good range of merchandise in both the team store and game-used kiosk. Bonus marks for various stalls selling empty mini helmets – if I'd noticed those before buying one filled with ice cream, I'd have gone for it. It's not quite enough to save its score though, with Washington's ballpark getting 6/10 here.

Atmosphere:

Credit to the fans – their team had been playing badly, and were up against an even worse side, but they came out in decent numbers and made some noise. The stadium holds over 40,000 spectators – decidedly middle-of-the-road in the context of the league, despite it feeling much larger than most I'd visited so far – and it was a little over half full, but it felt like a sellout crowd at times. Those in attendance cheered loudly every time the Nationals scored (which was several times during the game), and it felt like a very supportive atmosphere for players on the team.

Bonus marks are also given for the fans getting behind the Athletics' supporters' pleas for John Fisher to sell the team. Every game this season the Oakland fans have loudly chanted in the top of the fifth inning, and many Nationals fans joined in with this, creating an environment where teams didn't matter and both teams came together as one. On top of this, team staff were friendly, with the ushers in my section being particularly lovely, although security staff were slightly frosty when picking up on-field credentials, which went slightly against the feeling of the rest of the park. If it weren't for this, Nationals Park would get a perfect score, but I can't ignore it, and so it earns 8/10 here.

Weather:

There's no getting around it; Washington DC gets hot and humid (bordering on muggy) from June to August. I'm reminded of a former colleague who used to work just outside the capital talking of tourists standing out because of sweat soaking their shirts during the summer months, and I felt like I was suffering the same fate at times despite trying to stick to the shade. It's not quite as bad as some of the southern states, but it was significantly less comfortable than the Midwest, with only the later evening providing some respite from the conditions. Earlier in the season would be a sensible time to visit, but it's worth noting that American weather in general is more extreme than that of the UK, and it still gets chilly during spring nights.

It's probably something of a middle ground in the context of the country – Texas and Arizona get hotter, but some of the northwest is much cooler – so it's not getting a terrible score, but I think 7/10 is fair here.

Additional Features:

I've mentioned this already, but Nationals Park felt vast. It doesn't hold many more than others in the Major Leagues, but the seats had slightly more legroom and the outfield area was significantly more spacious, creating an enjoyable feel throughout the stadium. The team have leant heavily into their 2019 World Series success, with many displays around the club level (including several game-used jerseys and the trophy itself), but it would be nice to see this more accessible to all supporters rather than those who have paid more for tickets. I liked the Expos logo in the stairwell, but it felt hidden – this was the feeling I got for the whole park, with many of the interesting features being tucked away rather than on full display.

Before the game, the park felt alive, with a band playing in the outfield and a buzzing bar area on the approach to the stadium, and this was perhaps the main thing that set the park apart from others that I'd visited so far. It wasn't city-specific, though – and perhaps the only reference to the team's location was the mascot race which featured a number of giant former Presidents running around the field during a break between innings. I'd like to see more distinctive things around the park, and that's reflected in Nationals Park's score of 6/10 here.

Overall:

It's a lower score for the home of the Washington Nationals, with a total of 34/50 reflecting the ballparks' somewhat cookie-cutter nature. It was still an enjoyable place to watch a game, but the rest of the teams had set an incredibly high standard.

17

MINUTE MAID PARK

"You gotta love this team, well some people hate this team, but you gotta respect this team"

Dusty Baker

It seems that every sport has teams with certain characteristics. Whichever sport you follow, one team will generally be head and shoulders above the rest when it comes to trophies – in football (or soccer), you've got Real Madrid with 14 Champions League titles (double that of the second most-successful), rugby has Leicester with 11 Premiership wins and baseball has the New York Yankees, who lead the way with 27 World Series crowns. Success tends to breed further success, and eventually teams build up such a formidable reputation that they become favourites year after year.

Similarly, there are the perennial underdogs – consider Everton in recent years, or the Miami Marlins and Oakland Athletics; in fact, it's probably more impressive that baseball sides seem to be poor year after year since the draft system gives them the best prospects in exchange for finishing with the worst record. It's perhaps less surprising in international football; small nations such as Andorra and San Marino have been considered whipping boys for decades, but such countries have limited resources and players to choose from, making it a remarkable success that they can field competitive teams in the first place.

But you've also got teams who have periods of success despite overwhelming unpopularity. The best example of this in English sports is Leeds United; considered one of the biggest clubs in the country despite achieving very little for over twenty years, they had an eleven year spell during the sixties and early seventies in which they won three league titles and never finished outside of the top four (in addition, they won two minor European competitions and three domestic trophies). During this time, Leeds were incredibly controversial due to a style of football that was considered somewhat physical – it probably didn't help that defender Norman Hunter was nicknamed "bites yer legs", or that fans used to sing about how captain Billy Bremner "would break himself in two" for the cause.

Famously, legendary manager Brian Clough took over the managerial reigns and attempted to change this reputation, telling the players that they could throw their medals in the bin since they hadn't been won fairly. Clough lasted just one month in the role after the squad failed to subscribe to his school of thinking (I can't possibly imagine why) – being succeeded by Jimmy Armfield – and the whole affair is chronicled in the excellent book *The Damned United*, which was later adapted into one of my favourite sporting movies of all time. This marked the end of the side's period of success, but the fanbase and reputation remained and, still playing their fearsome brand of football, they won a few trophies towards the start of the nineties, including the final top-flight season before it was rebranded as the Premier League.

Perhaps the closest baseball side to Leeds United are the Houston Astros. I've already written about the controversy surrounding their 2017 World Series win, which still causes Yankees and Dodgers fans to froth at the mouth, but this allowed the Texas side to launch into a period of real success. The team's first win since they were formed in 1962 (in fact, only their second pennant in that time), they then went on to compete in three more World Series in the space of five years, cementing their position as one of the most successful sides in the sport.

And fans hated it. With baseball being played behind closed doors in 2020 due to the Coronavirus pandemic, the following year offered the first chance for supporters to make their feelings known to the players implicated in the 2017 scandal. Many dubbed it the "shame tour", and trips to New York in particular featured some extremely intense reactions from those in the stand. On the milder end of the spectrum some dressed up as trash cans to taunt Astros hitters, but others screamed obscenities at those most involved for the entire game; Jose Altuve came in for some of the worst treatment, even from fans of teams who were unaffected by the entire thing.

All of this made later successes even sweeter for Astros fans; the team went on to win it all in 2022 against the Phillies, and were therefore the reigning world champions for my visit to the city. The entire situation seemed to have created something of a siege mentality for both players and supporters, and this inevitably led to them making it clear how proud they were of winning the World Series twice in the space of five years. Branding around the ballpark was clear, and the Astros had some of the most active Twitter fans that I had seen on the trip so far. In fact, their fanbase reminded me of another English team; Millwall have created a similar feeling around their team after their fans had built up a reputation for causing trouble over the years, and are perhaps most famous for their chant "no-one likes us, we don't care".

Following seventeen consecutive days of watching live baseball I was completely exhausted, so the opportunity to have a rest day was most welcome. There was still an early flight from Washington thanks to scheduling, but after landing in Texas it was short bus ride to my hotel, which allowed me to check in and get to my room early. The Astros were actually playing that evening, but I had opted to go to the game the following day, and I spent the rest of the day catching up on admin work and resting up before getting an early night. I had made a quick visit to a local convenience store for some food and drinks, and the intense heat of Texas mixed with humidity hit me immediately, cementing in my mind that it was a wise decision to have a day off to catch up on sleep. Sunday's matchup was a day game, meaning I would have two consecutive days where I could get to bed at a reasonable time – something I was looking forward to following several days of late finishes.

Feeling refreshed the next morning, I embarked on the short walk to the ballpark. Minute Maid Park was only half a mile from my hotel, but in the late morning heat it could have been an hour away. I made the mistake of stepping into the sun at an intersection, quickly realising that it would be wise to stick to the shade after that. Mercifully, the gates opened just as I arrived at the stadium, and the air conditioned interior was sweet relief which made a huge difference immediately upon stepping inside. This was my first ever baseball game with a closed roof, and I was curious how this would change the feel of the stadium.

In all honesty, it didn't make a huge difference to the atmosphere of the place; the ballpark was cavernous and unless you looked directly upwards you barely noticed that it was enclosed. I collected my giveaway item – a set of cornhole bags, which were significantly heavier than expected (I immediately wondered how they'd fit in my luggage that night) – and made my customary visit to the team store, which was located in the historic Union Station. With gates opening two hours before first pitch, there was plenty of time to explore Minute Maid Park, and I'm glad I had such an extended period as there was simply so much to see (more on that later).

This was my second time watching the Angels as the visiting team on this trip, and once again I was excited to see Shohei Ohtani play. On the previous occasion I saw him, he hit a home run with the very first pitch he faced, but was unable to follow up with a similarly spectacular feat this time as the greatest player in the sport grounded out to second after working Astros pitcher Jose Urquidy to a full count. Urquidy recorded a perfect first inning, striking out Mickey Moniak and Brandon Drury either side of Ohtani's plate appearance, and repeated this in the second before giving up a double to Moniak in the top of the third, allowing Eduardo Escobar to score the opening run of the game.

By comparison, the Astros were scoreless through the first five innings, despite working Angels pitcher Chase Silseth through a number of pitches early on. The home side had won the first two games in the series but were looking unlikely to record a sweep, and this was made even more uncertain in the top of the sixth. After catcher Chad Wallach singled to left field, Moniak grounded into a double play and it looked like the score would remain at 1-0. Enter Shohei Ohtani, who hit a 448-foot home run to centre field about as casually as it's possible to do so, doubling the Angels' lead and making the score 2-0.

The Astros did respond in the bottom of the sixth, as a Jon Singleton hit was enough to allow former Giant Mauricio Dubon to score a run that halved the deficit, but that concluded the scoring for the game. Singles from Alex Bregman and Chas McCormick in the seventh and eighth innings respectively hinted at a comeback, but excellent pitching from the Angels bullpen – including three strikeouts in the eighth – put pay to any hope of this. Jose Altuve flied out to right field for the third out of the ninth inning, and fans left Minute Maid Park despondent at the defeat despite winning the series overall. It was another warm walk back to the hotel, where I was grateful to still have much of the afternoon to prepare for the rest of the trip.

Location:

Minute Maid Park is another stadium to be located on the edge of downtown; situated by the old Union Station, it's near the football (or soccer) ground and right next to a metro line, as well as having parking lots in the immediate vicinity. It was less than a ten minute walk from my hotel, and there were plenty of other accommodation options near the park.

The biggest downside would apply wherever the park was in the town though – Houston is simply not a city that's suited to public transit. There's no options for getting to the city from other nearby towns (in fact, there are just three train a week to the one station there) and the heat makes walking anything other than a short distance practically impossible. Considering this, the ballpark's in the best location it could be, and so it receives a score of 8/10.

Concessions:

I entered Minute Maid Park via the southwest corner – it was the nearest gate to my hotel, and offered the least time in the Houston heat – and was immediately met by the glorious smell of a barbecue. It's only a small kiosk, but its aroma permeates a large part of the concourse and makes a trip to the ballpark a much more pleasant experience. The rest of the food isn't too much beyond the standard for baseball (although the chicken was distinctly of the southern fried variety versus the plainer breading at other parks), but the Astros made up for that with a wide range of bars inside the stadium. Perhaps understandably considering the large crowd, queues were long – especially for ice cream after the seventh-inning stretch – and prices were slightly higher than others, but all the options I saw looked good.

On top of this, the ballpark had more full-sized merchandise stores around its footprint than anywhere else I'd seen so far. Union Station had been fully converted into the flagship shop, which offered a unique browsing experience, but all sides of the stadium had proper stores, with the lack of kiosks around the concourse being notable. There was an excellent range of products available, although it's worth noting that Minute Maid Park was another place that didn't offer game-used baseballs from that day's matchup. On the whole, there was plenty for fans to explore, but a few missing items – both memorabilia and food – limits its score to 8/10.

Atmosphere:

I've mentioned that there's something of a siege mentality surrounding the Astros, and the consequence of that is that the fans really get behind the team. The consistent success over the last few years has led to extremely healthy crowds, and they made noise throughout the game despite the disappointing result on this occasion. The downside of this is that some supporters weren't completely familiar with things; routine fly balls were cheered as if they were home runs, for instance. The club have made a real effort to put on a show using the lights and screen, which is helped by the indoors environment that allows them to control the lighting more than those whose parks are exposed to the elements.

Everyone is friendly too – although I'm not sure if this would still be the case if you were a Yankees fan wearing your team's jersey to the park. Brooke didn't need to collect a jersey for me but she did, and those who took photos of me holding the sign were genuinely interested in my journey so far. I get the impression that the team are proud of their success and love it when people are happy for them, despite the reaction they get from a lot of opposition supporters. I can't fault anyone I spoke to, so the Astros score 9/10 here.

Weather:

There's no easy way to say this – Houston is hot. Even compared to the muggy conditions that can plague the East Coast, it was astounding to feel just how warm it was after landing in the city. To tell the truth, it was uncomfortable but not unbearable in the shade – especially when you're in no rush to do anything – but the combination of heat and UV index made it downright dangerous to be in the sun for any extended period of time.

Thankfully, the Astros have built a ballpark with a roof and air conditioning. My first step into the stadium gave me a sense of relief as the oppressive heat turned into comfortable coolness, and the lack of direct sunlight inside meant there was no need for any form of UV protection. The team has plenty of glass forming the outfield wall, meaning there was still a good amount of natural light entering the field, and the strong amount of climate control inside meant it was a pleasant atmosphere to enjoy a game. I can't ignore the sheer amount of heat I experienced walking to and from the park though, and so Minute Maid Park scores 8/10.

Additional Features:

The main thing I look for in this category is something that makes the park unique, or representative of its hometown. Minute Maid Park has this in spades – interesting features include the train atop the outfield wall, which moves back and forth throughout the game and has an enthusiastic driver hyping fans up during games, as well as the arches below hosting an impressive hall of fame walk. The Astros also lean into the city's history of space travel with a giant astronaut statue near home plate, as well as an interesting display which links this with the team's City Connect jerseys.

Impressively, the club were able to link old with new when building this park. The stadium is located on the site of the old Union Station, part of which remains standing and now hosts the main team store in one corner of the ballpark. The World Series trophy is housed within this store, allowing all fans to see it, and there are similar displays of the team's success scattered around the park and offer multiple photo opportunities. Add in a number of bar areas and party decks and you've got a genuinely very good place to catch a game, completely justifying the fact that the gates open two full hours before each game (there's just so much to see). I'm struggling to think of a stadium so far that has as much for fans, and because of that Minute Maid Park scores 10/10.

Overall:

It's a strong score for a controversial team, with the home of the Astros earning an overall mark of 43/50 – the fourth highest on the trip so far. It was an excellent place to watch a game, and with the team challenging for another title the baseball on display is similarly enjoyable. I would be heading across the Lone Star State to watch another game before getting a chance to escape the heat, and was interested to see how the newest park in the league would measure up to Minute Maid Park...

18

GLOBE LIFE FIELD

"It is baseball time in Texas!"

Chuck Morgan

It's hard to believe that it's been more than three years since the entire world ground to a halt as a result of a global pandemic. Whilst things have generally returned to normal now, it wasn't that long ago that people were stuck indoors with lockdowns limiting any form of physical interaction, and international travel was seen as an unacceptable risk. I'm slightly surprised at how easily I forgot about the uncertainty and fear that struck many people at the outbreak of Covid, and how large the death toll loomed for so long, such was the speed at which it seemed to go back to normality after a few years. As a teacher, I was placed into the previously unimaginable position of working from home, delivering online lessons and only being in school on extremely rare occasions. Of course, many key workers did continue as normal, but the vast majority of adults changed their life significantly for several months, if not years.

Like most things, baseball was heavily affected by the pandemic. Whilst Spring Training had started and players were starting to prepare for the season before the entire world ground to a halt, they were not afforded the luxury of continuing to work out as a team, even in the form of a bubble. As the uncertainty began to give way to attempts at working out a route to normality, the question of starting the season raised its head. It was clear that the games would need to be played without fans – this was, after all, still early in the course of the pandemic and mass gatherings were several months away – but with the increased space this afforded and the outdoor nature of the sport the league started to come up with a plan to restart safely.

When you look back on it, it's a miracle that we got any baseball at all that year. Spring Training restarted in July – nearly five months after it would usually begin – and the Canadian government refused to allow the Blue Jays to play in Toronto (in hindsight, this was perhaps understandable; at a time when the vast majority were not allowed to travel, countless trips across the border would look tone-deaf at best). In fact, the schedule wasn't even known at the time that players reported back to their teams, and eventually at the end of July clubs started to play a significantly shortened 60 game season. In an attempt to reduce travel, each side played a reduced number of opponents; two-thirds of their games were against division rivals, and the other 20 were interleague games, meaning that teams only faced off against 10 others (compared to the usual 20, and now all 29 teams in the league).

The knock-on effect of this was that it became significantly tougher to judge which team was the strongest. In an ordinary year you could say with some certainty that the sides with the highest winning percentage would be the best, but with the season reduced to just 37% of its usual length and teams playing a smaller variety of opposition this became almost impossible. As a result, the league opted to expand the postseason from 10 teams to 16 (meaning it was easier to make the playoffs than miss out), with the top two teams in each division qualifying as well as a wildcard spot in each league. The roster was increased from 25 to 26 players (although the typical September expansion was virtually eliminated) and the designated hitter was introduced to the National League, which eventually became permanent – as did the introduction of a "ghost runner" in extra innings.

It wasn't a perfect solution – games did get postponed on numerous occasions due to players testing positive over the course of the season – but it was something. Looking back it's clear how unusual this season was, but at the time fans were glad to have some form of baseball to keep them occupied during the endless hours at home. As a result, many fans still dispute the legitimacy of the Dodgers' World Series crown that year, feeling as though they had failed to run the full marathon of a 162-game season which usually grinds many players down and forces them to show a different skillset to that which marks a 60-game sprint.

The postseason had another quirk too. Usually teams shuttle back and forth between their home cities in a playoff series, but with travelling still heavily restricted it was decided to hold the later rounds at neutral venues.

Whilst a handful were selected for the division series, the newly-constructed Globe Life Field in Texas was used for the National League Championship Series as well as the World Series in mid-October. It was certainly strange seeing such a modern venue for the first time without any spectators in attendance, but I was captivated – I watched much of it live, as lockdowns had ruined my sleep schedule at the time – and I knew that this would be a special stop on my journey.

After the previous day's game in Houston, I was relatively refreshed and ready to brave the slightly more manageable temperatures of the early morning. I had booked a coach to Dallas – at about four hours, it was no slower than a flight once travel to the airport and time waiting at the gate was taken into account, and it was significantly cheaper too. It was an extremely nice coach, featuring large reclining seats, and with only a handful of people on board the journey was quiet and relaxed. We pulled into Dallas early (it was just as hot as Houston, but marginally less humid) and after a short connection to my hotel I started to prepare for that night's game.

Arlington was a relatively hefty journey from downtown Dallas – the entire area is one large metro area in reality – but any reservations I had about the ballpark were removed as soon as I walked through the gates. Many people who had visited Tottenham Hotspur's new stadium have been wowed by the sheer scale and modernity of the place, and I had a similar first impression of Globe Life Field. It was vast, clean and built with comfort in mind, and despite many ballparks being relatively new this one stood out as being a class above. It was perhaps a touch too corporate for some, but as a visitor for a one-off game it simply blew me away.

Somewhat uniquely, the park is sunk into the ground, meaning the level that fans entered on was actually the concourse for the second deck. Spacious all the way around, I overheard another spectator suggest that it felt a little like a shopping mall, and I thought that was a good comparison. Every aspect of the supporter experience had been taken into account, with clear signage and various concessions arranged in a way that made the park feel easy to navigate despite its cavernous nature. After making my usual visit to the store and getting some photos, I noticed that Chuck Morgan – the team's iconic stadium announcer – had his booth located on the main concourse right behind home plate and was encouraging fans to come in and meet him before the game. He was interested to hear about my trip, and generously gave up his time to speak about it before posing for some photos.

I went down to the lower level after that, with my seat being located in just the third row along the first base line. This area felt luxurious, despite my ticket being relatively inexpensive, and it was a real treat to have access to a lounge area partially located under the field. The view from this lounge wasn't for me though, and I headed back up to get an incredible brisket sandwich before going back to my seat to watch the game.

It was an extremely one-sided affair; the Angels simply didn't show up and recorded their third defeat in as many games that I had seen them in. Failing to score a run all game – in fact, they only managed a solitary hit in the top of the second – a steady trickle of Rangers runs put the game beyond doubt fairly quickly. Sloppy play in the bottom of the first almost gave the home side the lead early on, but Patrick Sandoval rescued the visitors from a sticky situation. It was in vain though, as a Marcus Semien hit allowed the Rangers to score two runs in the second and a good third inning put them 5-0 up.

After another run was added in the sixth, the game went wildly out of control for the Angels in the bottom of the seventh. After Grossman doubled to lead off the inning, Martinez hit a single and a home run from Marcus Semien piled on another three runs before Garcia added two more with a moonshot of his own. Both prompted loud fireworks from the stadium roof, and the visitors seemed to give up, putting position player Eduardo Escobar in to pitch the eighth inning (and promptly giving up another run, making the final score 12-0). I left promptly after the final out, after securing the ball that put the first two runs on the board from the authentics store. It was an enjoyable evening at a modern park, and a great end to my time in Texas.

Location:

Despite being brand new, Globe Life Field is an absolute pain to get to. The Dallas-Arlington-Fort Worth metropolitan area is huge, but it has next to no public transport infrastructure, making it a nightmare to navigate. I was staying in downtown Dallas due to an early flight the following day, which made it necessary to pay for an Uber to the ballpark; even then we encountered significant traffic on the highway despite arriving early. To be fair to the team, this isn't a new problem; they'd made efforts to build the park directly opposite their previous home, which remains standing and is now used by smaller teams on rare occasions.

It's something of a sporting district, with the NFL stadium also visible from the Rangers' ballpark, and as a result there's a plethora of parking options nearby – this is clearly a place to drive to. There was also a small social area (Texas Live) in the vicinity, giving fans something to do before the game itself. Getting away seemed challenging, however; finding my Uber back to the hotel was tricky and there seemed to be no clear signage on where to go. The roads around the ballpark were gridlocked, although this cleared once on the highway, making it a relatively easy journey back. This doesn't make up for the lack of public transit though, and so Globe Life Field scores 5/10.

Concessions:

One of the benefits of building an entirely new ballpark is the total flexibility in design, including what food options you install and where you place them. The Rangers leaned heavily into the Texas food scene – various stands served tacos, nachos and Tex Mex as well as barbecued food. The Lone Star State is well-known for going big on food, and Globe Life Field doesn't disappoint here, with hot dogs and burgers measuring two feet in length. Add in all the standard options and this ballpark certainly pulls its weight.

Globe Life Field comes into its own in the lower level though. Wine bars, dessert stalls and restaurants line the concourse, and that's before you even consider the various suites dotted around. Prices weren't too bad even in this section, and considering the portion sizes it was a good value evening out. Bonus points to the ice cream stands for selling helmets separately – after eating an excellent brisket sandwich and chocolate brownie I wasn't sure if I had room for a sundae as well. I can't fault anything here, so the Rangers score 10/10.

Atmosphere:

The Rangers certainly had some extremely friendly staff – something which worked in perfect synchronicity with the more luxurious nature of much of the seating bowl. Guest services were outstandingly nice, giving me a bag of gifts for checking in with them as well as a scavenger hunt list of sights around the park. Staff in the store were engaging and struck up conversations with each customer, and ushers welcomed me to my seat as if I were an old friend. Hosts in the hospitality areas were noticeably laid back as well – I was expecting to be questioned upon arriving in the luxury level, but they were clearly used to fans from all walks of life having tickets for those sections, making sure that I didn't feel out of place.

Fans sitting nearby were similarly friendly, and it was great to talk all things baseball with those around me, as well as several others being really positive when they realised the aim of my trip (this includes Chuck Morgan, who made a real effort to speak not just with me but with everyone queuing to meet him). However, there was a lack of real atmosphere within the park despite the team's huge success this season – quite possibly due to the team's historic struggles and subsequent difficulty attracting a significant fanbase. With that in mind, Globe Life Field scores 8/10.

Weather:

Just like Houston, Dallas gets extremely hot, which led the Rangers to constructing a ballpark with a roof and air conditioning – in fact, this was the main reason for constructing Globe Life Field, with their former home lacking this and reportedly being an almost unbearable place to watch a game. Whilst this makes the ballpark similarly comfortable, it does suffer from the heat being a problem before walking through the gates, albeit with a touch less humidity than Houston receives. It wouldn't be fair to score this park any differently to Minute Maid, and so it also earns a score of 8/10.

Additional Features:

This park has it all. Upon entering, I realised how modern and high-tech Globe Life Field was, but there was also a slight reservation about how this might lead it to become somewhat corporate and soulless as a result. However, after visiting guest services and being handed a list of sights to see, I realised that the Rangers had made this stadium their own. The sheer number of eateries and suites – I suspect a large proportion of ticket holders will have access to at least one of these – transforms the ballpark experience into one with a touch of luxury, and whilst some may have concerns about the corporate nature of the concourses it allows for excellent circulation and small queues wherever you choose to go.

There are nods to the state around the park – from former player quotes and murals of various icons to plaques marking Chuck Morgan's iconic lines (I particularly liked the large sign stating that it was baseball time in Texas). Morgan's booth being so open to fans was another fantastic touch, and something I hadn't seen at any park so far. The scoreboard hanging from the roof was also something that the ballpark did differently to the others – as were the fireworks which launched horizontally after home runs, which were loud enough to scare me the first time they went off! It was almost perfect; my only reservation was that there wasn't any large standout feature that made the park stand out from the seating bowl, instead being scattered around the concourses. It's difficult when constructing such a modern park to do this, but Minute Maid Park shows that it can be done – and that therefore limits the Rangers' score here to 9/10.

Overall:

Adding these up gives Globe Life Field a total score of 40/50 – it's one of the best parks I've visited, but it's another stadium that's let down by a poor location. Next up would be a trip to my favourite of them all, and I was looking forward to seeing how I would view it in the context of so many   others   on   this   trip…

19

ORACLE PARK

"Remember the final two words in our National Anthem; Play Ball"

Tom Brokaw

My love of sport is not just limited to watching live games; like many people I enjoy playing video games based around football as well. In recent years EA has become more reliant on its sports arm, with the FIFA series becoming one of the most successful game franchises in the world. In particular, the Ultimate Team feature allows players to set up their own side – ostensibly limited by a pack-based system but in reality closer to a fantasy team style – and play against each other. Looking at it from the outside, it seems incredible that millions of people buy a new entry in the series with very minor differences each year, but this annual purchase is a symbol of the size of its fanbase.

But FIFA isn't the only game based around the sport. Far from it in fact; there are a plethora of options, including the gloriously nerdy *Football Manager* series, which allows players to take over the running of a club and role play as the titular manager. A game which has no clearly defined end goal, the player can control tactics, transfers and even individual training routines, all of which affect the individual games and success of the season.

It's often described by critics as a giant spreadsheet; everyone in the game has numerous attributes which fit together to form an overall squad profile, and a keen eye to detail is required to fit all the pieces of the puzzle together and form a winning team. Users are encouraged to tinker with tactics and adapt over the course of the season, and this comes together to form an incredibly addictive gaming experience – the lure of "just one more game" usually ensures gaming sessions are lengthy.

This has caused the game to gain a cult following. Many dedicated players become deeply familiar with effective tactics and individuals who progress to become stars over several seasons, and these names are often mentioned years later in deeply ironic ways. Few outside the community will remember Cherno Samba, Freddy Adu or Tonton Zola Moukoko, but those who play the game probably look back at them more fondly than Messi or Ronaldo. Indeed, one player discovered a randomly-generated character (referred to as a "newgen") called Ivica Strok, and dedicated many years to chronicling his fictional career online.

There was an excellent book written by Iain Macintosh about the phenomenon of this series a few years ago called *Football Manager Stole My Life: 20 Years of Beautiful Obsession*. It features stories from several gamers whose lives were affected by the games, and is a fun read for anyone interested in that sort of thing. However, the main thing that resonated with me was the second part of the title – the phrase "beautiful obsession" is a simply superb way to describe so many things in life, not least the support that sports fans have for their teams.

It was a phrase that I felt aptly described my love for the San Francisco Giants; since watching them back in 2017 my interest in the side had grown, and it was common for me to wake up extremely early in the morning to watch their games before work. I had seen them play a number of series on the East Coast since then – the shorter flights and less severe time differences making it easier to see them play in New York and Philadelphia – but I was incredibly excited to head back to the Bay Area for the first time in six years to see them play at their home park once again.

It was the final early start for a while as I woke up at about 4am in Dallas, getting a taxi to the airport and a chance to escape the extreme heat. Fort Worth was an enormous place, with multiple terminals, but it was extremely well-organised and after quickly navigating TSA I settled into a lounge and prepared for the week ahead. There was a quick connection in Salt Lake City – I was impressed to see the Utah airport had its own LEGO store and if I had luggage space I could have spent a fortune there alone – but before long I had landed in San Francisco and was in another taxi to the hotel.

My parents had flown out to California on their own holiday, and I was excited to see them again after several weeks away – not least because they had a generous baggage allowance and had brought an extra suitcase out for me, allowing me to swap out my growing collection of souvenirs for new clothes and create extra space in my own luggage. It would be their first baseball games in America, and I was looking forward to showing them the wonderful experience that the sport offered as well as explaining some of the intricacies that can confuse newcomers.

They'd booked a VIP pregame tour as a surprise, and we got to the ballpark early to make the most of this opportunity. After visiting the store – I got a new jersey with Patrick Bailey's name on the back after the rookie catcher was becoming more impressive by the day – we met the guide and headed out to the field for batting practice. Incredibly, she had spent time living in the same small city that I grew up in, and others in the group had the same surname as me. It felt as though this tour was some kind of fate.

We caught the end of the Giants hitting, and Blake Sabol was kind enough to spend time speaking to us and posing for photos, as was Gabe Kapler. Manager Kapler had the unenviable job of taking over from the legendary Bruce Bochy, and had done very well in his four years in the role, including a season where the side broke their record for most wins. Perhaps most impressively, he was unusually socially progressive, and had been outspoken in support of civil rights and the direction of the country – it could be claimed that he was a perfect fit for the notably liberal city of San Francisco. His open communication had won him significant praise from the players, and he felt like an incredibly modern manager for a team that needed a new direction after a few poor years.

Our tour guide then showed us some of the most spectacular views from various points in the park – including some gorgeous panoramas of the bay from the upper deck – as well as the exclusive Gotham Club, which was formed as a speakeasy in the prohibition days when the side played in New York. It's testament to the creative and luxurious designs of modern ballparks that this area featured bowling alleys and pool tables alongside various suites, and it would have been entirely possible for visitors lucky enough to have access to spend their entire time away from the action on the field.

Like all good things, the tour eventually came to an end and we headed back to the main concourse after seeing the media area and finishing with a look at the Giants' recent trio of World Series trophies. The team had won it all in 2010, 2012 and 2014 as manager Bruce Bochy created something of a dynasty alongside legends such as Buster Posey, as well as Brandon Crawford, who remained on the team. The gigantic trophies provided the perfect backdrop to the concourse, and we headed to our seats with a full awareness of what the club could be capable of again in the future.

It would be unlikely to happen this season, however, as the Giants were several games back from historic rivals the LA Dodgers, who had once again spent heavily and were running away with the division. San Francisco were by no means having a bad season though, and were comfortably second and a few games ahead of the wildcard spot, despite losing heavily to the visiting Tampa Bay Rays the previous night. They had blooded a number of rookies this year, with the aforementioned Patrick Bailey being the most promising, and Wade Meckler was the most recent to make the jump to the Major Leagues after making his debut the previous day. Meckler had only been drafted one year prior, and was just the fourth player from that year's class to make his MLB debut (the other three had come through the Angels' system).

He'd have his chance to make an impact on the game, but not for a while. It started slowly, with both sides scoreless through the first five innings. The Giants had opted to make this a bullpen game – in fact, they were operating with only two recognised starting pitchers, with Alex Wood relegated to a reliever role after several poor starts – and Jacob Junis gave them four innings with just two hits and one walk (plus an error in the third). The Rays were starting with former Giant Zack Littell, and he allowed just a single hit through five innings, before the game shifted significantly in the sixth.

With Sean Manaea pitching a good fifth inning, striking out two batters and inducing a ground out in addition to allowing a walk, he came in and kept the Rays scoreless in the top of the sixth. The Giants, however, blew the game open in the bottom of the same inning, with Thairo Estrada hitting the go-ahead solo home run to left field. After Lamonte Wade Jr struck out, Wade Meckler recorded his first Major League hit, singling to centre field and forcing the visitors to take Littell out of the game. Kevin Kelly came in to replace him, and immediately gave up a home run on the first pitch he threw – Wilmer Flores allowing Meckler to score as well and making the score 3-0.

Things got even better for the Giants in the seventh inning – Kelly continued to pitch, and after giving up a single to Michael Conforto he walked Patrick Bailey. A fielding error allowed Blake Sabol to reach base safely, and with no outs and the bases loaded it looked likely that the Giants would increase their advantage. By that point, we had walked round to the outfield to explore the park, and had a superb view from centre field as (after Brandon Crawford struck out and Michael Conforto was thrown out at home) another error allowed both Bailey and Ramos to score and increase the lead to 5-0.

In the eighth inning the Giants added another two runs on – a Michael Conforto double and Patrick Bailey single each allowing players to reach home safely – and a three-strikeout perfect inning from Luke Jackson earned San Francisco the win. It had been a perfect afternoon at Oracle Park (albeit an extremely long day), and after a taxi back to the hotel I went to bed happy with not just the win but the entire experience.

Location:

Maybe I'm biased here, but Oracle Park is perhaps the most perfectly located in all of baseball. Situated right on the San Francisco Bay, it has the scenic backdrop of China Basin (affectionately nicknamed McCovey Cove after legendary player Willie McCovey). This gives fans a rare chance to catch a boat to games, as well as the local MUNI metro system having a stop nearby (and the heavy rail system being a few minutes' walk away too). The ballpark is also a short walk from the central location of Union Square and Embarcadero, which offers BART connections further afield, and the Giants own much of the nearby land allowing them to operate several parking lots.

Getting to the game was extremely easy – although we were very early – and heading back to the hotel after was also fairly simple, with the major rideshare apps having designated pickup spots a couple of blocks away allowing for a better flow of traffic. There's nothing to fault here, and so the Giants get a score of 10/10.

Concessions:

Being on the West Coast and in the centre of the Bay Area, San Francisco's food scene is heavily focused on seafood. Oracle Park leans into this, with the Crazy Crab Sandwich being one of its iconic dishes alongside clam chowder and fish tacos. The Giants also take inspiration from the Bay Area's more progressive mindset, featuring organic food and gluten-free stands as well as a garden area where fruits and vegetables grown are sold within the park itself. Dessert options are headlined by the local Ghirardelli company, offering intricate sundaes as well as the more typical pretzels and waffles. This is, of course, in addition to the standard ballpark classics, combining to create an extraordinarily vast menu.

The Giants have come under some criticism for their pricing over the years, with many believing Oracle Park to be one of the more expensive in the game. There's been some effort to remedy this in recent times, however, and prices did seem a little more reasonable than I was expecting. It wasn't as cheap as Cleveland, but it was less than you'd pay in New York, and it seemed worth it considering the wider range of options available. Add in the excellent game-used memorabilia store and vast team shop and there's something for everyone at Oracle Park, meaning it earns a perfect 10/10.

Atmosphere:

Since I've started following the Giants, there hasn't been a vast amount to cheer about – the first four years I watched were all losing seasons, and even when they did finally make the postseason they fall at the first hurdle. Despite that, the team has historically been extremely successful, and as a result they draw a huge crowd. Once they started putting runs on the board the atmosphere became electric, and fans genuinely seemed like they were having a good time. Ushers were friendly as ever, and the tour guide certainly knew her stuff. It's once again a score of 10/10.

Weather:

What a contrast to Texas – after a few days in the sweltering heat of the Lone Star State, San Francisco felt genuinely cold. There's an oft-repeated quote from Mark Twain that states "the coldest winter I ever spent was a summer in San Francisco" and after walking around the outfield later in the game I could understand where he was coming from. The breeze from the Bay makes the climate extremely mild in the day (although the UV index is still very high, so suncream is a must) and chilly in the evenings; you'll need a coat at this park.

That said, it's not uncomfortable – it's easier to add an extra layer than it is to survive the heat – as long as you're expecting it. The fog rolling in over the course of the evening makes the park seem somewhat atmospheric, which is a nice touch, and it's a much drier city than much of the Midwest, but it's not quite the warm evening environment that sums up the American pastime. Taking that into account, Oracle Park drops its first points as it earns a mark of 6/10.

Additional Features:

Perhaps the best thing about Oracle Park is the view – just like

Pittsburgh, it's considered the defining feature – and the first time you see the San Francisco Bay from the upper deck it will take your breath away. Pine trees in left field add to the view, making it a real California landscape. There's also the giant Coca-Cola bottle (which have slides inside, allowing fans to do something fun before or during the game) and glove nearby, as well as the raised boardwalk along the right field line, with all these features combining to give a unique backdrop for a game of baseball.

The Giants have also made an effort to put the character of San Francisco into the ballpark. A replica trolleycar in the outfield offers an interesting section of seating, and the team mark home runs with jets of water and a foghorn (a welcome departure from fireworks) to represent the city's maritime history. Perhaps uniquely, fans walking along the pier can watch a few innings through a gap in the wall as well, and I've yet to see a fan offering as many as three World Series trophies in the same display cabinet in the main concourse. It adds up to a terrific fan experience, and therefore the Giants score 10/10 here.

Overall:

I'm sure there will be some accusations of bias, but Oracle Park is widely regarded as one of the best – and the total score of 46/50 is earned on its own merit rather than simply being the home of my favourite team. Next up was one of the least popular ballparks, and I was curious how it would compare to the home of the Giants...

20

OAKLAND COLISEUM

"If my uniform isn't dirty, I haven't done anything in the baseball game"

Rickey Henderson

Once in a while, you get a true sporting shock. It may be one that's somewhat surprising – think the Chicago Cubs overcoming their curse and winning the World Series, or Carlos Alcaraz beating Djokovic in the Wimbledon final – or it may be one that comes out of nowhere. Perhaps the most recent example of such a big upset came in 2016 when Leicester City, a historically provincial club, won the Premier League despite starting the season as favourites to finish bottom of the table, with bookmakers suggesting the odds were 5,000/1 (or 500,000 in Moneyline odds); an implied probability of 0.02%. Incredibly, this was the same year that the Chicago Cubs overcame the famous Curse of the Billy Goat and won their first World Series in over 70 years.

But neither of these come close to the story of Wimbledon Football Club. Emerging from the British non-league system into the fourth tier in 1977, the side surged through the divisions and ended up taking just three years to work their way up from Division 4 to Division 1 (the precursor to the Premier League) – unheard of in the modern game, and pretty unlikely back then as well. But that wasn't all. Fuelled by a tight-knit bond between the players, Wimbledon beat arguably the best club in the world at the time – the great Liverpool team of the late 1980s – to win the FA Cup. Legendary commentator John Motson famously declared that "the crazy gang have beaten the culture club", and every single football fan of a certain age will reminisce about what is regarded as the last great football shock.

However, the story of Wimbledon had a sad ending. Despite their success, they never built up a particularly large fanbase – English football fans are famously territorial, and other nearby sides had swept up the support of local fans before their emergence – and after a raft of new safety legislation came in during the early 90s the team could not afford to upgrade their stadium to meet the standards. After more than a decade playing at nearby Crystal Palace's Selhurst Park ground and effectively being run out of a portacabin (a sorry state of affairs for a club that had won the footballing world's premier domestic cup competition, and would go on to spend 14 years in the top flight), the club announced their intention to move 50 miles north to Milton Keynes in what would become the first (and, to date, only) significant relocation in modern English football.

Predictably, there was an outrage. Whilst the fanbase was not large in number, it was vociferous, and the traditionalists were understandably unwilling to travel such a large distance every week to watch their local team. Nevertheless, after a new stadium was designed and funding was secured, the team moved and were renamed as MK Dons. To this day, they remain one of the most passionately hated teams in football, with opposition fans bitterly referring to them as "Franchise FC". Wimbledon fans eventually created their own phoenix club – AFC Wimbledon – and after the former club's decline and the latter's eventual climb through the league pyramid, both teams now play at the same level.

By comparison, American sports teams seem to move fairly often. Indeed, the club I support famously relocated from New York to San Francisco nearly 70 years ago, and the majority of baseball sides have changed city at least once in their history. The most recent team to move (and, in fact, the only one in the past 50 years) were the Montreal Expos, who in 2005 moved to the US capitol and became the Washington Nationals. The decreasing frequency of these relocations seems to match the increasing hostility with which they are received, and there is no better indication of this than the Oakland Athletics.

The Athletics are one of the most storied franchises in North American sports. Formed in 1901 as the Philadelphia Athletics – one of the original eight baseball sides to set up the Major League system – they spent over 50 years in Pennsylvania before a relatively short 13-season spell in Kansas City. Following the Giants' successful move to San Francisco and the increasing popularity of baseball in California, the Athletics moved to nearby Oakland in 1968, and have remained at the city's Coliseum ever since. The team became one of the most notable in the late eighties thanks to the overwhelming power of Mark McGwire and Jose Canseco – nicknamed the "Bash Brothers" – who led the Athletics to the 1989 World Series trophy.

In the late 1990s, the side pioneered the "moneyball" concept, and their use of advanced statistics and clever player recruitment led to a historic 2002 season in which they set a record winning streak of 20 games on the way to winning the American League West before falling in the Division Series. Their approach was so successful and revolutionary that a book was written about the team, which was later turned into one of the most famous baseball movies of all time, starring Brad Pitt as the side's general manager Billy Beane.

But just like the story of Wimbledon, that of the Athletics don't look like they're going to have a fairytale ending. Other sides caught on to the data-driven approach and star players moved elsewhere as the side's winning percentage steadily declined, and after 2007 the team went on a run of just three winning seasons out of eleven. In 2016, the side was purchased by John Fisher, and whilst results improved the crowds continued to dwindle. Little investment was made in the Coliseum, which was now showing its age, and the team started to make noises about needing the city of Oakland to fund a new ballpark. The Raiders – the NFL side who shared the stadium – moved to Las Vegas in 2020, and left them with a ballpark which had been extensively adapted to play host to multiple sports.

Sure enough, rumours started to emerge about the Athletics also looking to move to Vegas. The silence from the club was deafening, and fans began to stay away in greater numbers as their fears looked likely to come true. In 2022, the Oakland Athletics and Major League Baseball announced their intention to move the team to Las Vegas as soon as possible, and I think it's fair to say that almost all fans across the sport were devastated by the decision. Attendances dropped to record low levels in a boycott of Fisher's ownership – it's now normal to see crowds of less than 5,000 at the largest ballpark in America, which should hold more than ten times that number – and fans reported a complete lack of interest from the ownership. It's a truly sad state of affairs for such a historic club, and I felt conflicted about visiting the Coliseum.

Upon arrival, the situation became even more apparent. With gates opening minutes after I stepped off the BART, I was expecting to see at least a few fans waiting to get in, but there was barely anyone around. The bridge linking the station to the ballpark had a couple of vendors – I picked up a "sell" shirt to show support to the fans and join the protest against the owners – but there was no issue walking to the gate. The mesh fencing around the bridge made the place feel a little like a prison, and I was reminded of Bristol Rovers' Memorial Stadium that had a similarly unwelcoming feel.

It was pretty obvious that those in charge had not even invested in a proper entry system, with ushers moving tape back and forth to allow fans passage through a ticketed area to reach the gates, and once inside the concourses were so quiet that you could hear a pin drop. After completing a lap of the stadium – the outfield areas didn't even have any concession stands open – I found my seat and settled down for the game.

To be honest, the Athletics didn't have a chance. The visiting Orioles had been completely transformed by key rookies Adley Rutschman and Gunnar Henderson, and the latter made an immediate impact by hitting a single before reaching third on an Anthony Santander hit and subsequent throwing error. Ryan Mountcastle and Cedric Mullins then reached base safely as well – the former on a single and the latter on a double – running the score up to 3-0 before the first inning was over. Whilst the hosts pulled one run back in the bottom of the inning, it was clear that they would be second best in this contest.

The Orioles continued to run up the score as the game went on – scoring two more runs in the second inning thanks to a Henderson home run (which also allowed Rutschman to score) and another pair each in the fourth and fifth – making the host's job significantly more challenging. The Athletics were by no means bad hitters, but horrendous pitching and fielding gave them a mountain to climb whilst the game was still in its early stages, and this made their four runs on twelve hits almost irrelevant. A huge number of fans had left before the fifth inning was over, and with the score 9-4 at this point they could hardly be blamed.

In fact, the scoring was completed after the fifth; whilst the Athletics did load the bases one inning later they were unable to capitalise, and the remainder of the game featured little action. This meant that BART was almost completely empty on the way home – those passing through would perhaps be unaware that a game had even taken place – and I arrived back to San Francisco with an overwhelming sense of sadness for what was taking place in Oakland. It's clear that there is a significant disconnect between fans and owners, and the looming move to Las Vegas isn't helping anyone right now. I think it's fair to say that the best thing that could happen is for the Athletics to stay in Oakland, and for those in power to listen to supporters.

Location:

Oakland is regarded as a slightly less attractive area than neighbouring San Francisco, but it's a busy place in its own right. Whilst the Coliseum is conveniently located directly adjacent to a BART station (connecting it not only to its own downtown but also to the rest of the Bay Area; in fact, it's less than 20 minutes from San Francisco's Embarcadero) it's not particularly central to the city itself. Anyone flying into Oakland airport will see the stadium; it marks the intersection of the rail link to the wider network, and a direct footbridge links this junction to the ballpark, meaning fans never have to step foot into the nearby neighbourhoods.

There are also the standard range of large parking lots in the immediate vicinity of the Coliseum, and with the Arena in the same location it creates a small entertainment district. It's pretty uninspiring as far as ballparks go though, and it's made even worse by the complete lack of any outfield view thanks to the construction of Mount Davis before the Raiders moved out. This limits its score pretty heavily to 6/10.

Concessions:

John Fisher comes under heavy criticism on a regular basis for the slow decline of the fan experience at the Coliseum, and the food offering is a large part of this. With crowds getting smaller all the time, half of the concession stands – even on the field level – remained closed, meaning that fans had few options to choose from. Most of the open stands only sold hot dogs (and the "Colossal" dog looked slightly sad) or pizza slices, with only one kiosk each selling burgers, chicken or fish. In fact, there was just one solitary stand for ice cream, hidden out in the empty outfield area, and even that was difficult to find.

The food itself was forgettable and on the expensive side of things; many fans choose to eat outside the park to avoid giving Fisher money, so there's little motivation to improve the quality of the offering. The flagship team store was the smallest I'd seen, with a limited offering – a very small range of pin badges and balls highlighted this – but bonus points for using various entry tunnels for separate options, including a clearance area offering cheap shirts. Overall though the catering and shopping options were limited and uninspiring, and so Oakland earns a score of 4/10.

Atmosphere:

It's really sad to see such a gigantic stadium so empty – the boycott has been in action for an extended period of time, and crowds rarely reach five figures, giving the Coliseum something of a muted atmosphere. Add in to this the fan theory that Fisher has instructed the ushers to enforce seating allocations strictly and you've got an experience that is far removed from the hospitality and accommodation provided by the vast majority of baseball teams. This game had fewer than 9,000 in attendance (comfortably the lowest crowd of any game on my trip so far), and for large portions the Coliseum was quiet.

Fans coordinate a protest each game; at the top of the fifth inning they all rise to their feet and chant "sell the team" in an attempt to get the message through to John Fisher, and this is a sign of how passionate Athletics fans can be. Indeed, in a bases loaded situation during the sixth inning the crowd made themselves heard, and for a moment the ballpark was as loud as any – the lack of atmosphere is in no way the fault of the fans. Ushers, on the other hand, are pretty officious at the Coliseum, with regular ticket checks even for fans who have been in their seats for the entire game. It makes for a fairly sterile place to watch a game, and therefore the Coliseum only scores 4/10 here.

Weather:

Oakland has a climate similar to San Francisco – although the geography of the Bay Area does create different conditions for locations only a few miles apart, both cities are located close enough to the water to receive a breeze that keeps temperatures much lower than the rest of the state. One benefit that the enclosed nature of the Coliseum has over Oracle Park is the lack of an outfield area exposed to the bay, meaning there's less opportunity for the wind to whip up and create uncomfortably cold conditions, but it's still far from warm even at the height of summer. Bring a coat for this one. I can't score it any differently to the Giants' ballpark, so Oakland gets 6/10.

Additional Features:

The Athletics have some nice branding around the park – murals of former greats adorn the entrances – but that's about it. The empty concourses and mothballed concession stands make the experience as bland as possible, and without a decent view through the outfield the seating bowl is bland. The Coliseum is old, and the ownership have neglected any improvements for so long that cracks in the concrete and sun-bleached seats make the place look unloved. I'm always hesitant to be negative about a ballpark, but there's so little to mention here that it's hard not to criticise it. With that in mind, it's a low score of 2/10.

Overall:

Unsurprisingly, the Coliseum receives the lowest total score of the entire trip so far, earning just 22/50. It's truly sad to see what's happening to the Athletics, and I can only hope that the ownership sees sense and keeps the team   in   Oakland.

21

DODGER STADIUM

"I'm not concerned with your liking or disliking me. All I ask is that you respect me as a human being"

Jackie Robinson

When you take a step back and look at it objectively, sports fandom is a very strange thing indeed. On a regular basis, thousands of supporters gather in stadiums, bars and front rooms to watch teams of people they've never met and have very little in common with play a game, with the result determining how they feel for the next few hours or days. The week following the match will usually entail breaking down minutiae of a player's performance, analysing each play or decision, even though the fan will likely have no particular expertise in the sport, and even though a defeat might have ruined his or her day they'll most likely come back and put themselves through it all at the next possible opportunity.

But really, it's not just about the game itself. Following any particular team gives you a sense of belonging; a camaraderie with other fans, and in many cases friendships that will last a lifetime. Reading Football Club have been pretty terrible for years now, and yet I keep going to their games – not for the quality of football, but for the opportunity to see family and friends in a relaxed environment. In a way, I've grown up at the Select Car Leasing Stadium, knowing the people who sit in nearby seats for over a decade, and it's these connections that make me return and cheer on the team week after week.

Baseball is the same. For generations, fathers and sons have bonded over a game of catch in the back yard and trips to the ballpark to watch their local team play. It provides an icebreaker at bars or on a bus, such is the ubiquity of the sport. It becomes a huge part of supporters' lives, and arguably a key part of their identities, as well as that of the cities that the teams represent. Places like St Louis are known for the Cardinals, and they provide a huge boost for the local economy, especially when the teams experience sustained success.

And of course, sports fans love a rivalry. With so much of a fan's identity tied up with the tribalism of their side, it's perhaps inevitable that they look to other teams to try and create a "them-and-us" mentality. The best rivalries are the ones that go back to the sport's origins. The sheer history of the Merseyside derby, for instance, is part of the fabric of football, and holds something of a mythical status amongst fans of both teams – simply put, it's part of their identity.

Perhaps the best example of this is the rivalry between the San Francisco Giants and the Los Angeles Dodgers. Uniquely, it's something that goes back to the nineteenth century, and crosses an entire nation. Both sides were formed in 1883 – the Giants as the New York Gothams and the Dodgers as the Brooklyn Grays. Whilst both teams eventually changed their names (the former quickly becoming the New York Giants, a moniker that has stuck for nearly 140 years, whilst the latter went through multiple name changes, including the Grooms, the Superbas and the Robins before settling on the Brooklyn Dodgers in 1932), the fact that both sides played in the same city meant that there was animosity from the start. The Yankees would not come into existence for another 20 years, such is the length of time that these two sides have been going at each other.

Perhaps the strongest indication of the rivalry enduring throughout the years was seen in 1956, when icon Jackie Robinson – a player with ten seasons of service for the Dodgers – was traded to the Giants for pitcher Dick Littlefield and a significant sum of money. Instead of taking the trade and playing for a team that his fans passionately hated, Robinson opted to retire from baseball altogether.

Two years later, both sides moved to California – the Giants to San Francisco, and the Dodgers a few hours south to Los Angeles. The first instance of MLB teams moving to the Golden State, this arguably kickstarted a new era in baseball (Billy Joel's song *We Didn't Start the Fire* includes a reference to "California baseball" amongst other historical events), and both sides doing so simultaneously ensured that the rivalry lived on.

The full tale of this rivalry is too rich and storied to be summarised here, but safe to say these are two teams that really do not like each other. The Dodgers have gone on to become one of the less popular sides across all of baseball with their recent heavy spending and dominance of the National League, although as a Giants fan I do somewhat enjoy their continued failure to make much of an impression on the postseason. They do, however, have probably had the last laugh so far, as despite this they beat the Giants in the 2021 National League Division Series, ending our playoff hopes at the first hurdle. Most fans also recognise the importance of both teams continuing to have success as well, which keeps the rivalry strong – a one-sided dynamic between the Giants and the Dodgers would be boring, and success on both sides allows each team to push each other on to continual improvement.

My visit to Dodger Stadium came on perhaps the most unexpectedly stressful day of the trip so far. Whilst travelling to the Coliseum the previous evening, I received a number of alerts for the following day. First came the email from Amtrak advising me that trains between Los Angeles and Anaheim – where I was staying for the game – had been cancelled due to the weather alert, and then the Dodgers announced that the weekend's games had been condensed into a Saturday doubleheader. The Angels followed suit, throwing my plans into chaos.

It transpired that California had received its first hurricane warning in nearly a century, and all three sides in the south of the state had hastily moved forward their Sunday games to avoid being caught up in the extreme weather. This meant that my plan to visit Angel Stadium that day would need to change, and on the 20 minute subway journey to Oakland I came up with a new plan involving an early flight and some form of travel between both Los Angeles parks to catch two games in a day.

The end result of this was an alarm waking me up just after 3 in the morning and a taxi to the airport to catch a 6:30 flight. I landed into Orange County just before 8 – thankfully my hotel was willing to store my bags even at that early hour – and rushed to the Amtrak terminal, which allowed me to get to Union Station in Los Angeles by 10:30, just 90 minutes before first pitch. Thankfully, a fleet of "Dodger Express" coaches were waiting to take fans to the ballpark, and I arrived just before 11, giving me time to explore the park. The team were handing out caps as the giveaway item, saving me money – although with the rivalry I only wore it for the photo I was getting at every park!

The game started promptly – understandable, given that there were to be two such matchups that day – and the first three innings went by quickly as neither team put runs on the board. In fact, there were just four hits in that time (the Dodgers managing just one of them), and I was starting to think I'd be watching an extraordinarily short game. In the top of the fourth the Marlins took the lead, with outfielder Bryan De La Cruz doubling to left field and allowing Jake Burger to score, and this would remain the only run through the seventh inning.

In the bottom of the eighth, the Marlins fell apart. It's fair to say that closer David Robertson hasn't had the best of times since being traded to Miami from the Mets, and after inducing a fly out from Chris Taylor he walked James Outman and gave up a single to Kike Hernandez, putting men on the corners early in the inning. Austin Barnes then bunted a single to allow Outman to score, and a throwing error from first baseman Josh Bell allowed Hernandez to reach third, setting things up for a Mookie Betts hit to send both runners home and give the Dodgers a 3-1 lead.

The home side threatened to make things worse for the Marlins as Freddie Freeman then hit a double, but two relatively quick outs followed and they got out of a sticky situation with just a two-run deficit. With just one inning left, they were unable to fix the mess, as Jazz Chisholm, Burger and De La Cruz each recorded outs on a total of five pitches combined, and the Dodgers recorded an improbable win from behind after just 2 hours and 10 minutes of baseball. I was pleased the game had ended so quickly, as it gave me more time to make the journey to Anaheim for the game that evening – more on that soon – but it had been an unexpectedly enjoyable time at Dodger Stadium.

Location:

Los Angeles is a famously car-centric city – relying on walking or public transportation is an extremely bad idea. It's also a sprawling metropolis which goes beyond the wildest imaginations of most visitors, and Dodger Stadium is a fair distance from many landmarks; for instance, it's nearly 20 miles from Santa Monica beach, and a similar drive from the Hollywood sign. As a result, the park is surrounded by parking lots and is nearly impossible to access without your own vehicle (especially when you consider the sheer number of hills nearby).

The team has done their best to make it accessible – the Dodger Express runs as a free shuttle from Union Station before and after games, although there's only so much capacity it can provide. Traffic cleared reasonably quickly after the matchup I attended, but this was partly down to the low crowd; I've heard there can be gridlock after well-attended events and Dodger fans are famous for leaving early to avoid this. On the plus side, the slightly more remote location affords attendees a spectacular view of the hills in the background, which combined with the palm trees lining the outfield gives the park an exotic feel. It doesn't save the stadium though, and it earns a score of 4/10 for location.

Concessions:

The Dodger Dog is arguably one of the most famous food items in baseball, rivalled only by the Fenway Frank. The endless debate about whether it should be grilled or steamed has led to it achieving a cult-like status at the park, and most concession stands stock both varieties. You've got the standard ballpark classics, but there didn't seem to be anything truly unique beyond that. It probably didn't help that the smaller attendance at the game I attended led to a few stands being closed – I'm sure these are open for the majority of games and offer a bit more variety.

The slightly confusing layout of the park (the hills outside mean there are entrances to pretty much every level from outside without the need for endless elevators or escalators) meant there was no obvious location for a main team store – instead, several smaller locations were scattered around various concourses. Approaching the end of the season, a number of items were sold out, including pins and certain styles of cap. The game-used store was also surprisingly poorly stocked, but I did like how New Era had dedicated kiosks around the stadium, redeeming this score to 6/10.

Atmosphere:

I've mentioned a few times how this was one of the smaller crowds that Dodger Stadium will have seen all year. The incoming storm and subsequent last-minute rescheduling of the game led to an inconvenient midday start time, and many would have had little opportunity to change their plans to make this game (especially with a more convenient one later that day). Taking that into account I thought the Dodgers fans made a good amount of noise and got behind their team; certainly later in the game when they took the lead it sounded like an almost completely full ballpark.

Their supporters do have a reputation, however, for arriving late and leaving early, and considering the traffic and location I can understand that. From what I saw, this seems overstated, with the vast majority of fans making it in time for first pitch despite the unusually early start time.

Everyone was friendly – even when I mentioned that I was a Giants fan – and the impression I got that the Dodgers had a passionate fanbase who loved the sport. With that in mind, they earn a score of 8/10.

Weather:

To clarify, I'm not taking marks off for a once-in-a-lifetime hurricane warning. Los Angeles is renowned for its weather – many move there for the climate and sun as well as the lifestyle – so I was a little disappointed to visit on such a cloudy day. The humidity was noticeable (more so here than anywhere else I'd visited on the trip, including Texas) but the heat wasn't excessive, making it a pleasant environment for watching baseball. The ballpark could do with a little more shade (the roof over parts of the upper deck feel somewhat makeshift) to protect fans from the sun, but otherwise it seems pretty nice, giving Dodger Stadium a mark of 8/10.

Additional Features:

This is one of the most historic ballparks in baseball – it's the third oldest, having been open for over 60 years – and despite recent refurbishment it hasn't lost any of its charm. The club level (which is open to all fans) has a vast collection of memorabilia from the past; my personal favourite was the old bullpen car. The outfield has a number of giants bobbleheads too, alongside child-friendly play areas – in fact, Dodger Stadium seemed to have a larger collection of outdoor spaces than anywhere else I'd been so far.

The scoreboards are smaller than other parks, but the unique shape makes them stand out, and alongside the palm trees and view of the hills the stadium captures the relaxed and vintage feel of true baseball nostalgia. Add in the range of colours used for seating, and despite being the home to my team's biggest rivals I can't dispute that this is a classic place to watch a game. I can't give it anything other than 10/10.

Overall:

A mixed collection of scores earns Dodger Stadium a total of 36/50 – slightly lower than others, but this is mainly due to a poor location and limited range of food and merchandise options. I was just glad to have made it to a game there after the stress of rescheduling at short notice, but there was no doubt that this was a memorable part of the trip.

22

ANGEL STADIUM

"I always wanted to see a Japanese player participate in the Home Run Derby. It happens to be me"

Shohei Ohtani

I vividly remember sitting in a maths lesson at school and being told the story of Srinivasa Ramanujan. A mathematical prodigy in the late 19th century, the Indian-born genius moved to England to study under GH Hardy before struggling to cope with the difference in climate and food. Upon visiting him in hospital one day, the socially awkward Hardy remarked upon his taxi having a boring number (1729) on it. Ramanujan famously replied that it was, in fact, a very interesting number (for reasons that I won't go in to here, to avoid the risk of you closing this page right now). This is perhaps the most notable instance of Ramanujan considering each number to be one of his close and personal friends.

You may be wondering why I'm starting an chapter about a baseball game in Los Angeles with a story about an Indian mathematician, but these two seemingly unrelated topics have one thing in common. As someone with a degree in maths, I've always found numbers to be somewhat reassuring (although not to the extent that Ramanujan did), and the plethora of data that baseball uses is strangely comforting. Humans like to categorise all sorts of things, and the use of various statistics allows us to rank players with comparative ease. Any argument in favour of a player can be strengthened by reeling off some form of data, especially if this ranks them as number one. You simply can't argue with numbers.

147

The endless debates over who might be the all-time greatest player (or GOAT) hinges heavily on this. Vanishingly few people alive today can say they watched Babe Ruth or Lou Gehrig line up for the New York Yankees, but they can see the numbers they managed to put up. Ruth in particular is said to have changed the game – before he started playing, Roger Connor held the career home run record with 138, and the Bambino blew past that on the way to 714 – but the fact that we can measure that numerically is what allows the current youth to recognise his impact and influence on the sport. There's a reason that players like Ruth and Mickey Mantle are iconic today, even to non-baseball fans on the other side of the Atlantic, and it's because of their dominance of the sport.

The Oakland Athletics' famous Moneyball approach allowed all of baseball to make significant steps forward in the use of statistics and analytics – the ubiquitous sabermetrics now being available not only to scouting teams but also everyday fans – and the study of MLB data is now a rabbit hole that you can spend an almost endless amount of time learning about. Some of my favourite measures of player performance are OPS+ and ERA+ – the "plus" indicating that the statistic is somewhat normalised and allows us to compare players from across various eras. There's also the oft-quoted *wins above replacement* (WAR), with a high number in this measure being a good indicator of a player's hall of fame chances.

All of this is a lengthy way to say that the Angels have a couple of players who are good – really good. Mike Trout is, unsurprisingly, one of those players. He was considered the best player in baseball for a number of years, and his nickname of "the WAR machine" might give you some idea of why this might be the case. Over his career so far, he's earned over 85 wins above his replacement – having him on your team would, in the long run, give you an entire season worth of extra wins. This is good for 52nd of all time (far and away the highest number out of all active players, with Miguel Cabrera a distant second for position players with 67), and he has several years left to increase this figure. Even though his performance has slightly dipped as he's gotten older and more injury-prone, his OPS+ touched 250 in the recent past (which would suggest he's 150% better than the average player). Even Trout's accomplishments in the past few years, however, fade into significance when you consider Shohei Ohtani.

It is simply impossible to state how good Ohtani is at baseball. Going into the all-star break, the two-way phenomenon led the entire MLB in home runs and OPS+, as well as letting his opponents have the lowest batting average when pitching to them and achieving the third most strikeouts in the league. Simply put, he's quite possibly the best hitter AND the best pitcher in the sport simultaneously right now. Babe Ruth was elite at one and good at the other, but Ohtani is a leader in both. The man is box-office entertainment, and crowds flock to Angels games to quite simply witness history whenever he plays. Opposing fans cheer his plate appearances, and when his Japan side beat the United States in the final of the World Baseball Classic, Americans seemed to feel more happiness for him to win than sadness that they had lost.

Hopefully this lengthy introduction goes some way to explain how much I was looking forward to visiting Angel Stadium and seeing these two icons of baseball play live. Sadly, Trout had been out injured for this trip – there's no real hardship having to schedule another visit to Anaheim in the future to see him play – but Ohtani had been setting the standard for the rest of the league, and I had already seen him hit two home runs in the previous three games I'd seen him play.

This was the second part of my long and hastily rearranged day after the incoming storm had put a spanner in the works. Thankfully, and against all odds, I had met some Brewers fans in San Francisco a few days prior who were doing their own tour of the California parks, and they were also making the journey from Dodger Stadium down to the home of the Angels. They kindly offered me a lift between the two parks – especially helpful as Amtrak had cancelled the only conveniently-timed train down to Anaheim – and so after the first game of the day had reached its eventual conclusion I jumped in the back of their car and we chatted baseball all the way down the interstate. Thanks to the prompt pace of play from the Dodgers we actually arrived in the Angel Stadium parking lot as their first game was finishing, so I had time to head to my nearby hotel and check in before going back to the ballpark.

Once I got there, I was astonished by the sheer popularity of Ohtani. I wasn't expecting him to remain anonymous, but it seemed as though everyone in the crowd was there for him, and branding around the ballpark matched this, with images of the two-way phenomenon plastered around the concourses and the team store appearing to only sell memorabilia with his name or face on it. After picking up a cap – which also featured his name on the side – I headed into the seating bowl to get my photos, before picking up some food and settling down for the game.

Just like the first game of the day, it started with a handful of scoreless innings – albeit more slowly. Angels pitcher Patrick Sandoval opened the game by walking Yandy Diaz and allowing Randy Arozarena to hit a single, before designated hitter Harold Ramirez reached first on a fielder's choice (with Arozarena being out at second) and Isaac Parades grounded into a double play to end the inning. The hosts, by comparison, received three quick outs as Zach Eflin needed just 14 pitches to sit down the hitters and set up the second.

The next two innings went by somewhat quicker, before the visiting Rays opened up the game in the top of the fourth. After Ramirez struck out, Paredes hit a single and Curtis Mead earned a walk, Osleivis Basabe hit a ground rule double and put one run on the board. Josh Lowe then grounded out to second, but Mead rounded home and made the score 2-0 as Jose Siri struck out to end the inning. This opened the floodgates – the Angels recorded three more quick outs in the bottom of the inning and in the fifth the Rays put four more runs on the board thanks to a succession of hits – Paredes, Mead and Basabe getting the key hits to send runners home.

This was enough for Angels manager Phil Nevin to take Sandoval out of the game, bringing in Jaime Barria to continue instead. He quickly ended the inning, bringing the Angels in to bat, and they finally pulled a run back as Hunter Renfroe hit a home run to make the score 6-1. That was as good as it would get for the hosts for a while, however, as the Rays piled on seven runs in the top of the sixth, and Barria was further humiliated in the seventh as they scored two more runs thanks to an Arozarena homer. He was taken out in the eighth inning – Jimmy Herget was his replacement – but his did little to mitigate the damage as another Ramirez hit sent home two more runners and increased the score to 17-1.

There was some respite from the Angels in the bottom of the eighth; Ohtani hit a double after Nolan Schanuel had already got a single, meaning Brandon Drury's subsequent home run pulled back three runs. This, in reality, meant nothing, but fans still celebrated wildly – they were, after all, just four grand slams away from being back in the game – even though this ended the scoring for the game, with a comparatively dull ninth inning ending with just one run for the Rays and concluding the contest at 18-4 to the visitors. I headed away quickly, knowing my hotel would afford me a better view of the post-game fireworks than the seats in the ballpark, and a spectacular display provided a perfect end to a long and tiring day.

Location:

Just like the home of their cross-city rivals, the Angels have a ballpark surrounded mainly by parking lots (albeit not as extensive or hilly as Dodger Stadium). The one advantage that the Anaheim side have, however, is the number of hotels within walking distance, not to mention the colossal intermodal transit centre almost directly across the road. Trains, buses and metro services aren't exactly frequent from here, but it offers some access by public transit, and the freeway running directly past the ballpark makes getting away easy (the Angels have even put a separate panel on the side of their scoreboard so passing cars can see the score).

It's still not perfect – much like other ballparks of this age it was built for cars more than anything – but at least there's been some effort to integrate travel options into the ballpark's location. The view from the outfield isn't quite as exciting as others though; you only really get a view of the intermodal station and the highway, and so the score is limited to 5/10 here.

Concessions:

I hope you like Shohei Ohtani – if you do, there's merchandise galore for you at Angel Stadium. The main team shop might as well be renamed the Ohtani store, with the queues to enter going far around the concourse and checkout lines snaking outside the stadium itself, but various other kiosks in the park provide alternative options. The game used store has limited options however – possibly because anything related to the main man would sell out instantly – but instead they stocked some impressive artistic memorabilia.

Food was once again slightly limited to the classics (it feels as though they're missing a trick not selling any Japanese food, such is the popularity of Ohtani and the number of visitors from his homeland that the ballpark attracts), but with a few slight twists on the regular options. I went for the Nashville Hot chicken strips, which had a nice kick and flavour to them to set them apart from the offering at other parks. My area also had at-seat delivery, and after scanning a QR code an usher brought a cookie and drink to me during the game, which added some luxury to the food offering. Overall, it wasn't bad, but lacked anything truly unique, meaning Angel Stadium earned a mark of 6/10.

Atmosphere:

There's a running theme here – the vast majority of fans were at Angel Stadium for Shohei Ohtani. Hit plate appearances were cheered wildly, but those of his teammates were significantly quieter, making them feel like a supporting cast rather than legitimate big league players in their own right. To be fair, the game was more a demolition of the Angels than a true sporting contest, which muted the atmosphere, and there were a number of fans near me who clearly knew what they were talking about, but it didn't feel like a real sporting crowd on the whole.

On the positive side, everyone at the park was friendly, and those working behind the scenes put a lot of effort into making the game feel like an event. The fireworks crew might be the best-paid staff there, with rockets being fired into the air after the national anthem and as each Angels player was announced, and home runs were met with a volley of explosions and blasts of flames in the outfield – all of this before the post-game display. This meant that both home runs were celebrated as though the team had won the game, and boosted the atmosphere significantly, also raising the score to a respectable 7/10.

Weather:

I can't really judge this any differently to Dodger Stadium – it's less than 30 miles from the home of the other Los Angeles team, and the climate is pretty much identical – so to spare you an extended paragraph musing about California's weather I'll jump straight to the point and give Angel Stadium an identical score of 8/10.

Additional Features:

To be brutally honest, the seating bowl is fairly generic, with only the rock garden in the outfield setting this area apart from most other parks in the league. It's an interesting feature – and now it's laced with firework launchers it's become the centre of attention when not watching the game itself – but it also serves to make the rest of the stadium look a little bland by comparison. The concourses are a little more interesting; there's a lot of team branding on the pillars, making them more attractive than the bare concrete that seems to blight a lot of other ballparks, and just like Dodger Stadium there are a number of outdoors areas, with the gated perimeter being moved further outside of the main structure.

Perhaps it's the outside of the ballpark that offers the most recognisable features though; the main gate is flanked by two gigantic Angels caps (they even feature the hat size on the inside rim; at 649 ½ inches they're a little bigger than those that most fans would wear), and at the edge of the car park is a huge team logo. The massive "A" is topped by a halo featuring an rotating screen, and draws fans in from the nearby freeway. However, when you're talking about a giant sign in the parking lot as a key feature, you know the rest of the park is lacking, and with that in mind Angel Stadium scores a comparatively low mark of 6/10.

Overall:

Another mixed bag of scores gives the home of the Angels a total of 32/50 – a little lower than nearby Dodger Stadium, and that's something that feels right considering it didn't have the same charm. Seasoned ballpark chasers consider this ballpark to be far from great, but it's not an objectively bad place to watch a baseball game; it's just a little bland.

23

PETCO PARK

"The weather, the people...everything's been great around here"

Eric Hosmer

On the face of it, baseball is an unpredictable sport. If you take the best team and pit them against the worst for a four-game series, it's fairly certain that the poorer side will manage to win at least one of those matchups – and it's not outside the realm of possibility that they'll win the series itself. This is perhaps best demonstrated by looking at the standings after a season is completed; the very best sides in the game will lose over 50 games, and the very worst usually win at least a third of their contests as well.

However, these things tend to average themselves out over the course of a season. After 162 games the best sides will tend to rise to the top of their division, and even though it's not a perfect way to compare teams (an unbalanced schedule ensures that) it's good enough to select the top few for a postseason playoff. One of the key consequences of the recent change to the wildcard places was that more teams than ever qualified for the postseason, and a number of sides who historically appeared only rarely in these playoff games were now able to make more regular appearances.

The unbalanced does result in each division having differing levels of predictability though. The East and West divisions are usually regarded as stronger than those in the middle of the country – and as a result some groupings have a more exciting race come the end of the season. For instance, the American League West this year features three sides (the Rangers, Astros and Mariners) within just three games of each other, whereas the perennially strong Atlanta Braves sit over thirteen ahead of their nearest rivals in the National League East.

Perhaps the most predictable of divisions, however, is the National League West. The Los Angeles Dodgers have been one of the most dominant sides in regular-season baseball for well over a decade, winning the division in nine out of the previous ten seasons (in fact, their most recent last-place finish was in 1992, giving them a 30-year streak avoiding this). As a result, the remaining sides (Giants, Padres, Diamondbacks and Rockies) tend to start out each season hoping to battle for a wildcard spot at best, limiting their ambitions – unless, like San Francisco in 2021, they have a record-breaking year and win well over 100 games.

But the San Diego Padres set out to challenge this. Only coming into existence in 1969 as an expansion team, they've generally been a side that have struggled towards the bottom of their division (except for a handful of wins in the late 1990s and mid 2000s) and between 2016 and 2019 they finished rock bottom three times. However, entering 2020 the side underwent a transformation to become one of the most ambitious franchises in the sport, thanks in part to the emergence of young superstar Fernando Tatis Jr and the big-money acquisition of Manny Machado. During the pandemic-shortened season they shot from fifth to second, clinching their first postseason berth in 14 years.

The following year, they became even more ambitious, bringing in some impressive starting pitchers in Joe Musgrove, Yu Darvish and former Cy Young winner Blake Snell, and the team looked like real challengers after surging to a 49-33 record by the end of June. However, this would not last, and one of the most significant collapses in the history of baseball followed as the team slumped to fall to a losing record of 79-83 at the season's conclusion. This included a run of just 5 wins in their final 23 games, with many questioning the dedication and spirit of the players when things started to get tough.

In response, the Padres doubled down, once again bringing in some big names (including Luke Voit, a player who had recently led the league in home runs) for the 2022 season, and once again started strongly. This time the team kept it going, maintaining a 57-46 record at a trade deadline in which they made headlines by trading for Juan Soto – regarded as the most outstanding young player in baseball – as well as slugger Brandon Drury and exceptional closer Josh Hader. The Padres kept things going, ending the season with 89 wins – good enough for another wildcard spot (the Dodgers once again set records, winning 111 games and denying any other side the chance to win the division). This time San Diego went on a promising postseason run, winning the wildcard game and Division Series before falling to the Phillies in the National League Championship Series.

As a result, hopes were high going into 2023, and fans were only more expectant after the signings of Xander Bogaerts and Nelson Cruz (a pair of players with eleven combined all-star appearances and nine Silver Slugger awards between them). However, the side never really got going, with the side failing to post a winning record after May 9th. With the emergence of the Diamondbacks as a competitive side during the season, the Padres slipped to fourth in the division entering my visit, with fan morale at an all-time low. It was clear that the side still needed a significant amount of time to become true contenders on a regular basis, and just like the failure of the Mets' season it was a timely reminder of how difficult it was to build a top baseball team.

After the hurricane warning changed my plans in Los Angeles, I had a free day on the Sunday, and after spending a few hours watching the weather channel I decided to stop focusing on the incoming storm, reasoning that it would only make me worried over something I couldn't change. As it happened, coastal California was only mildly affected by the extreme conditions, with downtown San Diego escaping mostly unharmed, so Monday was spent in my hotel before catching a lunchtime train down from Anaheim.

Amtrak is far from punctual, and even this short trip was affected by a 20-minute delay, but before long I was riding the wonderfully named Pacific Surfliner through southern California. There were some spectacular views of beaches, piers and the ocean, and after a couple of hours I arrived in San Diego. I checked into my hotel before taking a short walk to Petco Park, and was extremely impressed by what I saw once I entered. The ballpark managed to combine old and new with ease – the concourses were arranged on multiple levels and at varying distances from the seating bowl, there were plenty of trees and plants around, and everything smelt amazing.

Having picked up a ticket from a resale site that morning – the storm had made it too unpredictable to buy before that – I got a bargain, only paying $26 for a seat in the club level, giving me a padded seat and an astonishingly good view. It was San Diego Zoo night, and after a number of animal puppets were paraded around the field it was time for the game to start. Unlike a number of recent matchups, I didn't have to wait long for some action as the visiting Miami Marlins put men on base early on as Luis Arraez continued his outstanding season with a base hit before Josh Bell also got a hit. Ultimately though, three strikeouts from Michael Wacha ended the top of the first with no runs, allowing the Padres to flex their offensive muscles instead.

And what a start it was from the home side – leadoff man and fan favourite Ha-Seong Kim doubled after four pitches, with the following hitter Fernando Tatis Jr earning a walk. Juan Soto struck out, but with men on base and only one out Manny Machado only needed to hit a sacrifice fly to allow Kim to score, and as Tatis was thrown out after Bogaerts hit a single the Padres ended the first inning with a 1-0 lead. The Marlins had an unremarkable second inning, especially compared to San Diego's efforts in the bottom – after three consecutive walks from Marlins pitcher Ryan Weathers the table was set for Kim, who duly obliged with his first career grand slam. The fans went wild, making a huge amount of noise as fireworks went off and four runs were added to the score. At 5-0 in just the second inning, it felt as though the game had already been decided.

A scoreless third inning from both sides only deepened that feeling, and after Weathers walked Cooper in the bottom of the fourth he was removed from the game – but by that point the damage had been done. In the fifth inning Machado hit a solo home run to increase the Padres' lead to 6, making Bell's own homer in response during the top of the sixth something of a consolation, and even Jesus Sanchez's sacrifice fly (allowing Jake Burger to score) which made the score 6-2 felt like it was too little too late. In the end, that would be the case, as three scoreless innings later the game ended at that score, offering San Diego's fans some slim hope of making a wildcard spot after all. It had been an enjoyable game, but the ballpark experience had trumped that; Petco Park certainly felt like one of the best locations of the trip so far, and after a few days of weather-related stress it indicated that the journey was well and truly back on track.

Location:

After a few days of ballparks which were effectively surrounded by huge parking lots, it was a huge breath of fresh air to visit Petco Park. The Padres' home is located within the city's famous Gaslamp district and just minutes from the bay, allowing easy access to a number of bars and restaurants as well as having metro stops nearby. The centre of San Diego is relatively compact – I was staying near enough the opposite end of downtown and was able to walk to the park in under 20 minutes – meaning almost every hotel is close to the stadium, and this also means that whilst parking might not be available in the immediate vicinity it's extremely easy to leave your car fairly close nearby (as an aside, I read that the parking lots at Dodger Stadium took up the same amount of land as the centre of Nottingham in England – so you may actually be *closer* to Petco Park when parking downtown than you would be to Dodger Stadium when parking at an official lot!). There's little to hate about this ballpark; the only thing I would improve would be having the main Amtrak station closer, and so the Padres get a score of 9/10 here.

Concessions:

I'll start this section off by saying that Petco Park is the best-smelling place in baseball. I'm not sure how they managed it, but walking along the concourse you're hit by the wonderful scents of various foods that draw you in. There are classy options too – I noticed an Italian restaurant situated adjacent to a wine bar, and one area behind home plate houses a number of healthy options (it's actually the first time I've seen fruit for sale at a ballpark; a welcome respite from endless burgers and hot dogs). Specialties include tri-tip nachos and fish tacos, leaning into San Diego's food scene, and there's a strong presence from fast food chain Jack in the Box (including sponsorship on the foul poles).

The team store was well-stocked, but interestingly not behind home plate, and there was a comprehensive game-used section which offered some gorgeous framed photos as well as jewels from bases at reasonable prices. Bonus marks for getting balls from that day's game early on (I think the fifth inning might be the earliest I've seen so far) as well. There's very little I could think of to improve the offering here, so San Diego earns a perfect score of 10/10 for its concessions.

Atmosphere:

I thought the Padres drew a healthy crowd during my visit, but a number of fans I spoke to suggested that this was their lowest attendance in a while. This speaks volumes to the level of support the team attracts, especially considering their well-publicised struggles over the course of the season. Even without the team performing poorly though the support made for a raucous atmosphere, with cheering for routine plays and hits which built to a crescendo of noise for Kim's grand slam. This is clearly a fanbase that gets behind their team, and they really deserve a better level of baseball than they've had to witness this season.

Staff were friendly – especially those in the guest services kiosk, who engaged with everyone that visited, offering signs to hold up for photos – as were the fans that I spoke to (I even had a few offering to buy me a beer!). The city of San Diego seemed to have a relaxed vibe, and this was reflected in the ballpark, making it one of the nicest places in America to visit. Once again, I can't find fault in this section, so Petco Park gets 10/10 once again.

Weather:

If you ever read a list of the world's top climates, you're bound to find San Diego near the top. The city is noted for its near-perfect weather conditions throughout the entire year, with it seemingly never becoming too hot or too cold. Even the once-in-a-lifetime tropical storm that swept through the day before my visit seemed to leave it unscathed. Maybe it was because I'd spent time in the Midwest and Texas before visiting, but I found the Padres' home park a little cold at times – although nowhere near the chilly breeze that swept through the San Francisco Bay a few hundred miles north.

Nevertheless, it's clearly a comfortable place to watch a game, and it's unlikely you'll have to bring different clothing options to an April game or one in August. I'd probably have brought a light jumper or jeans with me though, considering it's not exactly baking hot in the shade. This might be controversial, but I'm giving San Diego a score of 9/10 for its weather.

Additional Features:

Petco Park might be the perfect way to build a modern stadium. It features a huge number of easter eggs in the concourses – my personal favourite was a collection of hats to represent schools in the local area – as well as a serene hall of fame in the left field area. The most notable feature, however, has to be Gallagher Square; possibly the only such place in a Major League ballpark. The large grassy area dominates the outfield, and a small hill allows fans to stand outdoors and watch the game in unique surroundings. There's a screen behind the scoreboard and commentary is played through speakers, allowing fans an immersive environment, and as it's still part of the park you can walk into the concourse and buy whatever food and drink you want.

Speaking of the concourses, they were open, airy and surrounded by plants, giving them a truly natural feel that set Petco Park apart from many of the modern ballparks. It's not all new though – the team have incorporated the Western Metal Supply Company building into the left field corner, with the 1909 construction being declared a historic landmark and forming a link to the past within the modern park. This blend of old and new made for an interesting location with something for everyone, and once again gives the Padres a strong score of 9/10.

Overall:

An extremely strong set of scores combine to give Petco Park an overall mark of 47/50 and put it in first place so far. It ranks among many people's favourites, and with only a handful of ballparks left to visit it looks as though it might be my top-ranked stadium too.

24

CHASE FIELD

"I think the sunsets here are fantastic"

Zack Greinke

We live in a world full of modern wonders. Some are small in scale – for instance, almost everybody now owns a smartphone more powerful than the device that landed a rocket on the moon; a device which allows us to access the sum total of human knowledge yet fits in the palm of our hand – but some are vast. Jumbo jets allow us to fly vast distances at incredible speeds, and the increasingly efficient manufacturing processes and designs mean we can do so at constantly lowering costs. If you went back in time 100 years and told somebody you could travel halfway across the world in less than a day, paying under a month's salary for the privilege, before using a pocket-sized device to hold a video call with loved ones, they'd be astonished.

As one of the younger countries in the world, the United States has largely been built up with technology in mind. From the silicon valley of northern California – where self-driving taxis are starting to roam the streets – to vast subway systems under the streets of New York City, many large cities are dominated by relatively modern conveniences. Perhaps the clearest indication of this are the vast skyscrapers that pepper the streets of almost all of these vast metropolises. This is in stark contrast to much of the UK, which is home to cities first populated thousands of years ago – cities such as York and Durham are dominated by ancient structures instead.

There's no better example of this in my mind than Phoenix in Arizona. It would have been unthinkable in the past to build a city in the middle of a desert – the blistering heat, lack of water and sheer remoteness of such a location would traditionally have made it uninhabitable – but Americans found a way. Indeed, the indigenous population abandoned the place about 600 years ago after several droughts, despite their attempts to create water channels through the settlement, and it wasn't until nearly 50 years ago that the entire urban area was limited to under a million residents.

Now, with the invention of air conditioning and modern building techniques, nearly five million people call the Phoenix area home. A vast collection of cities, it has become a popular retirement destination, and arguably is one of the spiritual homes of baseball, with half of all Major League teams travelling out every February for spring training, taking part in the gloriously named Cactus League (the other half go to Florida and play in the Grapefruit League, enjoying similarly warm winter climates).

With a rapidly growing population, it became clear that Phoenix would need some sports teams. Even though a large proportion of residents moved to the area having already chosen their side, it was almost unthinkable that such a large area would be devoid of sports. Originally playing host to basketball side the Phoenix Suns, later years saw other franchises move to the city – the St Louis Cardinals (not to be confused with the baseball side) bringing football to the state in 1988 and the Winnipeg Jets of the National Hockey League moving in 1996, becoming the Phoenix (later Arizona) Coyotes.

At that point, only baseball was missing from the major North American sports. However, with the league containing 28 sides by the late 1990s, it was decided that two new franchises would be added to make an even 30. As one of the fastest growing areas in the country – not to mention one with significant baseball infrastructure already in place – Phoenix was chosen, and in 1998 the Arizona Diamondbacks entered Major League Baseball. They were placed into the National League West, and have remained there ever since, being geographically close to the three California sides (albeit a little further from Denver, as are most sides).

You'd expect a new franchise to struggle in their early years as they find their feet and adapt to the demands of Major League Baseball, despite acquiring players from other sides via the expansion draft. This was true of the Diamondbacks' first season – although a .401 winning percentage wasn't a complete disaster – but the following year they saw a significant improvement. Fuelled by the free agent signing of Randy Johnson, the team went on to win 100 games in the regular season, placing first in the division, before losing to the Mets in the first round of the playoffs. Johnson won the Cy Young award that year – the first of a record four consecutive triumphs for a man who would go on to become a franchise legend.

Two years later, the team would go on to win it all. Ending with a 92-70 record, the Diamondbacks once again won their division (an impressive second time just four years after coming into existence) before overcoming their postseason demons and beating the Cardinals, Braves and Yankees to win the 2001 World Series. As a comparison, the Tampa Bay Rays (the other side to have entered the league in the same expansion) finished rock bottom of their division for nine out of their first ten seasons – finishing fourth by three games in the other one – and are yet to win the World Series after 25 years.

The Diamondbacks had fallen away somewhat in more recent years – the 2011 season saw them win the division for the fifth time in 14 years but they have failed to clinch top place since then – and three consecutive bottom-two finishes between 2020 and 2022 saw the franchise in a difficult place. The unique nature of North American sports, however, prioritises the draft system and allows struggling sides an opportunity to recruit the most promising youngsters, and after bringing in Corbin Carroll in 2019 trading for rookie Gabriel Moreno in 2022 they started to look towards a brighter future. The pair have been pivotal in 2023, as has the emergence of Zac Gallen as one of the game's best pitchers (and possibly their first Cy Young winner since Brandon Webb in 2006) as the side briefly took first place in the division again after an unexpectedly strong start to the season.

I would only be making a short visit to Phoenix – as with most other stops on this trip, I would be limited to 24 hours in the city – but was interested to see how such a new team had built up an impressive record of success in such a short space of time. It was a short flight from San Diego, and thankfully the hotel was able to check me in a few hours early – even a quick trip on the metro rail from the airport was enough to show me that it was just as hot as people said, and it would be a poor decision to spend too long outside – and I was able to have a quick nap and freshen up before heading to the ballpark.

Upon entering Chase Field, two things hit me; the air conditioning made it immediately more comfortable, but as one of the older enclosed ballparks it felt pretty dark. Globe Life Field was more than 20 years younger, and the home of the visiting Texas Rangers had made the most of improvements in lighting technology (as well as using vast walls of glass effectively). My eyes soon adjusted to it, but it made the stadium feel old. I was a little surprised – 25 years might be close to a ballpark's lifespan in the US, but in the UK that would make for a modern sporting venue; indeed, my own team opened their ground at the same time and it's still regarded as new location.

I was looking forward to the game – Gallen was starting for the Diamondbacks, facing off against Jon Gray for the Texas Rangers. I had seen the Rangers demolish the Angels one week prior, and was interested to see how they would fare against more capable opposition. They started reasonably strongly, with Corey Seager hitting a single in the top of the first in between three strikeouts, and Gray retired the three Arizona batters in just eleven pitches to end the inning.

However, they started to crumble in the second. After a promising start to the inning (in which Gallen gave up two more hits), the Rangers were unable to capitalise, and would go on to regret this just minutes later as the Diamondbacks' offence stirred into life. Christian Walker hit a single to left field before Lourdes Gurriel Jr hit his own to right, and Alek Thomas earned a walk to load the bases with no outs. Whilst Jace Peterson grounded into a double play, it was enough for Walker to open the scoring, and Moreno's single immediately afterwards doubled the home side's lead. A Geraldo Perdomo walk kept the inning going, and Carroll's subsequent single combined with an error led to a third run scoring, giving the Diamondbacks a commanding lead early in the game.

The Rangers continued to get hits in the third – Marcus Semien getting in on the action to lead off the inning – but once again the side were unable to capitalise, and in the bottom of the fifth notorious hothead Tommy Pham hit a single that allowed Perdomo to score another run before Gurriel's sacrifice fly meant Carroll could make it 5-0. This inning saw three separate Rangers pitchers – manager Bruce Bochy was notorious for his seemingly endless pitching changes during his time as Giants manager – with Gray taken out at 3-0 before Grant Anderson was removed after giving up two runs himself.

In the top of the sixth the visitors finally got one back thanks to a Mitch Garver home run, but once again this was the extent of the damage and the Diamondbacks drove home another in the same inning; Corbin Carroll once again doing the damage, with his sacrifice fly sending Moreno home and making the score 6-1. In the top of the seventh the Rangers threatened to mount a comeback as Seager's double allowed two runners to score, but this would be the extent of their scoring and the game was settled as a 6-3 contest.

The eighth inning, however, brought a personal highlight. The stadium announcer had got in touch via social media and offered me a chance to appear on the big screen between innings, and during the middle of the eighth I was taken down to just behind the dugout and shown alongside an explanation of the trip. It was a great opportunity, and even better was the chance to move to the best seats in the house – right at the front of the ballpark just next to the dugouts. I had a fantastic view of the final few innings as the Rangers tried their best to tie the game up in the ninth, but ultimately it wasn't to be.

There was a slight tinge of sadness, as this meant the Diamondbacks overtook the Giants in the division standings, but I could hardly complain as they had put on a good display of both hitting and fielding to win this match. It was a quick walk back to the hotel, and I got off to sleep quickly, well aware of an early flight to Atlanta in the morning.

Location:

Chase Field is located in something of a sporting district within Phoenix – the Suns' arena is pretty much next door, and the close proximity of two sports venues has led to the inevitable proliferation of hotels nearby. The city lacks the vast number of skyscrapers that dominate other skylines, partly due to the huge area a desert affords planners, meaning things are a little more spread out, but there are a number of nice hotel options within a 10 minute walk of the ballpark. There's also a light rail stop directly outside, with frequent services running directly to the airport (curiously called a Sky Harbour instead, however), and a number of parking garages in the immediate vicinity.

The short walk between the two sporting venues takes you past some small restaurants and bars, which feature outdoor air conditioning systems spraying a mist of cool water over the street, as well as larger fan areas attached to the ballpark by a footbridge. To be honest, it was too hot for me to explore the immediate area, but it did look as though the team had worked with the city to create an attractive and well-connected location for the stadium. The light rail does offer limited capacity for getting away quickly after a game, however, and that limits the score slightly, meaning Chase Field earns 8/10 for location.

Concessions:

The food options are slightly limited; the same two or three concession stands seemed to pop up repeatedly on the concourse. To be fair, Phoenix doesn't really have its own identity when it comes to food, but as a ballpark located in the southern region of the country I was surprised not to see many Mexican-based options. Prices were reasonable though, with the Diamondbacks being one of the few teams to offer a value menu, allowing fans to get popcorn and other snacks for under $3. I went for Chick-Fil-A after failing to find anything truly interesting.

The team store was relatively well-stocked, although the Diamondbacks joined Cincinnati as just the second team not to have 9Forty caps which was a little disappointing. The game-used store was also somewhat lacking, mainly being filled with balls from previous matchups instead of having a diverse range, and later in the game they had only received two balls from that evening's game (with the cheapest one being $175, I decided to pass). This section therefore lets Chase Field down a little, and I can't justify a score above 5/10.

Atmosphere:

The Arizona Diamondbacks have dubbed themselves the friendliest team in baseball, and clearly pride themselves on the fan experience. I can't really fault the staff that I encountered, especially when being given the opportunity to feature on the big screen. The ushers who I spoke to were also very friendly, offering to take photos for me and talk about the team's history, as were fans before the game. It was a little surprising to be asked to show my ticket whilst the game was in progress though.

The team struggles to draw large numbers though – most living in the area have already got a favourite side, and as a result the Diamondbacks tend to see big crowds only when facing the more popular sides. It's a shame, as they've been a relatively successful franchise during their short existence, and with this game taking them to second in the division they deserve to be playing in front of more fans. It makes for a strange environment, with more noise being made for the visiting side than the home team, and as a result I'm giving them a score of 5/10.

Weather:

I'm repeating myself when I say this, but Phoenix is in the middle of the Sonoran desert. Regarded as one of the hottest places in the world, it's astonishing to me that people manage to live there – and without air conditioning, I doubt they would. That said, it's a dry heat, and so the conditions outdoors don't feel significantly worse than Texas (although in both locations you're probably going to be outside for a limited amount of time). If you're relaxed and in no rush it's just about tolerable, but going about your day-to-day life in those oppressive conditions would be painful.

Thankfully, Chase Field is indoors. It's got a retractable roof – the very start and end of the season might just take place during more comfortable evenings, but even this is unlikely – and vast pipes above each section provide air conditioning. The upper deck is warmer (after all, hot air rises) and the sheer number of people in one place provides some humidity, but by and large it does its job and the ballpark is a pleasant environment to watch a game. I suspect the vast majority of attendees will either be staying a short walk from the stadium or using air conditioned transport to get home, so the impact of the heat is limited, but I can't really score it any differently to the Texas ballparks, meaning it earns a mark of 8/10.

Additional Features:

The Diamondbacks have a challenge here; as the newest team in the league, they don't have an extensive history to reference around the ballpark, and as a city made up primarily of transplants from other locations there isn't a particularly strong culture to draw from either. However, they've leaned heavily into making the stadium a family-friendly environment. In the upper deck there are numerous play areas, as well as my personal favourite feature – the STEM dugout. As a maths teacher and STEM lead within the school, it's great to see such a huge organisation promoting this aspect of education, which will hopefully inspire future scientists and engineers.

Beyond that, there are opportunities for fans to create a free bobblehead of themselves and get virtual photographs with players in the outfield area, as well as exhibits from previous All Star games (the team-branded Mickey Mouse is a particular highlight). There are a few old bullpen cars dotted around by the main entrance too, but the most famous attraction in Chase Field is probably the pool out in right field. Sadly it's now a suite area, meaning the vast majority of fans don't have access to it, but it's still something that sets the stadium apart from others in the league.

I also need to give a mention to possibly the most intimidating mascot in the league – a giant cat that looks like it's ready for a fight at all times. It's certainly unique! However, on the whole there still seems to be limited features around the park compared to others, and the lack of windows make it feel quite dark, so I'm going to be a little harsh and give Chase Field a score of 6/10 here.

Overall:

A mixed bag of scores results in the Diamondbacks earning a total of 32/50 – towards the lower end of the scale so far. Sadly, it feels accurate; the place could do with some renovations and a larger fanbase, despite the friendly   welcome   I   received.

25

TRUIST PARK

"Everything we do moving forward, everything we've done so far, we're doing it for our fans"

Ronald Acuna Jr

The Major Leagues have undergone several expansions over the years – as late as 1960 there were just sixteen teams competing, with the following year seeing the first two new teams entering the competition. Since then, it has been a semi-regular occurrence to see sides joining the big leagues, with two more clubs entering in 1962, 1977, 1993 and 1998 (four teams entering in 1969 as well). It's a distinctly American concept to see new teams being formed and entering the top level of a sport straightaway, in comparison with the European model that sees newly-formed entities starting at the bottom and needing to work their way up. I had seen the newest side – the Arizona Diamondbacks – the previous day, and was impressed by how they had achieved success so quickly and felt like an integral part of baseball just 25 years into their existence.

The Atlanta Braves stand in stark contrast with the Diamondbacks, being one of the most historic franchises in Major League Baseball. Formed in 1871 – coincidentally the same year as my football team Reading – they're over 150 years old, making them the second oldest team in the league (second only to the Chicago Cubs, and the Wrigleyville side have just a year on them). As a result, the side became a founding member of the National League, in which they have remained since its inception, but their history has much more to it than that.

Indeed, the team's roots stretch back even further; the Braves are in fact closely linked to the first ever professional baseball team. The Cincinnati Red Stockings (unrelated to the modern-day Reds) were established in 1866, becoming professional three years later once the sport's governing body permitted sides to pay their players. After going perfect with a 57-0 record (the only such season in baseball history) and embarking on a nowadays unthinkable 81-game winning streak, they disbanded citing high costs involved with player wages.

The team's player-manager, Sheffield-born Harry Wright, remained undeterred by this, and moved across a still-young United States to Boston at the invitation of Ivers Whitney Adams to form a new club. This would become the Red Stockings, and the team stayed in the city for over 80 years under various guises, including the Beaneaters and the Rustlers, before finally settling on the Braves in 1912. Babe Ruth represented the side in his final playing season, and the team experienced great success (including a World Series crown and fourteen pennants) before moving to Milwaukee in 1953. Boston's current team – the historic Red Sox – arguably pay tribute to this franchise's roots with their similar name.

The team spent just over a decade in Milwaukee (in which they won a second World Series title), in a rare gap between various franchises (each called the Brewers) occupied the city, before moving in 1966 to Atlanta, where they remain over 50 years later. The side have had mixed fortunes since then, but following Ted Turner's purchase of the team in 1976 they became perhaps the most widely broadcast area in the country, earning them the moniker of "America's team". A third World Series followed in 1995, and two years later they moved into Turner Field, a stadium constructed for the Olympic Games held in the city.

2017 saw the side move once again to the north side of the city, with Truist Park (originally called SunTrust) representing a significant shift in baseball stadium design, thanks in part to the simultaneous construction of The Battery (more on that later). After an underwhelming opening season in their new home, the Braves went on to win five consecutive division titles – and look on course to win a sixth this year – alongside yet another World Series title in 2021. The side continue to feature a young core, spearheaded by superstar Ronald Acuna Jr, and are likely to be perennial favourites for the foreseeable future.

After leaving the Arizona desert, I had once again underestimated the sheer scale of the United States and found the three hour flight to Atlanta tiring. Thankfully, I was spared the struggle of a long journey across the city as Ryan had been following my trip online and kindly offered me a lift to the ballpark – during which we stopped off to visit some of the Braves' former homes. I was staying just a few minutes' walk from the stadium, and so after he dropped me at my hotel I quickly dropped my bags and headed across to Truist Park, where he showed me around various features. With a large crowd in attendance, the stadium staff prepared a similarly impressive display, with the national anthem concluding with a helicopter flyover and pyrotechnics from various positions in the outfield.

Charlie Morton was starting on the mound for the Braves, coming off the back of two excellent games in which he had given up no runs – and he got to work quickly, striking out Mets leadoff hitter Brandon Nimmo in just four pitches. Morton went on to record seven strikeouts in the first three innings, only allowing one baserunner (Francisco Lindor was hit by a pitch), with fireworks going off for each one. The loud bangs punctuated the raucous atmosphere in the stands; with Marcel Ozuna hitting a single for the home team in the bottom of the first and a fielding error from the Mets, the Braves were able to take an early lead which they never surrendered.

In fact, the visitors would have to wait until the fifth inning until another one of their players could reach first base. DJ Stewart actually went one better, hitting a one-out double to left field, and he was joined two batters later by Rafael Ortega as Morton hit another Mets player with a wild pitch. Stewart, however, was picked off at second base to end the inning, and the New York side were unable to capitalise on their promising position.

They would pay for it in the bottom of the sixth, as a succession of hits extended the Braves' lead to an unassailable status. With Austin Riley leading off the inning with a single, Ozuna's double was enough to make the lead 2-0, and he would score himself on a Sean Murphy single. Both Murphy and Michael Harris II then went on to extend the lead to five after Vaughn Grissom hit a triple, and whilst Acuna fouled out Atlanta's position was looking strong. They would go on to make it 7-0 the following inning as a Matt Olson single was followed up by an Ozuna home run, and this ended the scoring as the Mets were unable to find any more luck against the Braves bullpen.

It wasn't the end of the evening for me, however, as Ryan had secured on-field passes for photos after the game. It was great to once again stand on a Major League dirt track, and the staff were keenly interested in my trip after hearing about the challenge. It was a perfect end to an enjoyable game, but I wasn't looking forward to the early wake-up call for my trip to Florida the following day...

Location:

This is a real mixed bag. On the plus side, Truist Park arguably pioneered the concept of a ballpark district, with The Battery offering a wide range of dining and social options for fans attending the game. It's a vibrant area, and even a significant amount of time after the game had ended there were still a number of people milling around, making the place feel truly alive – an impressive feat for an out-of-town park. It's also home to a number of apartment complexes (and if you're a sports fan, is there a cooler place to live than just outside your team's stadium?) and a handful of hotels, giving a sporting identity to the entire neighbourhood.

On the downside, it's almost completely inaccessible by public transport. Atlanta as a city is a little like Los Angeles in that it's dominated by the car – my journey from the airport to the ballpark would have taken nearly two hours if I was relying on buses or trains, but thanks to Ryan's kindness it took a little over a quarter of that time. This is clear when you walk around the area; vast parking lots flank the perimeter of The Battery and major highways run through the immediate vicinity, making it easily accessible to those who drive. For tourists, however, it can be a bit of a nightmare, and this harms the location score significantly, with Truist Park earning 6/10.

Concessions:

With new ballparks comes the option to introduce unique food items, and the Braves certainly made the most of this opportunity. One of the most iconic symbols of the sport's culinary decadence is the Cleanup Burger – a gigantic concoction of meat, cheese and hash browns served between two huge waffles and cut into four, with a portion of fries stuffed into the centre. I was considering trying it, but when I saw the sheer size (and price) of it I was put off. Size was a theme at Truist Park – there were entire buckets of chicken on offer alongside foot-long hot dogs. I was impressed to see a barbecue stand in the outfield, which apparently was even better than the ones in Missouri and Texas, and the park also had the standard ballpark options at fairly reasonable prices.

There were a couple of large bar areas in the corners as well; the Chop House is perhaps the most well-known, offering excellent views of the field as well as an extensive area to eat food purchased around the park. There were a few well-sized team stores dotted around each concourse in addition to the gigantic main shop, and the game-used stand was extensively stocked (getting balls in earlier than any other park I've been to – I was able to pick up one that Morton had pitched to Alonso in the bottom of the fourth inning). Just like Globe Life Field, the Braves had set up a rotating rack of shirts for custom printing, and I liked how they would text you when it was ready to collect. They could have done with a few more truly unique food options, but otherwise it was an outstanding park, meaning Truist Park earns a score of 9/10.

Atmosphere:

It's easy to draw a crowd when you're the best team in baseball, and Atlanta have been experiencing success over an extended period now. I was very impressed by the level of attendance, even though a number of fans told me the park was comparatively empty for this game. Supporters were clearly proud of their team, turning out in large numbers and making plenty of noise for even routine plays and hits. The staff displayed the famous southern hospitality, with ushers being helpful and the back office going out of their way to give me a welcoming gift, and that doesn't even begin to mention how amazing it was for Ryan and his season ticket rep to sort me out with on-field access after the game.

There's some controversy around the team's use of the "chop" – I've written briefly about the debates surrounding sports teams' use of Native American heritage – but there's no doubting that it creates an impressive moment when the opposition make a pitching change and the lights go out. In fact, the stadium operators make good use of the park itself, with fireworks going off after the National Anthem as well as for home runs and strikeouts (with the way Morton was pitching, I was starting to wonder if the team would run out of pyrotechnics), plus a helicopter flyover before the game. It's certainly a great experience going to a Braves game, and with that in mind they score 10/10 for atmosphere.

Weather:

Atlanta might be the warmest place in the United States to have a ballpark lacking a roof – apparently at the time of Truist Park's construction the technology didn't exist to offer air conditioning for a building of that size. It could certainly do with something though, as the city gets extremely warm for much of the baseball season – well over 30 degrees for my visit – and that's not to mention the intense humidity that makes it feel even hotter. There are some fans embedded in the concourse roofs, but this does little once you're in your seats, and the team have resorted to giving away small signs upon entry that many use as personal fans during the game.

Once the sun goes down and the match enters the later innings it becomes a little cooler, and temperatures approach comfortable conditions for a game, but it doesn't quite make up for the first few hours. I was glad to have spent some time researching which sections were in the shade, as I couldn't think of much worse than sitting in the blazing heat of the bleachers for anything more than a few minutes. It's unfortunate that this detracts from the experience, and as a result I have to give Atlanta a lower score of 4/10 for its weather.

Additional Features:

One of the real benefits of a modern ballpark is that you can built it up with fan amenities in mind, and Truist Park has this in spades. My personal favourite area of the entire park was the hall of fame and mini museum behind home plate, which was an area of tranquility just steps away from a busy main concourse. Featuring exhibits such as original jerseys from the team's Boston days alongside interesting information boards and World Series trophies, it's a nice way to spend an extended period of time before the game, and has taken on an extra level of poignance after Hank Aaron's recent death.

There's also a decent children's area in the outfield section, including a climbing wall and mini baseball field as well as arcade machines. It's certainly a contrast to the bars flanking it! The other standout feature has to be the previously mentioned Battery area – whilst this technically isn't in the ballpark, the two locations are closely linked to each other and the social space forms a large part of the game day experience. It's one of the better parks in this regard, but some of the upper decks could benefit from more references to the team's history, so I'm limiting this score to 8/10.

Overall:

Truist Park earns a total score of 37/50 – it's a nice modern ballpark but is heavily let down by poor public transit links and some oppressive weather conditions.

26

TROPICANA FIELD

"We have a great team here, and it's going to be fun to watch all year"

Brandon Lowe

I've written about how Phoenix is largely a city of transplants, but Florida goes one further by doing that as an entire state. With similarly challenging weather conditions – it's not as hot, but the incredible humidity makes it challenging to live there – the entire area was mainly home to ranches until air conditioning made it significantly easier to move to the state in the 1950s. With the state being home to just over 2 million residents in 1950 (incredibly low, considering it's only slightly smaller than the island of Great Britain), it's grown to over 22 million in an extremely short space of time, now being the third most populous state.

Its growth is almost unheralded, and it's now one of the most interesting states in the country. Home to Disney World (almost an entire city in its own right) as well as NASA's main hub, it's become an incredibly popular tourist destination thanks to the year-round heat. Just like Phoenix, the state is one of the homes of Spring Training, with 15 teams heading to the southeastern corner of the nation every February to prepare for the upcoming season. It was perhaps inevitable, therefore, that after Miami became the first team to represent the state in Major League Baseball in 1993 that another city would receive a side in the expansion just five years later.

Unlike the Diamondbacks, however, the Tampa Bay Devil Rays had a difficult start to life. Beginning with six consecutive last-place finishes in the

American League East, you'd be forgiven for thinking that they might have been happy with ending the 2004 season fourth in their division – also being the first time they managed to win 70 games in a year. After slightly rebranding in 2008 to drop the "Devil" from their name (allegedly at the request of Christians who objected to such a word), they saw a significant boost in results, winning the division at the first attempt and reaching the World Series before losing to the Phillies. Future franchise hero Evan Longoria went on to win Rookie of the Year and manager Joe Maddon won the award for Manager of the Year as well.

This kickstarted a much more successful era for the Rays – they went on to win three more division titles as well as qualifying for four more postseason campaigns through the wildcard system, once again making it to the World Series during the pandemic-shortened 2020 season. One of my clearest memories during that year was Brett Phillips making a huge hit in that campaign, with Randy Arozarena rounding the base to score a walk-off run against the Dodgers and providing an iconic moment in the history of the franchise. This helped to establish the Florida side as one of the most dominant teams in the division – an impressive achievement when you consider they're up against such powerhouses as the Yankees and the Red Sox.

It was unsurprising, therefore, that the Rays headed into this matchup against the struggling Colorado Rockies as heavy favourites. After an extremely early start (against my better judgement I had booked onto the 7am flight from Atlanta, in case of any delays, meaning I landed into Tampa not long after 8 in the morning) I found myself in a taxi heading across an extremely long bridge into downtown St Petersburg – the Rays' home not actually being located in the Tampa area, after the adjacent city opened the park in 1990 to try and attract various other franchises to move there. They were unsuccessful, and the existing home helped Tampa win the right to an expansion team eight years later.

The home team had already won the previous two games and were going for the sweep, although they were forced to run it as a bullpen game thanks to injuries to various members of their pitching staff. Shawn Armstrong was chosen to open the contest, pitching two scoreless innings and allowing just two hits in the top of the first. The Rays took the lead early on, as Luke Raley hit a home run to lead off the bottom of the second inning. Raley would go on to dominate the game, hitting a triple in his next plate appearance in the fourth, before an Osleivis Basabe single allowed him to score the second run of the game.

The game shifted in the Rockies' favour in the fifth inning, however, as Brenton Doyle hit a leadoff double and Charlie Blackmon followed up with a single of his own to put Rays pitcher Erasmo Ramirez in a difficult position. It would get worse though – Brendan Rodgers (no relation to the former Reading, Celtic and Liverpool manager) hit a three-run homer to give the visitors a 3-2 lead and give the Rays a mountain to climb. The fans were relaxed, however, as they had been behind in the two previous games of the series before scoring heavily late in the game to come back and win.

And so it would prove again. Isaac Paredes hit a solo home run in the bottom of the sixth to tie the game, and Josh Lowe knocked one of his own out of the park in the eighth to make the score 5-3 after fan favourite Arozarena had reached base earlier in the inning. Closer Pete Fairbanks came in to the game in the top of the ninth, throwing some serious heat to strike out the side, allowing just one hit in a drama-free end to the game.

I was slightly dreading the logistics of the rest of the day – I needed to get back to the store a mile away where I'd stored my bags (walking in the peak heat of the day) before getting a taxi to the airport for a late flight to Miami, but thankfully a fan who I'd been chatting to for the game kindly offered to drive me there himself. A lawyer by trade, he had told me lots about the team's culture and history, and he proved himself to be one of the best people out there after returning my phone to the check-in desk after I absent-mindedly left it on charge in his car during the journey. It saved me a huge amount of stress, and meant I could breathe a huge sigh of relief as an extremely long day came to an end.

Location:

One of the biggest complaints that fans have about Tropicana Field is how difficult it is to get there. Located across the bay in St Petersburg – making the Rays possibly the most misleadingly-named team in baseball – it can take those living in Tampa over an hour to get to games due to heavy traffic on the various bridges connecting the cities. Adding to this, there's a complete lack of public transit options; it's simply impossible to get to the Trop from the Tampa area unless you're willing to make several connections and spend half a day travelling (or pay through the nose for an Uber).

At least there are some hotels nearby; St Pete is becoming something of a hub itself now, and for drivers there are a range of reasonably-priced parking lots attached to the ballpark. It did feel like a strange location for a modern stadium however, and I can understand why this is the source of much fan dissent. It meant I had to make a very short visit to the area rather than staying and exploring, and I'm limiting the Rays' score for location to 3/10.

Concessions:

This was a bit of a mixed bag too – the Rays have made some attempt to connect with the Florida food scene by including a wide range of seafood at their park, with poke bowls and calamari for sale alongside fish and chips. The outfield area featured an attractive bar with build-your-own food counters, and I also liked how the ballpark organised their concession stands into first and third base food districts rather than being dotted around the concourses. Both sides were identical, featuring burgers, chicken and pizza – these were relatively pricy, but the chicken bowl that I ate was probably the best of the trip so far.

The main team store was located just inside the entrance and was extremely well-stocked, with a number of smaller stands by each food area, and the game-used store had an astonishingly wide range of memorabilia for sale. I was tempted by a mystery jersey bag, but $165 was a little too much for me, instead opting for my usual purchase of a ball from that day's game. It had more of a mystery element to it than I'd have liked, with customers having to purchase before the match started and getting handed a sealed box after the ninth inning – so I'll have no idea what ball it is until the details get uploaded to the MLB database. Overall, the park had a good enough range for the low attendance, but there wasn't anything truly unique and prices were on the higher side, so Tropicana Field earns a mark of 7/10.

Atmosphere:

Florida, being a state that's only hosted a significant population for a few decades, is hardly a traditional baseball powerhouse – most of its residents have grown up supporting other sides. As a result, the Rays struggle to draw a big crowd, just like the Diamondbacks. It's a shame, as the side have been one of the most successful in the sport for a while now despite sticking to a lower budget, and they deserve to be playing in front of more fans. This meant the atmosphere was limited, with those in attendance making limited noise. The game felt more like a social occasion than a big sporting event to be honest, despite the stadium staff's best efforts.

Ushers were relatively friendly, although they were strict about checking tickets. I had to show mine multiple times even when getting photos over an hour before first pitch, which did feel excessive considering the low crowd in attendance. The fans were much better; a group that I sat nearby spent the entire game telling me about the team and its history, and made me feel extremely welcome at the park – one of them even gave me a lift to the airport afterwards! This elevated my experience, and means the Rays' score is perhaps higher than it might have been, giving them a mark of 6/10.

Weather:

I seem to have left the hottest and most humid locations until the end of the trip; Florida struggles so much with these conditions that it was almost completely unoccupied until air conditioning made it easy to live in any environment. Tampa was experiencing slightly cooler weather than usual during my visit, and the 20 minute walk from the bag storage location was bearable when in the shade, but in the sun it made for extremely sticky conditions.

Thankfully, Tropicana Field is air conditioned, like almost all parks that feature a roof. Indeed, the cooler air hit you immediately after walking through the door, and the more intimate nature of the stadium meant everywhere in the seating bowl was afforded the same luxury (unlike, say, Minute Maid Park, where the air conditioning in some of the busier areas struggled to cope with the sheer number of people radiating heat). I'll have to go with the same score for the Texas and Arizona environments and give Tampa a mark of 8/10 for its weather.

Additional Features:

This ballpark receives a lot of criticism for its permanently closed roof – it's the only permanent one in the league – but I liked how the team had incorporated it into the game day experience. Lights had been installed at the peak of the dome, with various colours flashing at different points during the day and providing a surprisingly atmospheric experience. The catwalks were distracting – although I didn't see any balls hit them – and the batters' eye was bland, but Tropicana Field was nowhere near as bad as I was expecting it to be.

The standout feature is probably the stingray tank out in centre field, with fans being able to pet the marine creatures before and during the game. It's surrounded by educational display boards explaining the wildlife in the area, and it was a nice place to spend some time – if I ever return, I'd like to spend a couple of innings watching from this area. The team also heavily promote their mascots, with Raymond and DJ Kitty greeting those entering through the main hallway as well as having their own section of the concourse to meet fans. Overall, the park felt like a fun place to watch a game, albeit one that was very different to the traditional baseball experience. I can understand why some fans hate it, but I enjoyed my visit, and so it scores relatively highly here, getting a mark of 8/10.

Overall:

Whilst Tropicana Field receives a relatively low mark of 32/50, this is mainly due to its poor location and atmosphere rather than any inherent flaws with the park itself. If the area was built up more, got some better public transit and a larger fanbase, it could become one of my favourite ballparks in the league. I was interested to see how it would compare to its same-state partner in Miami the following day.

27

LOANDEPOT PARK

"Don't let people tell you what you can't do"

Kim Ng

Whilst planning the trip has dominated my year, I've still found time for other sports. Indeed, just weeks before flying out to begin the journey, I was able to watch a few pre-season football matches. One of the first evenings of the season was spent at Melksham Town, my hometown ground, watching Forest Green Rovers. Ordinarily this would be an unremarkable game – as a fan of Forest Green I'm probably one of the most engaged people in the stadium – but this year it was different.

There's been a growing movement in European football towards gender equality; women's leagues are becoming increasingly popular (England now sell out Wembley on a regular basis – unthinkable just a few years ago when they were struggling to shift 20,000 tickets at regional grounds) and calls for pay equality are becoming ever louder. With Forest Green taking pride in doing things differently – under chairman Dale Vince they became the first ever vegan football club, and have given advice to the UN on making the sport carbon neutral – it was perhaps of little surprise that they became the firs team to appoint a woman as first-team manager, with Hannah Dingley taking charge for the Melksham friendly.

This annual game usually attracts a couple of hundred fans, but as a result of Dingley making history there were nearly that many just from the media – there was even a hastily-arranged press conference after the game using the club's bar. It was certainly interesting to witness such an event, and it got me thinking about how other sports had similarly embraced gender equality. I was certainly aware of the San Francisco Giants' hiring of Alyssa Nakken in 2020 – becoming the first full-time female coach in MLB history (two years later also becoming the first to take the field after Antoan Richardson's ejection against the Padres) – but I was surprised to learn about the Marlins also making history.

Florida is generally considered to be one of the most strongly Republican states in America, so I wasn't expecting a team from the Sunshine State to be at the forefront in this regard, but in late 2020 the Miami side hired Kim Ng as general manager, marking the first time a female had been hired in this capacity in the history of major North American sports. Ng had worked as assistant to Brian Cashman of the New York Yankees for three years, followed by twice as long in the same role with the Dodgers, so she was clearly qualified for the job. Her role was part of the motivation behind the team designating this game as Women Empowerment Night at loanDepot park, which was set to draw a significant crowd.

It was looking like it would be a good game, with Braxton Garrett starting on the mound for the Marlins against Joan Adon of the Nationals – I had seen Adon struggle against the Athletics when visiting DC two weeks prior. However, both pitchers started relatively strongly; whilst Garrett gave up a run in the top of the first after CJ Abrams hit a single and capitalised on some productive outs to start the game, Adon threw a clean inning and allowed just one baserunner (a fielding error allowing Jorge Soler to reach first base with one out).

The game moved quickly, remaining a 1-0 contest through the fifth inning, but Garrett began to struggle as it entered the two-thirds mark. In the top of the sixth Kelbert Ruiz hit an infield single to reach base safely, and immediately afterwards Carter Kieboom knocked the ball out of the park to triple the Nationals' lead and make the score 3-0. Ildemaro Vargas followed this up with a double, but the side could not capitalise on another baserunner and Garrett saw out the inning with no further damage.

He was removed in the seventh, with former Giant Steven Okert replacing him, finding things similarly difficult. After Alex Call led off the inning with a fly out to centre field, Michael Chavis hit a double to right and advanced to third base after Abrams grounded out. Lane Thomas earned a walk, and with runners on the corners Okert could do little about Joey Meneses' subsequent double, which allowed both baserunners to score. Ruiz then singled, allowing Meneses to score, and the inning ended with the visitors 6-0 up.

The Marlins did fight back in the bottom of the seventh – after Jake Burger and Bryan De La Cruz both hit singles Jesus Sanchez' triple pulled two runs back – but even with Nick Fortes hitting a ground rule double to make it 6-3 it felt like too little too late. Jazz Chisholm Jr grounded into a fielder's choice and allowed Fortes to score another run, which made things interesting for a while, but with the Nationals hitting another run in the top of the eighth the contest fizzled out.

Similarly disappointing was a notice on the scoreboard around this time informing fans that the postgame drone show had been cancelled (I was secretly quite pleased as it allowed me to get back to my airBNB sooner and get more sleep ahead of an early start), and this began an exodus of fans as the Marlins fell to a 7-4 defeat. It had been a reasonably entertaining game, and I had been surprised to see the Nationals win a second game on the trip considering their struggles in the standings.

Location:

After a few days of out-of-town ballparks, I was glad to visit a more central location. The Marlins have built their new home in a largely residential area with much easier access to downtown; I stayed at an airBNB nearby but there were a few hotels within walking distance as well. It was far from perfect – it's probably closer to Milwaukee's situation than Denver – but you can justifiably stay near the stadium or access it by public transit without too many problems. There were a few pharmacies and takeaways in the surrounding streets, but otherwise houses dominated the neighbourhood.

Parking wasn't a problem – there were four large multi-storey car parks just across the road – and, like much of the United States, you've got a highway within a couple of blocks of the ballpark, allowing a quick getaway (although I question how long it would take to get out of the car park itself if you were on the top floor). It's far from perfect, but it's much better than those located out of town or surrounded by what seems like miles of parking lots. I'll have to give loanDepot Park a middle-of-the-road score for location, and so it earns 6/10.

Concessions:

Uniquely, loanDeport park had placed the main team store outside of the concourses. This worked, however, since the entry gates were outside of the stadium perimeter, and fans could leave the building itself to access the shop. This wasn't really necessary though, since there were a handful of medium-sized satellite stores dotted around the concourse, each sporting a wide range of options. On the downside, the Marlins did become the third team to not stock 9Forty caps, and I was also unable to get a logo ball, which was a shame, as was the minuscule size of the game-used section (which was little more than a cupboard with a few racks of jerseys, also charging a whopping $100 for a ball from that day's game).

Food options were a little more varied, with Caribbean options included alongside Cuban sandwiches and quesadillas, reflecting the more Central American nature of the city. Perhaps most impressively, the Marlins had committed to fan-friendly pricing, with a few sections offering a "305" menu (charging $3 for the majority of items and just $5 for a beer). This, combined with low ticket prices, makes a visit to loanDepot park a surprisingly affordable experience, albeit one where you might not be able to get all the merchandise you want. It's a mixed bag when it comes to concessions, and it results in a score of 6/10.

Atmosphere:

Much like their Florida neighbours, the Marlins struggle to attract large crowds, in part due to the state's relatively recent growth. Unlike the Rays, however, Miami have failed to find success in recent years, relying on their previous World Series titles to promote the team. As a result, the ballpark feels a little sterile – even on a Friday night there weren't that many people there to cheer on the side, and those that were in attendance seemed to spend more time in the concourses eating and drinking than actually watching the game.

Stadium staff were a mixed bag too – whilst the two ushers at the front of my section noticed the sign and were interested in chatting about the trip, many others employed by the Marlins seemed to be somewhat disinterested in the crowd, making the place feel a little less welcoming than other ballparks I'd visited. It wasn't hostile by any means, but the staff were noticeably less engaged than at a lot of other parks. Fans I spoke to were really friendly by comparison though, and that redeemed the Marlins' score somewhat, ensuring they get a mark of 6/10 for the atmosphere.

Weather:

It's difficult to give Miami a score too dissimilar to Tampa; both are located in the hot and humid state of Florida, with sticky outdoors conditions meaning an enclosed and air conditioned ballpark was a necessity. The key difference is that Miami is in the southeastern part of the state, meaning it's a little more susceptible to the storms that the region is famous for – indeed, an unforecast bout of rain coming through the city led to the drone show getting cancelled after the game. This means that the Marlins are slightly worse off than the Rays, and as a result I'm giving it 7/10.

Additional Features:

Ironically, the most famous part of the ballpark has been moved outside. The home run sculpture is either iconic or monstrous depending on who you ask – a giant monument featuring dolphins, flamingoes and pine trees set against a colourful backdrop used to grace the outfield until Derek Jeter moved it to an outdoors location (I can't possibly think why). As a result, the left field area is now somewhat bare, but it does mean fans get a clear view through the glass wall of downtown Miami – something that's almost unique for a fully-enclosed ballpark. The monument's removal has also allowed a pleasant standing room deck to be placed in that area, and it was certainly popular during the game. Next to that is a small children's section featuring video games and an opportunity to meet the mascot, and on the other side is a museum corridor with relics from the team's former triumphs.

The right field area is host to another small play area for youngsters, as well as a bobblehead museum that seemed to be a fairly big draw. Further round the concourse was a large bar that doubled up as a social gathering space, but despite all of these options there wasn't really anything that represented the city of Miami itself. This was a nice ballpark, but it could well have been anywhere in the country, which harms its image in my view. As a result, I don't think I can give it anything higher than 6/10 here.

Overall:

The home of the Marlins was a fun place to watch a game, but struggled to stand out in many ways, and this is reflected in its overall score of 31/50, putting it towards the bottom of the pile.

28

CAMDEN YARDS

"We come to the park every day and expect to win, and that's not a feeling we've had in a long time"

Trey Mancini

There are many ways that sports can be categorised, but one of the most common is grouping them into individual disciplines and team games. The former tends to be more popular during the Olympics – athletics is front and centre during these festivals of sport – but the latter tends to draw significant crowds year-round. It's interesting, therefore, that team sports tend to generate the biggest superstars, considering that they rely on others in the side to help achieve success. Nevertheless, some footballers manage to become so dominant within the game that they can almost win trophies on their own – Lionel Messi seemingly leading Argentina to the 2022 World Cup through sheer force of will being a notable example of this.

Baseball is unpredictable in this respect though. Take, for instance, the Angels, who currently boast two of the greatest players to ever take the field in Mike Trout and Shohei Ohtani – but even these generational talents aren't able to get the team to even a wildcard spot, such are the struggles of the rest of the roster. On the other hand, Buster Posey showed his importance to the Giants when his retirement after an astonishing 2021 season caused a noticeable slump in results, and a handful of sides this year have experienced a significant upturn in fortunes with the emergence of exciting rookies.

One of the best examples of this is the Baltimore Orioles. Formed in

1901 as the original Milwaukee Brewers – and reaching Maryland via a 52-year spell in St Louis – the side have traditionally been one of the lower-ranked teams in the majors; save for a run of success around the 1970s they've only won six division titles in their history. Since 2017 they've failed to finish higher than fourth in the American League East (although this is arguably one of the toughest divisions in baseball, with the historically dominant Yankees and Red Sox battling it out with the Rays and Blue Jays for a shot at the postseason), and have finished bottom eight times since the turn of the millennium.

However, the Orioles made a massive improvement coming into 2023. Spearheaded by Adley Rutschman and Gunnar Henderson – both of whom made their debuts midway through the previous year – the team shot straight to the top of the pile, and through the three-quarters mark boast the second best record in baseball. It's difficult to understate how significant this is for Baltimore; there hasn't been this much of a buzz about the city since the debut of a certain Babe Ruth (having said that, he played for the minor league team of the same name – his debut coming later that year for the Boston Red Sox).

Rutschman may have taken the headlines this season – in the top ten across baseball for walks, he leads the team in on base percentage – but Henderson has knocked in more than 20 home runs as well. Add in the improving performances of youngster Ryan Mountcastle and it looks like the Orioles have found a recipe for success. They entered this game as heavy favourites against a struggling Rockies side (I had seen them lose just three days earlier against the Rays) and had won the two previous matchups in the series. Fans were hopeful of a sweep to strengthen their grasp on the division lead, and with great weather forecast it was set to be an exciting day of baseball action.

Having kept in touch with Joel from my earlier trip to the nation's capital, he had offered me a lift to Baltimore as he would also be attending the game. After meeting him outside my hotel, we made the short trip up the highway and arrived in Baltimore by late morning. We headed to the nearby Babe Ruth birthplace and museum – the great Bambino had roots in the town, and started his baseball career with the minor league team that played there before the Orioles came to town in 1954. It was interesting to learn more about his life, with various items telling the story of iconic moments such as his called shot in the 1932 World Series.

From there, it was a short walk to the ballpark, with fans beginning to head inside as we approached. Whilst it was the 28th stop on my trip,

Camden Yards was actually the final park I needed to complete visits to all 30, having been to Philadelphia and Boston the previous year. It was slightly overwhelming entering through the gates and walking down Eutaw Street, realising that I had fulfilled a personal bucket list item at last, and it hit me how it was a beautiful stadium to visit to mark that landmark. Opening in 1992, it marked a departure from the multi-purpose stadia that dominated the previous era, with the retro-classic design ushering in the nostalgia that now characterises modern ballparks. After visiting the store and exploring the field level, we found our seats and got ready for the game.

Jack Flaherty was the Orioles' starting pitcher – he was due to start in London for the Cardinals before being scratched due to injuries, and had been traded before I got to Busch Stadium earlier in the trip – and he opened the game by giving up a hit to Rockies leadoff man Charlie Blackmon. This was followed up by Ezequiel Tovar grounding into a double play, and Ryan McMahon lined out to third base to end the top of the first. The bottom of this inning saw former Giant Ty Blach pitching for the Rockies, and he had a similarly clean outing in just 13 pitches.

One of the great things about baseball is that every game features something new. After several thousands of matchups over more than a century you'd be forgiven for thinking everything that could possibly happen had already occurred, but new records are constantly set and fans are regularly surprised by events on the field. During the first inning, I was astonished to see outfielders move away from their positions due to a swarm of bees heading towards the bullpen – what followed was an almost unimaginable "bee delay". As far as I can tell, this was just the fourth such instance in MLB history, and as interesting it was to see I was glad it was over within just five minutes.

The game continued scoreless through three innings – neither side managing a hit during this time – but after Tovar singled and stole second in the top of the fourth, Brendan Rodgers' hit allowed him to score the opening run. The Orioles were unable to respond in the bottom of the same inning, and in the fifth the visitors made them pay as Michael Toglia homered to double the lead. Cedric Mullins did the same for the Orioles just a few minutes later, but Jorge Mateo was unable to continue the rally, with the home side still down 2-1 through five.

This set the tone for an entertaining contest, albeit one that would have been frustrating for Orioles fans. The Rockies restored their two-run advantage in the sixth inning after McMahon's double was converted into a run after debutant Hunter Goodman secured his first MLB hit, which was followed in the bottom of the eighth by Ryan O'Hearn's two-run homer to tie the contest at 3-3. At this point, the fans were beginning to believe that the home side could win from behind and sweep the series, but Goodman wasn't finished yet – after reaching second base on a single and a throwing error, he stole third base on Toglia's ground out and managed to score his first run after pinch hitter Elias Diaz made another productive out.

The Orioles were unable to respond in the ninth, with two strikeouts followed by Adam Frazier's line out to end the game and halt the team's four-game winning streak. As the game ended, we headed back to the car, and Joel drove me back to Washington. It had been an enjoyable day – but with just two more parks to go the end of the trip was in sight.

Location:

Thanks in part to *The Wire*, Baltimore has a pretty bad reputation – its crime rate is significantly above the national average, and many tend to avoid the city. Like most places, however, the area around the ballpark is perfectly safe, and with large crowds, nice hotels and a direct tram link to the station you're unlikely to run into any trouble. There's a lot of baseball history in the neighbourhood – most notably the Babe Ruth birthplace and museum only a block away from the northern edge of the stadium. The Bambino is one of the most iconic players not just in baseball but all of American sport, and it's well worth spending an hour or so before a game visiting the site dedicated to the great man.

Between this museum and the ballpark is Pickle's Pub, which sees large numbers gathering ahead of each game, and on the south side is M&T Bank Stadium (home of the NFL Baltimore Ravens). As a result, there's a significant number of parking lots in the immediate vicinity of both sporting arenas, all of which have pretty easy access to the highways. It's not quite downtown, but Camden Yards is in the next best area (in fact, it has some pretty good views of the city's skyscrapers alongside the warehouse that dominates right field), mixing the best of both worlds – as a result, the home of the Orioles earns a score of 8/10 for location.

Concessions:

You know you're off to a good start when you get handed packets of old bay seasoning upon entering the park – the Baltimore-created spicy salt goes great on any food served at Camden Yards. The Orioles also pay tribute to their iconic crab-based dishes with a popular seafood stand in left field – the shrimp and crabby fries were particularly popular. Also notable is

Boog's barbecue; former MVP Boog Powell serving gigantic portions of meat alongside beans, coleslaw and chips, with the man himself often there to meet fans as well. This was all alongside the standard ballpark classics, although it was particularly disappointing to note that this was the only place so far to not have mini helmets for ice cream.

The team store, located on Eutaw Street, was impressively well-stocked, but incredibly busy and slightly challenging to navigate. The smaller versions in the main concourse could be a better option if trying to avoid crowds – there were a handful along each side and were larger than the kiosks that most parks offer. The Orioles also had one of the nicest game-used shops in the league; I could have spent hours looking at the various memorabilia on offer. Balls from that day's game appear in the seventh inning and disappear incredibly quickly – they'd pretty much all sold out just five minutes after going up for sale. Overall, there was something for everyone, but the overcrowding in the main store and lack of helmets were real negatives, meaning the Orioles get 7/10 for concessions.

Atmosphere:

The American League East has been turned on its head this season, with Baltimore experiencing significantly more success than they've recently been accustomed to. Crowds have increased as a result, but for a weekend game it was a surprisingly low attendance. Those who did turn up were friendly, as were the majority of the staff – although a couple of the concession stand staff were a little grumpy. The Orioles can't score too highly here, but it wasn't awful, so I'm giving them 6/10.

Weather:

After spending the best part of a week in some of the hottest parts of the country, I was glad to be heading to slightly nicer conditions on the east coast. It's far from cold, however – Baltimore experiences warmer weather than the UK, and there's some humidity that makes it feel hotter still. Fans were noticeably avoiding seats in the sun, with shaded areas being significantly busier. In fact, when out of direct sunlight it's what I'd describe as perfect conditions for a ballgame, with conditions becoming warm but not uncomfortable. Because of this, evening games would provide a nice environment, but day games require careful seat selection to avoid baking in the sun. It would be unfair to score Camden Yards any differently from the nearby Nationals Park, so it gets a mark of 7/10.

Additional Features:

The ballpark is best known for the iconic warehouse – the former factory for the Baltimore and Ohio Railroad now dominates the right field view. The longest brick-built building on America's eastern coast, it forms the boundary of Eutaw Street, which acts as an exterior concession area for Camden Yards. This whole area provides one of the park's highlights – it's truly joyous to walk down the busy street before a game, taking in the sights and smells (you can walk through arches to the bleachers) before accessing the seating area. The Orioles also use this space to mark home runs; any home team hitter to knock one into this part of the ballpark gets a plaque to show where the ball landed. It's fun to spot them – Ken Griffey Jr's one went so far that it's embedded in the wall rather than on the ground.

There's also a nice area outside centre field with a number of statues, and nearby is a wall of fame – the franchise has a lot of history, and this is a nice way to pay tribute to it. The nearest seating area to this is the splash zone, with fans sprayed with water pistols after exciting moments in the game. It sounds like a fun way to cool down throughout the game, although it requires sitting in direct sunlight during the day. On the downside, the concourses are slightly empty, with the park's age showing a little – newer locations have used this space to showcase references to their teams' pasts. It lets Camden Yards down a little, but not significantly, meaning it scores 8/10 here.

Overall:

Combining these marks gives Camden Yards an overall score of 36/50. It's regarded as a seminal location in ballpark history, and it still has a lot to offer, but it's beginning to show its age a little and the team deserve bigger crowds.

29

CITIZENS BANK PARK

"Philly fans are great. Everybody complains about them being the meanest – that may be true, but at the same time they're great"

Michael Strahan

One of the biggest differences between sports in the US and the UK is how the fanbases treat games. In America, every match seems to be seen as a big event – supporters tend to arrive extremely early, using the time before a game starts to eat and drink as well as exploring the stadium and enjoying the pregame show. Breaks in play are usually accompanied by entertainment on the big screen – videos like the cap shuffle and various races are cheered on almost more loudly than the sports themselves, and cheerleaders usually make an appearance at some point to throw shirts into the crowd.

By contrast, British sports fans are much more focussed on the action on the field. Many attempts to add to the gameday experience in soccer, for instance, have been met with strong resistance – the cap shuffle would be loudly booed in a UK stadium and probably never featured again. Indeed, the tribalism of such fanbases mean there's no mixing within the stadium; visiting supporters are given their own fully segregated area of the ground, which leads to even more animosity throughout the game (even if it is somewhat artificial). This often means British fans are regarded as being much more intense, but to be honest it's all down to a fundamentally different approach to watching live sports.

Perhaps the intense fanbase in American sports is that of Philadelphia –

much like St Louis, the city seems to revolve around sport. However, unlike the Ohio town, Philly has an incredible amount of history as well; often regarded as the birthplace of the United States, significant moments in the nation's beginning happened in the southeastern Pennsylvania hub. I'd argue that this makes it even more impressive that many people know the city more for supporters of its sports teams, with the NFL Eagles being passionately cheered on and even the relatively serene game of baseball becoming a noisy and exciting event on an almost daily basis.

Whilst my own personal checklist of 30 teams had been completed the previous day in Baltimore, I still needed to visit the final two ballparks to complete the trip, meaning a revisit to Philly was on the cards. Thankfully, the two cities were extremely close, meaning I had the luxury of a much later start and the opportunity to avoid yet another flight – after taking 19 of them in the space of five weeks I was starting to tire of airports. Unfortunately though, Amtrak was having one of its bad days, with the train delayed by over an hour (despite the trip being around 100 minutes in length) and no information provided to passengers.

Even after it had arrived at the station, gates to the platform remained locked and the carriages sat empty for an extended period of time before we were allowed to board, making for an extremely stressful travel experience. Eventually, however, I made it to Philadelphia, making my way to the hotel and before long setting off to the ballpark. This was my second trip to Citizens Bank Park – I had visited the previous year to watch the Giants play a series against the Phillies – and having now been to the other 29 in the league I was interested to see it from a new perspective rather than as a comparative newcomer to the game.

Unfortunately, the Phillies had gone for the same policy as the Guardians in opening the gates extremely late. Whilst the vast majority of ballparks open 90 minutes before first pitch, Citizens Bank Park opted to do so just an hour before the game started. Vast queues formed before this time, such is the fanaticism of Philadelphia sports fans, meaning that once I had actually reached the front of the line and entered the stadium there was limited time to explore – much of this time was spent in the shop and getting photos. I gave up on my original plan of purchasing a cheesesteak (the iconic food of the city) and grabbed whatever was closest to my seat before settling down for an evening of live sport.

This matchup featured Taijuan Walker on the mound for the Phillies, who started the game in uncertain fashion as Angels leadoff hitter Nolan Schanuel was hit by just the third pitch thrown. Schanuel had been drafted earlier in the year, and made headlines a few days previously when he had been called up to the big leagues just 40 days after being selected by the Angels. He advanced to second after Shohei Ohtani managed a single, and after Brandon Drury and Mike Moustakas both recorded successive outs Luis Rengifo hit another single to allow Schanuel to score. Mickey Moniak then bunted to allow all baserunners to advance, but Logan O'Hoppe's out was enough to end the inning and get Walker out of a tough situation.

The Phillies weren't behind for long, however. Whilst Kyle Schwarber struck out to begin the bottom of the first, the next man up was Trea Turner. Turner had experienced a tough start to life in Philadelphia – one of the best players in the game whilst with the Nationals and Dodgers, he had struggled since signing a $300 million contract the previous offseason. Despite this, fans had rallied around him, notably giving him a standing ovation earlier in the month after his season had hit a low point. This had proven to be a turning point, with Turner going on a hot streak immediately after this, and it continued as he hit a home run to level the game at 1-1. Whilst Bryce Harper and Nick Castellanos recorded outs to end the inning, things were looking a little brighter for the home side.

The next two innings were comparatively devoid of action, but in the top of the fourth Drury's single allowed Randal Grichuk and Schanuel to put the visitors 3-1 ahead after Ohtani was intentionally walked (I guess that plan didn't work out). True to form, the Phillies levelled straight away, as Turner earned a walk to lead off the inning and Harper followed up with a two-run homer to centre field. Turner hit another home run of his own in the bottom of the fifth, with Jake Cave also scoring to put the home side ahead for the first time in the contest, as the home team went 5-3 up.

In the top of the seventh the Angels would have an opportunity to fight back – but they were only able to half the deficit as Moniak's single allowed Rengifo to score. An inning and a half later, the Phillies ensured that this would be for nothing, as Brandon Marsh hit a single to drive home Alec Bohm; this was actually the only run of the game that the home side would score that didn't rely on a home run. By this point, the noise from the crowd was unbelievable, and closer Craig Kimbrel had the support of over 30,000 people in the top of the ninth as he retired the side in just seven pitches to secure the win. It was an easy journey back to the hotel, and I went to sleep having watched an enjoyable contest, but also looking forward to finishing the trip the following day.

Location:

Citizens Bank Park is perhaps the only example of a well-located ballpark that isn't in downtown. With Philadelphia being one of the most historic cities in the United States, it was inevitable that there would be no space in the centre to construct a new stadium; instead the team looked to the southern boundary. This has become a true sporting district, with the Eagles' Lincoln Financial Field located across the road alongside Wells Fargo Center, home to the Flyers, 76ers and Wings. It was a smart move – by building all of the city's sports venues in one place, it maximises the use of parking lots, and it'a also allowed for the pregame hub of Xfinity Live to spring up and offer dining and drinking options for fans.

Despite being a few miles away from the heart of Philadelphia, this area is well-connected. There's a metro line that runs frequent services to downtown – the trains are lined up after games to ferry fans back to the centre – as well as ample space for buses and taxis to line up and offer a swift exit. It also allows for a wide range of parking lots without being intrusive to pedestrians, and the way the entire place was aligned means that there's still an excellent view of downtown Philly through the outfield. It's not quite perfect (there's only one hotel on site, so you're almost certainly going to have to make a journey there and back) but it's the next best thing, meaning Citizens Bank Park earns a score of 9/10 for location.

Concessions:

Can you really visit Philadelphia without getting a cheesesteak? In my case, yes. I wanted to get one but the queues at both Tony Luke's and Campo's – the two locations that sell them – were frankly unbelievable, snaking beyond the organised system and filling the entire outfield area. The queues were a common feature around the ballpark; with gates opening just one hour before the game started, fans had little time to get food, meaning they all had to line up at the same time. I ended up going to Federal Donuts before the game (I'd heard good things about the stand), and the chicken strips were simply incredible, blowing those from other parks out of the water.

I did go back to Ashburn Alley – the formal name for the centre field district – during the game to see if the queues had died down, but if anything they'd grown longer. I noticed the line for crab fries was moving much quicker, so went for those instead, but even that took me nearly 20 minutes. On the plus side, the team store was excellent – the upstairs area having multiple sale items, and downstairs featuring series-exclusive pin badges – and the game-used area was one of the better stocked ones in the league (I was able to pick up a ball that was hit by Ohtani, so was understandably delighted). Overall, the concessions at the ballpark was good, but no meal is worth missing an inning of the game for, which really hurts the Phillies' score here – they earn 7/10. It could have been perfect if not for the queues!

Atmosphere:

In case you haven't realised yet, I'll say it again; Philadelphia sports fans are cut from a different cloth. They show up in huge numbers, cheer their team relentlessly and create an atmosphere that's difficult to beat. It's in the city's DNA; the Eagles are regarded as one of the best-supported sides in the NFL, and I'm sure that the players get a significant boost from hearing the fans throughout the game. Despite their reputation of being intense, I found those I spoke to to be friendly and knowledgeable about the game, with a good number of them planning to travel to London next year for the games against the Mets.

Ushers were friendly – although it would have been nice to see them be more proactive in asking people to wait whilst players were in the batter's box (I almost missed part of Ohtani's first plate appearance due to people taking their time getting seated) – and concession staff took the long lines and disgruntled customers in good humour. I know some visiting fans have reported getting heckled in the past for wearing opposition jerseys, but it never spills into violence, and most supporters would rather talk about the game with you instead. It's a good place to visit in that respect, and it means the Phillies get a score of 8/10.

Weather:

I've been to Philadelphia twice, and experienced different conditions each time. On my first visit – at the very start of June in 2022 – it was swelteringly hot and extremely humid, making the day game uncomfortable but the evening matchups significantly more manageable. In fact, it was during that trip that I realised how nice it was to sit in the shade on a warm evening and relax by watching a baseball game. Compare that with this visit; it was quite a bit cooler towards the end of August, and if you're used to the warmer parts of the United States I'd go as far as to say you'll find Citizens Bank Park a little chilly in the shade. On the plus side, there was a gorgeous sunset view, and it never got to the point that you wished there was air conditioning at the park. It's as good as it gets on the East Coast, so it scores 8/10.

Additional Features:

The most popular part of this ballpark is undoubtedly Ashburn Alley – the centre field area features a number of the stadium's best food options as well as some amazing standing room viewpoints (including positions just above both teams' bullpens). It also features a children's area – with a climbing wall allowing kids to reach the top and ring the bell – and a casual bar, behind which are gigantic replicas of the team's two World Series trophies.

Entrance gates on both the first and third base sides also feature large outdoor bar areas (which seemed to have shorter queues than most of the concession stands inside the park itself), and the huge LED Liberty Bell gave the main seating area a local feel. Despite that, there wasn't a vast amount in the concourses to tell you that you were in Philadelphia; the park could perhaps do a little better in that respect. It certainly had more to it than places like Yankee Stadium and Globe Life Field though, which means it earns a score of 7/10.

Overall:

With a total score of 39/50, Citizens Bank Park is firmly in the middle of the pack. The intensity of the fanbase elevates this stadium above many others, and the uniquely good out-of-town location helps to make it an easy and enjoyable place to visit for a game.

30

FENWAY PARK

"I came to love Fenway. It was a place that rejuvenated me after a road trip; the fans right on top of you, the nutty angles. And the Wall. That was my baby, the left-field wall, the Green Monster."

Carl Yastrzemski

Things always seem to be better when they reach their conclusion. Arguably the most popular series of films in recent years has been the Marvel Cinematic Universe; the superhero flicks making an indelible mark on the pop culture landscape over the last decade – and nearly two dozen of them culminated in *Avengers: Endgame*. As the series had introduced a wide range of characters seemingly with the sole purpose of building up to this finale, it became something of a cultural event, transcending cinema and at one point becoming the highest grossing movie of all time. This wouldn't have been possible if it weren't for the ten-year buildup, and whilst it might be the best example of an epic finale it's far from the only one.

Perhaps the first example of this phenomenon was in 1991, when the TV series *Dallas* drew over 22 million viewers. Something similar happened when *Only Fools and Horses* finished in 1996 (when nearly 25 million saw Del Boy and Rodney finally become millionaires), and many regard the final few episodes of *Breaking Bad* to be amongst the finest hours in television history. Clearly things matter more when there's a buildup.

I'm not claiming my trip to be anywhere near the quality of those films or programmes, but it meant the world to me. It had been my life for the past month; almost every day I had woken up, travelled to a new city and crossed another ballpark off the list, and whilst it had been an incredible few weeks it was inevitably building up to the final stop. For the last few stops I could barely stop looking ahead to Boston, knowing that it would represent the conclusion of an incredible journey, and the anticipation of ending at the country's most historic ballpark became stronger as each day passed.

Once again, I was catching a train, meaning I had a slightly later start. Whilst Amtrak isn't perfect, it's certainly nice not needing to wait in a departures hall for two hours, especially when the station is significantly more central. The Acela Express took about five hours to make the trip to Boston, running at nearly 150 miles an hour for parts of the trip, and I had a table to myself the entire way. As a result I arrived into the Massachusetts capital refreshed and relaxed, quickly dropping off my luggage at the hotel (Boston is possibly the most expensive city in America to find accommodation, but I had treated myself for the final night of the trip) before heading across to Fenway Park.

This was another revisit – I'd been to see the Red Sox play the previous year, catching two games against the Orioles before heading down to see the Giants in Philadelphia – so I knew how special this ballpark was. I wanted to get there early to take in the atmosphere around the park, and upon arrival I was instantly reminded why many regarded Fenway as the best stadium in the league. Although it was more than two hours before first pitch, the entire neighbourhood was a buzzing hive of activity, and the unmistakeable smell of hot dogs permeated the air, giving me a wonderful reminder of the pure Americana of baseball. I was overcome with a sense of pride, safe in the knowledge that I had fulfilled the purpose of the trip and finally watched a game at all 30 ballparks in a single journey.

After queuing at the gate I headed straight for the team store. I wanted to get a custom printed jersey to mark the conclusion of the trip, and after filling in the appropriate form I was told to come back to collect it once they had made it up. I took the opportunity to purchase a hat and get the usual photos, taking plenty of time to explore parts of the park that I had missed on my last visit. There's simply so much at Fenway Park that it's impossible to see it all in one go, so there was plenty more to see, including an old bullpen car and the oldest World Series trophy I'd seen at any ballpark, dating back from 1912. By this time, my jersey was ready, so I headed back to the store (via Autograph Alley, where I was lucky enough to meet former Red Sox pitcher and 1973 MVP Bill Lee) to collect it – I used it to pose for another quick photo before settling down to watch the final game of the trip.

The final two starting pitchers I'd see on this adventure were Brayan Bello of the Red Sox and JP France from the Astros. Both players were in their rookie year, and whilst they weren't aces for their teams they were both having relatively impressive seasons. Whilst the Red Sox were having a poor year, they still harboured hopes to sneak a wildcard spot, and were taking some solace in the fact that their bitter rivals in New York were having one of the worst seasons in their history.

By contrast, the Astros were aiming for a third World Series trophy since 2017, but after a poor run of results were locked in an incredibly tight race for the division title after the Seattle Mariners had embarked upon an incredible winning run. In fact, the American League West had been a fascinating division all year; whilst Angels and Athletics were having poor seasons (the Angels having placed close to 20% of their roster on wavers that same afternoon to get salaries off the books, and looking all but guaranteed to lose Ohtani at the end of the season) the other three sides were neck-and-neck in an almost unprecedented fashion.

The visitor's hopes received a much-needed boost early in the game. Whilst Bello managed to strike out Jose Altuve to start off the contest (most impressive, since Altuve had hit for the cycle the previous day), he could only watch as the next two batters knocked in solo home runs – both Alex Bregman and Yordan Alvarez blasting the balls high above the Green Monster to give the Astros an early 2-0 lead. This initial volley of hits meant they almost didn't mind when Kyle Tucker and Jose Abreu grounded out to end the inning, and their day got even better as France retired Alex Verdugo, Rafael Devers and Justin Turner without allowing a single hit or walk.

The game continued scoreless until the bottom of the third – an error by Bregman allowed Verdugo to score, with Devers reaching third safely after Turner grounded into a fielder's choice, the three Red Sox players combining to make some amends for their earlier outs. That would prove to be the home side's only runs until the sixth though – and one of just two in the game – with Adam Duvall's left field homer giving the Boston side some faint hope but ultimately not enough to win the game, thanks to Bregman getting two RBIs in the top of the fifth after Abreu and former Giant Mauricio Dubon had reached base safely earlier in the inning.

The Astros piled an some insurance run in the seventh as well; Abreu grounded into a fielder's choice and allowed Bregman to score. Incredibly, this result put the Houston side joint top of the American League West in a three-way tie with the Mariners and their cross-state rival the Texas Rangers, setting up a memorable end to the season. From a personal standpoint, it was a great way to end the trip, with light rain coming down towards the game's conclusion and providing a truly atmospheric scene at one of the most iconic locations in world sport.

Location:

Teams have two options when building a modern ballpark – do you construct one in the middle of a city, taking advantage of public transit links and local landmarks, or do you go for an out of town location and build parking lots and destinations around it? The Cardinals and Twins went for the former, but the Braves and the Rangers (the two newest parks) opted for the latter option. There's no such dilemma for the Red Sox, with Fenway Park being built up long before modern city planning became so crucial.

With Boston being a significantly smaller city at the time of its construction, it's far from remote, with subway and rail stations nearby as well as the interstate running directly past the outfield. In fact, the history of this is evident when you consider that the team have to close Jersey Street (formerly Yawkee Way, the road has now been renamed due to the former owner that gave it its name allegedly refusing to hire black players in the 1940s) and incorporate it into the ticketed area to provide sufficient capacity.

It's not quite central, but that doesn't really matter; the area around the park has taken on a life of its own, with countless bars and eateries popping up over the years (not to mention the iconic Sal's pizzeria and numerous sausage stands). The streets around Fenway Park are almost as iconic as the stadium itself, and the gameday atmosphere is second to none. Not even Wrigleyville or St Louis' ballpark village comes close – it's the only park I'd purposely arrive at even earlier than the gate opening times to soak up the atmosphere and take in the sights and sounds (as well as the smells). It may not be a typical modern day location, but this is no typical ballpark, and I can't fault anything about it, so it earns a score of 10/10.

Concessions:

As the most traditional park in baseball, it's fitting that Fenway Park has a hot dog named after it. The Fenway Frank is a must-have for any visitor to the stadium, but there's so much more on offer too. Jersey Street hosts a number of pop-up stalls which arguably provide the most interesting items, but the main concession stands sell all the standard ballpark classics alongside more unique offerings, such as crab cake sandwiches and avocado fries. The Red Sox are aware of their reputation, with a large number of items being served in souvenir helmets – popcorn, nachos, fries and ice creams all allow you to take home a branded novelty after eating your dinner.

The stadium's limited space makes it impossible to fit a main team store inside, so the team built one directly opposite – and with Jersey Street being part of the park during the game you can visit it after getting your ticket scanned. This proved to be a stroke of genius; it's by far the largest shop I saw across the league, and despite being overwhelmingly popular it never felt crowded. The game-used kiosk is inside (and exceptionally well-stocked), as well as Autograph Alley, which allows fans to meet a former player at select home games. There are two things that stops the Red Sox from getting another perfect score, however; prices are fairly high (a team-branded ball costing almost twice the price of some other parks, for instance) and the seemingly exclusive deal with '47 preventing New Era caps being available. It's not a dealbreaker, but it does mean the team end up scoring 8/10.

Atmosphere:

There's just something about Fenway Park that makes it the perfect place to watch baseball. The fans are noisy and passionate, the staff care about your experience, and there's an almost indescribable magic in the air – you know you're somewhere special. No group of supporters do anything as well as Boston's singing Sweet Caroline in the eighth inning; even when the team are playing awful baseball it's something incredible to witness. Impressively, they tend to arrive on time and stay to the end too, which is a rarity amongst modern baseball fans – but then, this isn't a modern ballpark. I'd love to see a Yankees game there one day; if the atmosphere is this good against another side, I can only imagine how great it would be against their rivals. It's another perfect score here, as the Red Sox get 10/10.

Weather:

This has been the pitfall of the best parks so far, and unsurprisingly it's where Fenway stumbles a little. Boston is one of the wettest cities in the United States, with winds coming in from the north east making forecasts unpredictable; indeed, both of my visits to the city included rain and a wide range of temperatures. Somehow this doesn't matter here though – part of Fenway's charm is that you're not in a modern ballpark with countless luxuries, so sitting in the warmth of a setting sun would almost go against the place's atmosphere. I'm not excusing it (I'm sure sitting in the bleachers during a downpour would be miserable), but my tolerance for drizzle was much higher here than anywhere else. It doesn't get uncomfortably hot or stupidly cold, so it's fine by me – meaning the park gets a mark of 7/10.

Additional Features:

I could write a book just about everything inside Fenway Park – indeed, many others already have – but it's probably enough to say that the place is packed full of history and character. The most obvious feature is the Green Monster; the iconic wall in outfield was originally constructed to prevent ticketless fans from watching games outside the ballpark, but is now one of the most recognisable sights in the game. Whilst some complained when the team put seats atop the landmark, it's certainly better than its original appearance; it would be ruined if it were still covered in colourful adverts. One place that is covered, however, is Peskey's pole – the yellow foul pole in right field being filled with signatures of those who have visited the park over the years (you can bring your own Sharpie and write your name on there too – they don't mind you leaving your mark on the park).

There's so much more to see even if you don't have tickets for the monster; the concourses are bursting at the seams with objects and displays from the team's past. The original clubhouse is marked with several plaques alongside a replica of the 1912 World Series trophy (noticeably different from its modern appearance), and the original ticket booths have been preserved along the third base line. That's before I mention anything about the ballpark's exterior – ushers on stilts parade around Jersey Street, and that's probably not in the top 5 strangest sights nearby.

You could almost get lost exploring everything at the park (and that's not just because the concourses are on a number of different levels), and I'd strongly recommend taking a tour before going to a game. Fenway Park really is baseball heaven, and I couldn't possibly give it anything less than 10/10 – even a perfect score feels like I'm underselling it.

Overall:

The iconic home of the Red Sox ends up with a combined score of 45/50, good enough for joint-third in the rankings. To tell the truth though, it's simply incomparable – it's such a different place to any modern ballpark, making scores almost irrelevant. Do yourself a favour and get yourself to Boston as soon as you can.

FINAL THOUGHTS

"Baseball is more than a game. It's like life played out on a field."

Juliana Hatfield

Finishing the journey brought with it a mix of emotions. On one hand, there was an overwhelming sense of elation and relief to have finished the trip, and done so without any major drama. I had anticipated something unavoidable coming up – visiting all 30 parks was such an ambitious goal that the odds of everything lining up perfectly was slim. However, the hurricane passing through California had been the only real hiccup, and some quick rebooking meant that was only a minor inconvenience.

Despite this, a slight sense of sadness passed over me as I woke up the next morning. This challenge had been my entire life over the past five weeks, and a return to everyday life seemed like an anticlimax against the backdrop of constant travelling and meeting new people. I had hired a car for the drive back to New York – aware of the previous unreliability of Amtrak and the urgent need to get to JFK for my flight that evening – and I spent most of the drive through New England in quiet reflection. The relatively short drive was still a marathon by British standards, and the passing landscape was one that had felt like home for over a month, only to return to being part of a distant shore by the next morning.

I had originally planned to make a mental list of my favourite parks, with the intention of slowly returning and revisiting the very best over the next few years. But with each stop offering something new and exciting, the list had grown to cover nearly every single team in the league. Instead, I decided, I'd keep an eye out for the Giants' schedule each year, and try to make second visits to each park as and when my team played a road series at the parks. This especially looked appealing considering 2024 would see them visit DC – an easy trip compared to some of the Midwestern teams in smaller markets, and a chance to visit some of the more iconic sights that I had missed out on this trip.

The other benefit of this would be the opportunity to keep in touch with the many friends that I had made on this adventure. The overwhelming positivity and generosity of the baseball community struck me from the minute I started publicising my trip, and it was this that I would miss most about the adventure. Whilst I set out to watch baseball, I quickly realised that the real purpose of the journey would be to connect with others and hear their stories. Yes, baseball is a sport, but it's also a true American pastime – something that brings us together.

OVERALL RANKINGS

It was inevitable that, wherever I went, the minute I explained my trip to people they'd ask what my favourite park was. As previously mentioned, it's only human nature to want to assign a numerical value to things, and an extension of that is ranking them to decide a best or worst. Therefore, I created a final table of all the scores I gave to parks:

	Location	Concessions	Atmosphere	Weather	Features	Total
Yankee Stadium	7	10	6	8	5	36
Citi Field	7	9	9	8	8	41
Rogers Centre	10	10	9	9	7	45
PNC Park	10	6	8	9	7	40
T-Mobile Park	6	7	7	9	7	36
Kauffman Stadium	4	9	8	7	9	37
Coors Field	9	9	7	6	9	40
Busch Stadium	10	9	10	6	9	44
Target Field	9	10	8	7	7	41
American Family Field	5	6	7	9	9	36
Wrigley Field	9	9	10	7	10	45
Guaranteed Rate Field	7	8	6	7	6	34
Great American Ball Park	8	6	7	9	9	39
Progressive Field	8	8	6	8	4	34
Comerica Park	7	6	8	7	10	38
Nationals Park	7	6	8	7	6	34
Minute Maid Park	8	8	9	8	10	43
Globe Life Field	5	10	8	8	9	40
Oracle Park	10	10	10	6	10	46
Oakland Coliseum	6	4	4	6	2	22
Dodger Stadium	4	6	8	8	10	36
Angel Stadium	5	6	7	8	6	32
Petco Park	9	10	10	9	9	47
Chase Field	8	5	5	8	6	32
Truist Park	6	9	10	4	8	37
Tropicana Field	3	7	6	8	8	32
loanDepot Park	6	6	6	7	6	31
Camden Yards	8	7	6	7	8	36
Citizens Bank Park	9	7	8	8	7	39
Fenway Park	10	8	10	7	10	45

The immediate thing that stood out to me after seeing these scores all in one place was simply how strong they were across the board – with the exception of Oakland, every team had something to shout about (everyone scored at least 7 out of 10 on one of the ratings criteria), with 10s appearing on even some of the middle-of-the-road parks. However, there were some clear stand outs…

Joint-3rd – Wrigley Field, Fenway Park and Rogers Centre. It's fitting that the two oldest parks in baseball are tied in third place; whilst their relative lack of concessions and windy conditions harm them a little, there's very little to fault about the truly traditional experiences. Toronto surprised me early on in the trip too, and I'm excited to go back after the lower deck has been renovated.

2nd – Oracle Park. OK, I'm biased, but the San Francisco Bay is the perfect place to watch a game. Sort out the weather and this is the best stadium in all of sports.

1st – Petco Park. Not a surprise, perhaps, but the Padres took the Giants' home and somehow made it better. Maybe they're lucky that San Diego experiences better weather than San Francisco, but the park is slightly more modern as well – plus I'll never forget how good the place smelt.

Honorable mentions go to the atmosphere at Busch Stadium and Truist Park – getting perfect 10s (despite, in the case of the Cardinals, the team having a terrible season).

GLOSSARY

Much like other sports – and, indeed, any area of life – baseball has developed a rich vocabulary over the years, and several terms might be difficult to understand for someone new to the game. Many of the phrases and rules make baseball seem needlessly complicated to newcomers, so I thought it might be helpful to define some of these:

Ace: The best pitcher on a team.

At Bat: The number of times a hitter has been up to bat – but only counting those that end in a hit or a standard out. A plate appearance that ends in a walk or a sacrifice play would not count as an at bat.

Balk: If you understand this one, you're doing well. Generally speaking, if a pitcher does something to trick a baserunner, they will have given up a balk, which allows every baserunner to advance to the next base. Usually very controversial and the subject of intense debates.

Ball: A batter is not expected to swing at every single pitch they face. Sometimes the pitcher might throw the ball too high, low or wide for it to be hit, at which point a ball is awarded. Get four of these and you get to walk to first base for free.

Baserunner: A hitter who has reached a base safely, and is ready to run to the next base after the current batter has managed to get the ball into play.

Bases Loaded: A situation where all three bases are occupied. Generally considered a very dangerous situation for a pitcher, as any form of hit or sacrifice play will usually result in at least one run being scored.

Battery: The combination of pitcher and catcher.

Batting Average: Sometimes simply referred to as "average" or *AVG*, one of the most ubiquitous statistics for a hitter. This is the number of hits divided by the number of at bats. Represented as a three-digit decimal, if you're batting over .300 you're doing very well indeed. Most players will hit somewhere between .240 and .280.

Bloop: A hit that goes over the heads of the infielders, but not far enough to be caught by the outfield. Something of a fine art, but risky, since too much or too little power will turn it into an easy out.

Bullpen: This has two meanings, which are closely linked. Firstly, it can refer to the area in a ballpark where the relief pitchers warm up during a game, to ensure they're ready to replace the starter at a moment's notice. It can also refer to the collective pitching staff (minus the starter) itself.

Bunt: A hitter can attempt a bunt by holding their bat sideways and not swinging it, allowing the ball to bounce off it and roll along the ground. Considered cheap and easier than a normal hit, but can be an art form when done properly as it will make it incredibly difficult for the defensive team to make a play in time. Because of the comparative ease of bunting, one that goes foul does count as a third strike.

Can of Corn: A phrase that harks back to old fashioned stores, where a shopkeeper would grab products from the top shelves with a stick and catch it easily in their apron. A player is said to have hit a can of corn when they send out a fly ball and make it straightforward for the defensive team to catch it and send them back to the dugout.

Changeup: Any pitch that isn't a fastball – could include a slider, a curveball, a sinker or Kodai Senga's "ghost fork". Most (if not all) pitchers will have at least one good changeup pitch, and usually throw it a good percentage of the time in an attempt to keep batters guessing what they will face.

Check Swing: When a batter stops his swing before it becomes a meaningful attempt to hit the ball – usually because they know the pitch won't be a strike. Officially this is when the bat doesn't cross home plate, but it can depend on the quality of the umpire. Done correctly, it won't count as a strike.

Closer: Usually the best relief pitcher on a team, someone who is called in to pitch the final inning of a game in high-pressure situations. Mariano Rivera is probably the most famous example and popularised the role, and nowadays many closers are cult heroes, such as Edwin Diaz (whose entrance to Timmy Trumpet's *Narcos* went viral in 2022).

Complete Game: A relatively rare occurrence, this occurs when the starting pitcher throws the entire game. Rarer still is the Complete Game Shutout (CGSO), where he will allow no runs either.

Count: The running total of strikes and balls that the batter has faced. The first number refers to the number of balls, and the second the number of strikes. For instance, a *3-1 count* means that there have been three balls and one strike – another ball would award the batter a walk.

Curveball: A slightly slower pitch than a fastball, which is challenging to hit not because of its speed but its trajectory. A curveball will, as the name suggests, tend to "curve" away from its intended path and fool the batter into swinging at thin air.

Cycle: Another rare but celebrated occurrence, a player is said to have hit for the cycle if they manage to hit a single, double, triple and a home run in the same game. This has happened less than 350 times in the history of the sport, and no player has done it more than three times. An interesting piece of trivia is that Christian Yelich of the Milwaukee Brewers is one of those players, but the only one to do it against the same team all three times. The Reds must really hate playing against him.

Dead-ball Era: An early period of baseball, when the game was centred more around strikeouts and the home run was a rare event. Generally considered to have ended when Babe Ruth turned up and decided it would be fun to hit balls out of the park a lot. Most players have very different statistics to the current era, so comparisons need more advanced measures.

Defensive Indifference: One of my favourite terms in all of baseball. This only really occurs late in a game which has a one-sided score, but it refers to a baserunner stealing a base without any real resistance from the defensive team. This is usually because the team is so far ahead or behind that they simply don't care. It also means that the runner doesn't get credited with a stolen base.

Designated Hitter (DH): Originally something that only happened in the American League, but expanded to the National League in 2022. This is a player that doesn't play any defensive role, but only bats. This means that the pitcher does not have to hit – unless they're really good at it (for instance, Shohei Ohtani).

Dinger: Another word for a home run. It's just much more fun to say that a player has hit a dinger. If you don't believe me, search YouTube for "Big Al". The lad just loves hitting dingers.

Double: When a batter hits the ball and is able to reach second base safely. This doesn't count if they would have only hit for a single if it weren't for a defensive mistake.

Double Play: A fielding team records this when they manage to record two outs from a single play. Most commonly, a batter will hit a weak ground ball, which is picked up by an infielder. This is thrown to second (or third) base to force the baserunner out, and immediately thrown to the first baseman, who will ensure the original batter is out. Usually done in a matter of seconds, it's an immensely satisfying thing to watch.

Earned Run Average (ERA): The equivalent of battering average for pitchers, this common statistic is usually the first thing you'll see next to their name. An *earned run* is one that the pitcher has given up that a competent defence wouldn't have prevented – for instance, if a batter should have been out but the first baseman drops the ball, allowing them to make it to the base safely, them scoring would not count towards a pitcher's ERA. It's calculated by averaging out the number of earned runs they give up every nine innings (a complete game). A good pitcher is probably going to have an ERA under 4, and the best ones in the game hover around the 2-2.5 mark.

Error: Linking into ERA, an error is basically a defensive howler. Think a player dropping the ball or throwing it into empty space.

Fan Interference: A spectator is not allowed to reach into the field of play to grab a baseball – if it lands in the seats, it's fair game and they can take it home as a souvenir, but reach over that invisible wall between that area and the field, and it's likely you're going to get kicked out of the ballpark. If it happens in a big game, it's a good way to make yourself public enemy number one too.

Fastball: The bread and butter of a pitcher's arsenal, this pitch is usually just a way of throwing the ball really quickly. Sometimes called "heater", the best pitchers will get their fastballs somewhere around the 100mph mark.

Fly Ball: A ball hit at a large angle, resulting in it reaching a high altitude.

Foul: A ball that goes outside of the regulation field – that is, outside of the lines that extend from home plate towards the foul poles. You can be caught out on a foul ball, but you can't start running after hitting one. These count as a strike, unless it's your third.

Foul Tip: A foul ball that catches the hitter's bat and goes straight into the catcher's glove. This counts the same as if an infielder or outfielder were to catch the ball, and it's an out.

Full Count: A 3-2 count; that is to say a count that cannot go any higher. The next pitch, unless it's fouled off, will end the plate appearance, either with a walk or the ball being put into play.

Grand Slam: When a player hits a home run with the bases loaded, resulting in 4 runs being scored.

Ground Rule Double: Every park has their own unique set of rules – for instance, if the ball hits the catwalks in Tampa Bay's Tropicana Field, it could be called either a home run or stay in play (depending on which catwalk it hits). The ground rule double is universal though – if a ball bounces out of the field (a little bit like a 4 in cricket), it counts as a double. This can also happen when the ball is accidentally thrown into a dugout.

Hanging Slider: The cardinal sin for a pitcher. A slider is meant to move in the air, but sometimes a badly thrown one won't do so. This combination of a straight path, ideal location and lower velocity makes it significantly easier to hit, and will frequently result in a home run. Gives rise to the phrase "You hang 'em we bang 'em".

Hit: A player is said to have recorded a hit when they are able to reach a base after their bat makes contact with the ball.

Hit by Pitch: This one hurts. If you're a batter, and the pitch hits you, you get to walk for base for free – as long as you're not too badly injured (a fastball can break bones). Usually this is a genuine mistake, but it can be deliberately done in retaliation for some perceived injustice. Also called *getting beaned*.

Home Run: Another obvious one – when a player hits the ball so hard it goes out of the field of play, allowing them to run round all 4 bases and score (as with anyone that's already on base). You do get the much rarer inside-the-park home run, where it's hit so well that they have time to round the bases before anyone gets it back. Sometimes called a *dinger* or a *homer*.

Infield: The central part of the field of play, generally considered to be the area enclosed by the bases plus the dirt around it. The four position players (first, second and third basemen, plus the shortstop) are collectively referred to as *infielders*.

Infield Fly Rule: One of the strange subtleties of the baseball rulebook. Normally, a fly ball has to be caught for the batter to be out, but if it's hit in such a way that it would fall in the infield, and a fielder should be able to catch it easily (the official phrase is "with regular effort"), the hitter is automatically out regardless of whether it's caught or not. This only happens if there are runners on first and second – and if there are fewer than two outs in the inning. I told you it was a strange rule.

Inning: Nine of these (or more, in the event of a tied game) make up a game of baseball. Each team has to record three outs to end an inning. The away team always bats first (so that the home side have the opportunity to come back at the end of the game), and their turn batting is called the top of the inning. The second half, in which the home team bats, is called the bottom of an inning. For instance, the *bottom of the third* would be the second part of the third inning, during which the home team would be hitting.

Line Drive: A ball that is hit hard and at a fairly low angle, meaning it tends to travel in a straighter path than one hit higher (which would follow an arc). The lower angle means that most of its velocity is in the horizontal direction, allowing it to travel a great distance at high speed. Players – and fans – have been injured and even killed by line drives.

Maddux: Named after one of the all-time great pitchers Greg Maddux, who specialised in being economical with his pitching, a player is said to have thrown one of these if they record a complete game shutout with less than 100 pitches. It's much more impressive than a casual fan might realise.

NOBLETIGER: No outs, bases loaded, ending with team incapable of getting easy run. OK, this one isn't official, but it's an amazing acronym, and represents possibly the most frustrating offensive failure in the game. A team is said to have committed a NOBLETIGER if, like the name suggests, the bases get loaded without any outs, and the next three batters all end up making outs instead of getting a hit or a walk. It should be straightforward to score at least one in this position after all.

No-hitter: A celebrated and rare feat for a pitcher, this happens when a pitcher throws an entire game without allowing a single hit. Players are allowed to reach base on walks and errors (otherwise it would be a *perfect game*). Sometimes called a *no-no*, there have been a touch over 300 in MLB history, averaging about 2 or 3 a season. Superstition dictates that you shouldn't talk about a game being a no-hitter until it's completed, lest you jinx it.

On Base Percentage (OBP): Very similar to batting average, but takes into account walks as well. Instead of simply recording hits and at-bats, this records every time a hitter reaches a base safely (whether via a hit, a walk or being hit by a pitch) and divides it by their number of plate appearances. Because walks are fairly common, players will usually have a higher OBP than their AVG, but not by much. This measure, like the walk itself, is somewhat undervalued by many.

On Base Plug Slugging (OPS): The sum of a player's OBP and SLG, generally considered to be the best single measure of a player's offensive output as it takes into account their hitting power as well as their consistency in reaching bases safely. The most elite players will be looking to hit .900, and you'll get a few over 1.000 every season.

Outfield: The majority of the field of play – simply but, the part that isn't the infield. Three defensive players are considered to be *outfielders* – simply referred to as left, right and centre fielders.

Perfect Game: Considered to be one of the rarest feats in professional sport, a player is said to have pitched a perfect game if no opposing player reaches base at all – all 27 plate appearances end with an out. There have only been 24 perfect games in Major League history, and none at all between 2012 and 2023.

Pitch Clock: Newly added for the 2023 season to speed up the pace of play. Pitchers now have 15 seconds to throw a pitch (or 20 seconds if a runner is on base), otherwise they are said to have committed a *pitch clock violation* and automatically give up a ball. Batters must be engaged with 8 seconds remaining, otherwise they give up a strike. There are some other subtle rules, but these two cover the bulk of it.

Pitcher: Arguably the most important player in a game, the man who has to throw the ball and try to get hitters out. Often the highest-paid players on a team.

Plate Appearance: Every appearance at home plate, where a batter will try to hit the ball. Differs slightly from an at bat, since a plate appearance can also include those that end with a walk, sacrifice play or hit by pitch.

Run Batted In (RBI): A measure of how many players are able to score as a result of a player's hit (or walk) – in effect, a run created by the player's offensive output.

Rundown: The most common way to get a player out is by stepping on a base with the ball in your hand before they can reach it, but you can also "tag" them whilst holding the ball. If a baserunner is caught between two bases and starts running away from the fielder, they are said to be caught in a rundown. Often hilarious in a Benny Hill-like way.

Sacrifice Play: When a batter hits a ball in a way that gets them out, but creates sufficient time for baserunners to advance (or, ideally, score), the idea being that they have sacrificed their own chance to score in order to help the team out. This isn't counted as an at bat, and is sometimes called a "productive out".

Scoring Position: A baserunner is said to be in a scoring position if they're on second or third base – the logic being that a batter hitting a fair ball will allow them to score a run.

Seventh-inning stretch: An example of baseball being a romantic sport. During the middle of the seventh – approximately two-thirds of the way through a game – everyone in the crowd stands up, stretches and sings *Take Me Out to the Ball Game*. A callback to simpler times.

Slugging Percentage (SLG): A measure of how hard a player hits the ball. This is calculated by adding up the total number of bases (i.e. a triple counts as three) achieved by a batter of the course of a season, and dividing it by the total number of at bats. In theory, this could go as high as 4.000 if a player hits a home run every time, but in practice anything over .500 is considered to be really good.

Sticky Stuff: It's really difficult to throw a ball quickly and exactly where you want it. Pitchers, therefore, tend to use some form of sticky substance to help them with this. Various things have been used in the past, such as pine tar and a mix of sunscreen and rosin. Technically against the rules, the league turned a blind eye to it for a long time, until in 2021 there was a significant crackdown on what is and isn't allowed.

Stolen Base: The game isn't just about hitting the ball and getting on first – you've still got to get around the bases and score. If you're fast, you can try and run to the next base while the pitcher is throwing his pitch. Do it successfully, and you've stolen a base. If the pitcher – or catcher – notices this and throws you out, you're said to be *caught stealing*.

Strike: This is something that a batter doesn't want. If a pitch is thrown within the strike zone (broadly speaking, between your kneecaps and the letters on your uniform vertically, and about half that distance horizontally), and you fail to hit it into play, it counts as a strike. It can also be recorded by a hitter swinging and missing, or batting it into foul territory (unless it's the third strike). As the best-known rule in the sport states, three strikes and you're out.

TOOTBLAN: Thrown out on the basepaths like a nincompoop. Like the NOBLETIGER, this is not an official Major League stat, but one created by the baseball community because not only does it keep track of bad baserunning, it sounds funny too.

Triple: Somewhat rare, a player hits a triple if they are able to advance to third base after hitting the ball. Usually, this takes more time than a competent fielding side will allow, but some ballparks have quirky areas (such as Oracle Park's "triples alley") that make it very difficult for a fielding team to get hold of the ball and throw it back in time.

Unwritten Rules: Some of the quirkier rules of baseball, and often those that produce the most controversy. There are many, but some of the most notable include not swinging on a 3-0 count, admiring a home run that you've just hit, or bunting when the pitcher is on course for a no-hitter. A lot of these are arguably in place to protect the pitcher's feelings, and some teams have started to abandon following these rules altogether. Do so at your peril though – you're liable to get beaned by a very angry pitcher.

Walk: Also known as a "base on balls" and scored as such (BB), a batter is allowed to walk to first base for free when the pitcher throws four balls (non-strikes) in a single plate appearance. Some players with a strong reputation for their offensive prowess are frequently given *intentional walks*, where the pitcher indicates that he simply doesn't want to pitch to him, and everyone is spared the rigmarole of watching four pitches intentionally away from the strike zone.

Wins Above Replacement (WAR): Calculated by what seems to be magic (there are, in fact, three main websites that calculate this figure, all of which do so differently and therefore produce slightly different values), this number indicates the number of games a team has won over what they would be expected to do so with a league average player in his place. It takes into account offensive and defensive performances simultaneously, and is a fairly good way of determining the best players each season.

For the Love of the Game

ABOUT THE AUTHOR

Matthew Morris is a mathematics teacher in the South West of England. Having grown up in Hertfordshire, he quickly found a love of sports, following Reading Football Club through some of the best years in their history before experiencing some of the pain that best defines supporting any team. Having moved to Bath to complete his degree, he realised he loved the landscapes and quieter life away from London, and stayed there to complete his teaching qualifications. Matthew visited the United States in 2017 and fell in love with baseball, and returns on a regular basis to watch the San Francisco Giants, who inevitably lose when he gets the chance to catch a game.

Printed in Great Britain
by Amazon

45027562R00129